Call Centers and the Global Division of Labor

Call centers have come, in the last three decades, to define the interaction between corporations, governments, and other institutions and their respective customers, citizens, and members. The offshoring and outsourcing of call center employment, part of the larger information technology and information-technology-enabled services sectors, continues to be a growing practice amongst governments and corporations in their attempts at controlling costs and providing new services. While incredible advances in technology have permitted the use of distant and "offshore" labor forces, the grander reshaping of an international political economy of communications has allowed for the acceleration of these processes. New and established labor unions have responded to these changes in the global regimes of work by seeking to organize call center workers. These efforts have been assisted by a range of forces, not least of which is the condition of work itself, but also attempts by global union federations to build a bridge between international unionism and local organizing campaigns in the Global South and Global North. Through an examination of trade union interventions in the call center industries located in Canada and India, this book contributes to research on post-industrial employment by using political economy as a juncture between development studies, the sociology of work, and labor studies.

Andrew J.R. Stevens is Assistant Professor of Human Resource Management and Industrial Relations in the Faculty of Business Administration at University of Regina.

Routledge Advances in Sociology

Call Centers and the Global Division of Labor

A Political Economy of Post-Industrial Employment and Union Organizing

Andrew J.R. Stevens

Routledge
Taylor & Francis Group

LONDON AND NEW YORK

First published 2014 by Routledge

2 Park Square, Milton Park, Abingdon, Oxfordshire OX14 4RN
52 Vanderbilt Avenue, New York, NY 10017

*Routledge is an imprint of the Taylor & Francis Group,
an informa business*

First issued in paperback 2020

Library of Congress Cataloging-in-Publication Data
Stevens, Andrew J. R.
    Call centers and the global division of labor : a political economy of
post-industrial employment and union organizing / Andrew J.R. Stevens.
        pages cm. — (Routledge advances in sociology ; 120)
    Includes bibliographical references and index.
    1. Call centers.   2. Call centers—Canada.   3. Call centers—
India.   4 Telecommunication—Employees—Labor unions.
5. Telecommunication—Employees—Labor unions—
Canada.   6. Telecommunication—Employees—Labor unions—
India.   I. Title.
    HE8788.S74 2014
    381—dc23
    2013027778

ISBN13: 978-0-415-65913-0 (hbk)
ISBN13: 978-0-367-60105-8 (pbk)

Typeset in Sabon
by IBT Global.

To Jen, Liam, and Logan

Contents

Figures

Acknowledgments

There are a great many people to thank for bringing this book to fruition. My time as a graduate student at Queen's University was full of illuminating experiences that helped me write the dissertation that is the foundation for the book. Most of these experiences were positive. Vincent Mosco, my supervisor, could not have provided better guidance and support throughout the entire research and writing phase of this project. I can't thank Vinny enough for the mentorship he has shown me and countless other students in the ways of critical scholarship, and for the importance he placed on the role of academics as public intellectuals. A deep appreciation is also owed to Frank Pearce who has been a tremendous influence on me throughout grad school and beyond. Few academics parallel his love for social theory.

From a researcher's standpoint, many thanks go to all of the members of UNITES, UNI, the USW, the ITPF, the YPC, and Unite the Union who generously offered their time to indulge an aspiring scholar trying to make sense of their organizations. Of course, my political and scholarly interest in trade unionism is due to the handful of union campaigns that I am proud to have been a part of at Queen's University. In 2010 Public Service Alliance of Canada Local 901 emerged as the representative of graduate teaching assistants and fellows at Queen's University after years of hard work. The union drive of 2008 will forever be my reminder of how much time and personal anguish organizers and union members put in to these campaigns. On that note I have to thank Christopher Wilson, a staff representative with the PSAC, for believing that we could do it, even if it took two tries.

Finally, a great deal of gratitude goes to my family for their never-ending encouragement. Even though many of them didn't really know what it was I did, or why it took me so long to do it, they never questioned my motives or dedication to the work that I enjoy. My parents were a special blessing and a constant reminder of the strength of working people—they were an inspiration throughout. I wish my Dad could have been here to see me reach the end of the task. I'll never forget the love for reading he taught me so many years ago, long before I appreciated it.

To my wife, Jen, I owe so much. It can't be easy putting up with the anxiety and stress (and petty complaints) that accompany being a graduate student and academic.

I am grateful to the Department of Sociology at Queen's University, the Blakely Fund, the Ontario Graduate Scholarship, the Surveillance Project, the Dean's Travel Award, and the Shastri Indo-Canadian Institute for their generous financial support. Of course, to my supportive colleagues in the Faculty of Business Administration at the University of Regina, thank you.

1 Introduction

This is a book about the political economy of call center work and trade unionism. Research began in 2006 as recognition of India's role as the world's digital back office was gaining momentum in Canada and the United States. By the time field research commenced in 2007, interviews with industry representatives, call center workers, and trade unionists were full of apprehension about the looming economic crisis. Near the end of 2008, there was fear in India among the benefactors of information technology (IT) globalization that Barack Obama's imminent presidential victory might signal tough times for high-tech industries dependent on offshoring business from the United States. In Canada, call centers that provided services for American companies and consumers were beginning to see the effects of the country's rising currency exchange rate as labor costs were losing their competitive edge. And, because of the pace at which information technology enabled employment globalizes, the Philippines surpassed India as the leading offshore destination for call center work around 2010 as this study began to come to a close (Macaraig 2010). Much has transpired over the past ten years.

The first decade of the new millennium held promise and apprehension for those workers and industries affected by the globalization of information technology. Excitement over India's high-tech prowess reached new levels as the Indian Space Research Organization (ISRO) successfully launched an orbital lunar satellite in 2008. Coincidentally, ISRO veteran Kiran Karnik headed the National Association of Software and Services Companies (Nasscom), India's premier information technology and business process outsourcing (BPO) industry organization, between 2001 and 2008. Around the same time, Canada was experiencing record low unemployment rates and oil and resource companies, the jewels of Western Canada's economy, were reveling in record commodity prices. Most importantly, the country's currency had rebounded from its 1990s status as a "northern peso". These were exciting times for two of the world's leading destinations for call center work.

Despite their obvious differences, both Canada and India rank as leading destinations for call centers and investment in services. To capture the economic and social conditions that characterize work and the global division of labor, political economy, or more precisely the political economy of knowledge work, is used in this study as the platform for analysis. What I argue is that call centers have become one of the most instrumental workplaces and industries in post-industrial capitalism because they function as a principal mechanism through which businesses and governments interact with customers, clients, and citizens, at least for now. Most of us know these ubiquitous and faceless workers by a number of designations: "customer service agents" and "customer service representatives", "callers", "telemarketers", and "emergency services operators". But how did the call center become so central in our interactions with complex organizations? Why are "offshoring" and "outsourcing" so synonymous with a workplace that has as its origins the humble telephone operator, dispatcher, and reservation desk? Is it accurate to describe call centers as industries or sectors in their own right?

Thomas Friedman (2005) popularized the idea of a global call center industry with his now-infamous "flat world" treatise. For Friedman, the international promulgation of call centers was made possible by open economies and revolutions in technology. Of course, his account is also known for its subservience to a deterministic vision of information technology and the extent to which his writing appeases a corporate vision of globalization. For these reasons Friedman has been described by critics as the "court philosopher" for financial capital-driven globalization (see Chakravartty 2008). Such accounts of the call center's development, however, are closer to the end of the story than the beginning.

What my book asks is how political economic conditions precipitated the rise of call centers as a particular development in the history of telecommunications and knowledge work. The study departs from the idealistic depictions of call centers as utopian post-industrial workplaces, but simultaneously problematizes uniform characteristics of employment in IT enabled services. Third, the book situates labor and unionism as the cornerstone of investigation. The foremost question here is: *what are the challenges facing trade unions in Canada and India in their attempts at unionizing call centers?* Canada and India have been selected as comparative studies because of their prominence as leading destinations for call center services. Cases and participants have been drawn from a handful of organizations that reflect the types of trade unions and professional associations that have come to represent workers in the information technology (IT) and IT enabled services (ITES) sectors, which include call centers. Specifically, the United Steelworkers (USW) in Canada, the Union for ITES Professionals (UNITES), the IT Professionals Forum (ITPF), and the Young Professionals Collective (YPC) in India, Unite the Union (Unite) in the UK, and the Swiss-based Union Network International (UNI), are used to construct a narrative of global trade unionism.

What the book maintains is that post-industrialism has not resolved the contradictions or crises within capitalism, nor have such developments deflected the deterioration of working conditions in seemingly prestigious industries. Such a perspective on theories of post-industrialism and knowledge work also suggests that the globalization of call centers *vis-à-vis* offshore outsourcing is not as seamless as populists like Thomas Friedman suggest. Attempts by multinational corporations to establish call centers in Mumbai, Bangalore, and the National Capital Region of India, for example, are met with a host of economic, social, and even cultural barriers. In the past four years, a growing number of British, American, and Canadian firms have even recalled their call center labor forces back to "home shores". Major players like BCE Inc., American Express Canada, Sears, and others have brought thousands of call center jobs back to Canada from facilities in India and the Philippines. There is even talk in the United States of an "insourcing" boom as American corporations bring production, mainly in manufacturing, back to domestic shores because of a sinking standard of living and stagnant wage rates among the American working class (Fishman 2012; *The Economist* 2013; Bounds 2013; Silcoff 2012). Some of this return is, however, only symbolic and does not signal an end to the offshore experiment.

For labor, often a neglected subcategory when compared to marvelous technologies that seemingly define this post-industrial era, the question of organizing and unionism, as a means not only of resistance to employer power but also a mechanism of channeling collective action into institutions of regulation, remains important. Workers are as much a part of this political economic conjuncture as the businesses that employ them and the technology that controls them. And the term "worker" is used here deliberately. As the case of attempts in India to organize IT and ITES workers suggests, labor organizations have been forced to contend with how the making of identities, in E.P. Thompson's (1963) sense of the process, has meant a departure from "worker" to that of "professional". This is not an act of false consciousness, itself a vulgar generalization of how collectivities and individuals are capable of understanding their social world, but a feature of how the call center industry selects to present itself and its employees. In fact, identity and professional monikers are part of the global division of call center work.

POST-INDUSTRIALISM AND THE CALL CENTER IMAGINATION

The business imagination has been particularly enamored with the promise of India, as the internationalization of capital and investment have moved substantially toward services after decades of being centered on manufacturing and primary commodity sectors. Indeed, the common conception of the offshoring and outsourcing of work is one determined by the idea of distant shores and foreign labor—as well as the decline of "domestic" opportunities and greater promises abroad—as *the* manifestation of globalization. Call centers are quintessential in this regard. In 2006, *Time* magazine featured on its cover an image of a female employee, presumably of Indian decent, dressed in a traditional dancer's outfit donning a telephone headset. The 2006 release of *Outsourced*, a film depicting the story of an American call center manager sent to India to train staff in the company's new offshore facility, further popularized a particular image, albeit comical, of Indian call center life. Four years later NBC aired a sitcom based on the movie of the same name. In India call centers have similarly entered the popular imagination through novels like Chetan Bhaghat's (2005) *One Night @ the Call Center*, itself released as a feature length film in 2008.[1] Thomas Friedman (2005) had written earlier of the Indian back office and customer service agent as prototypes for his vision of the new global economy, staffed by eager and highly skilled workers who were helping to make the world a flatter and less expensive place in which to conduct business. For those who seek to embrace the riches that service offshoring has to offer, and on the other side of the debate those who lobby for restrictions on the use of foreign workers, India has become a convenient poster child for such causes.

Behind the imagery of India as the back office and call center hub for the world's businesses and, increasingly, governments, is a complex and more "nearshore" reality of call centers. For years, Canada grew in prominence as a world leader in the offshore and outsourced call center business, along with other wealthy economies that make up the OECD (Organization for Economic Cooperation and Development), like Ireland and the UK. As I show, the financial crisis that began in 2007–2008 upset the existing patterns of outsourcing and offshoring by moving more investment and jobs toward emerging economies, like India. Still, the flow of trade and investment are strongest between the most privileged and advanced capitalist countries (UNCTAD 2004, 2006). Only since 2009 have developing and transitional economies, another term used for developing countries that are experiencing massive economic growth, begun to receive a near-equal share of foreign direct investment (FDI), although this growth in prosperity has been made more uncertain by the ongoing global economic crisis (UNCTAD 2012).

In 2009, almost 75 percent of FDI outflows originated in the developed economies, down from nearly 85 percent in 2008, prior to the financial crisis (UNCTAD 2010). This is especially true for the higher valued business and IT services trade. A shift has occurred in recent years from these higher cost destinations to places like India and the Philippines, but the economic terrain of offshoring and outsourcing is hardly one where the so-called peripheral economies have been the only recipients of value-added services and employment. Earlier accounts point to the United States as home to more call centers than any other country, employing over four million workers in excess of 60,000 facilities (Head 2003; Holman, Batt, and Holtgrewe 2007). As in India, the expansion of the call center industry in

Canada has been conditioned by technological innovations in telecommunications that have developed in tandem with changing regimes of regulation. The reproduction of inequalities and issues of underdevelopment in advanced and emerging economies also accompany such transformations. It is no coincidence that Canada's Atlantic provinces, notably Nova Scotia and New Brunswick, were at the forefront of recruiting call centers as an answer to the region's economic stagnation throughout the 1990s. A similar claim can be made of India's emergence as a call center hub, despite the obvious differences between the two countries.[2]

Amidst the uncertainty in how the story of call center, information technology, and service occupation offshoring will unfold, it is important to consider the rate of economic development taking place in India and, to a greater extent, China. The Italian political economist, Giovanni Arrighi (2007, 1), noted in his final book that the changing contours of world systems can be described as an "economic renaissance of East Asia" because of the growing significance of the region in the world economy. An increasing flow of investment to the region from the developed economies is one feature of this transition. The conditions for this renaissance, Arrighi argued, have been building after a long and gradual revolt against the West's hegemony in the world economy, with signs of social and economic empowerment starting to bear fruit throughout Asia. Arrighi positioned an interpretation of Adam Smith's *Wealth of Nations* as a foundation for his analysis of the shift in global power and economic relations from West to East. The release of his work was timely because it was published on the precipice of the 2007 financial collapse, which created conditions for nations like India to take further advantage of an integrated global economy.

Along with these cultural images attached to call center employment are the conditions of work in information technology enabled spaces. Our interaction with call centers, part of the broader ITES and business process operations (BPO), or business process management (BPM) as it is now called in the industry literature, is ubiquitous. At times these exchanges are banal, sometimes frustrating, and at other moments pressing and necessary, as might be the case with telehealth or emergency services. But how often do we, as users of call center services, consider the conditions of employment, the access to wages and benefits these workers possess? What about the recognition of these workers as unionized employees? Equally significant is the fact that much of our interaction with major institutions is now mediated through a telecommunications network that is in many ways as old as commercial telephony itself, despite our thinking of call centers as a relatively new phenomenon. There is much activism and literature on offshore garment and textile sweatshops, but the condition of service work is often overlooked. How often does it cross our minds that prison labor in India, China, and even the United States is used to staff outsourced call centers? Would consumers tolerate this of a garment manufacturer? Similarly, there is acceptance in the consumers' eye that textiles and manufactured goods need to be produced in low-wage economies for these products to be affordable, but there is offense to interacting with foreign workers for customer service.

What the global division of call center work signifies is not just a process of globalization, but an evolution in corporate capitalism. Businesses are agents in creating economic conditions that demand a shift in accumulation, the use of foreign labor markets, and how organizations interact with customers. As the size and complexity of corporations expanded, so too did the need for more sophisticated models of organizing production and human resources. Even before the introduction of advanced communication and information technology in the workplace, the growing scale of markets demanded a scientific and professionalized class of managers to oversee national and international operations (see Chandler 1977). Call centers developed to provide efficient and technological-enabled interactions with vast numbers of customers in increasingly large organizations. Banks and telecommunications companies pioneered the use of call centers as a dedicated instrument to interface with customers in the late 1970s, but it was not until the 1980s and early 1990s that call centers became the ubiquitous means by which utilities, healthcare providers, transportation and freight companies, social service agencies, travel and entertainment providers, and sales firms conducted their core and non-core activities through inbound, outbound, and "blended" customer-contact centers (Russell 2009).

Call centers are defined as dedicated operations in which employees receive inbound or make outbound telephone calls, with those calls controlled and processed by an automatic call distribution (ACD) or predictive dialing system. The operations, which constitute call center processes, permit customer-employee interaction to occur simultaneously with the use of display screen equipment and instant access to information. For leading scholars in the field of call center studies, like Phil Taylor and Peter Bain (1999), as well David Holman (2005), this technologically mediated interaction between agents and customers helps distinguish this type of work from other working. environments. Furthermore, what differentiates *call* centers from *contact* centers is the former's reliance on voice-based interactions, whereas the latter depend on other technologically mediated processes, such as email, social media, or fax.

Since the late 1990s, call center employment has been the subject of debate among labor scholars, with much of the discussion stemming from the literature on computer-assisted employment a decade or more earlier. As the field of call center studies matured, a general consensus emerged that call center work could be described as repetitive, heavily scripted, and routinely surveilled. These conditions were accompanied with a long list of physical and mental strains that are characteristic of this type of employment (Zweig 2005). Employee selection criteria have subsequently been designed to recruit prospective workers who are mentally and physically capable of dealing with these strains (Callaghan and Thompson

2002). Such features make call center labor processes consistent with the elementary aspects of scientific management, as initially conceived by American engineer and stop-and-motion man, Frederick Winslow Taylor (2005/1911). This is why sensationalist monikers like "electronic sweatshops" and "Roman slave ships" have been used by labor organizers and scholars to describe the industry (see Garson 1988; Remesh 2004a, 2004b). Claims of "proletarianization", "cybertariat", and "cyber coolies" are similarly used to describe these new factory workers of the 21st century (see Norling 2001; Huws 2003; Remesh 2004a, 2004b). For many reasons there is justification for using pejorative language to classify work in the sector. The use of underemployed and marginalized populations is a practice routinely used by the industry as a means of keeping wages low. A globalized division of labor has enhanced the comparative advantage of lower wage regions like India.

For these reasons much of the literature on call center work is indebted to the work of Harry Braverman (1974) and his seminal book, *Labor and Monopoly Capital*, which launched the field of critical labor process theory. Braverman advanced the idea that the intrusion of scientific management into the labor process, originating in the work of F.W. Taylor, was a pivotal historic moment whereby labor was deprived of its control over the processes of work. Richard Edwards (1979) and Michael Burawoy (1979) furthered Braverman's political reading of work and management practices some years later. While these and other studies of the labor process are not without critics, the principal aim of labor process scholarship has been to establish a political economy of work that ties together technology, social relations, and regimes of control with the study of labor. It is a perspective that Michael Burawoy (1979, 1985) has labeled the *politics of production*.

While the focus on knowledge work is underdeveloped in the works of Braverman and the earlier Burawoy, they nevertheless set the stage for future treatments of post-industrial labor that effectively capture the nature of knowledge labor processes specifically. But there has also been a decidedly activist bent to much of the research in the area. Ellen Cassedy and Karen Nussbaum's (1983) *9 to 5* helped to account for the gendered nature of work as well as to dispel myths surrounding post-industrial employment. As a politically charged "how-to" guide for working women, *9 to 5* acknowledged trade unionism's importance to office workers as the ranks of largely female service employees grew. Their work eventually gained public fame when Hollywood star Jane Fonda produced a film of the same name in 1980 depicting the lives of women who had taken enough from their patronizing male boss and locked him away in his own mansion as revenge. Most importantly, Cassedy and Nussbaum spoke about the rationalization and reorganization of supposedly professional categories of employment just as call centers were an emerging workplace in the rapidly expanding post-industrial economy.

Near the end of the 1990s, two contrasting portrayals of call centers had entered the public consciousness. The sector's proponents presented exciting images of a call center, staffed by contented, professional workers talking with customers in a pleasing and skilled manner. Opposed to this vision, commentators offered an alternative perspective whereby electronic surveillance made total the supervisor's power over labor; perspectives that were supported by sensationalized depictions of call centers as "new sweatshops" and "dark Satanic mills" (Fernie and Metcalf 1998). While the severity and extent of these dismal depictions have been justifiably challenged (see Bain and Taylor 2000), technological advances have indeed enhanced the capacity for managerial control over the work performed in call centers (e.g., computer monitoring programs, CCTV, etc.). As early as the 1980s, scholars were beginning to identify the ubiquitous nature of electronic surveillance in the workplace as computerization was taking hold (Garson 1988; Zuboff 1988; Zureik 2003; Zureik, Mosco, and Lochhead 1988; Lyon and Zureik 1996; Stevens and Lavin 2007). Indeed, as surveillance scholars argue, various methods of supervision have always been crucial features of capitalist enterprises, with monitoring and control argued to be at the center of economic activity (Ball 2003; Lyon 2001; Rule 1996). But what makes call center work unique is that the general characteristics of employment, and the fundamental processes of labor, are *constituted by* a particular form of managerial control *vis-à-vis* electronic monitoring and the physical configuration of work that gives advantage to management by facilitating spatial, technical, and social control (see Batt 2002; Baldry, Bain, and Taylor 1998; Baldry 1999). From the construction of workplace culture, to the content of voice interactions with customers, and even the entry and exit to call center facilities, surveillance is a fixture in the arrangement of space and the labor process. Human resource management practices and philosophies ordered around flat hierarchical structures, constant surveillance, streamlined customer service interactions, and lean production systems have also been tuned specifically to meet the requirements of this type of post-industrial employment.

When information technology entered the workplace, Taylorism was well suited to the task of regulating this new economy, exemplified in management scholarship starting around the early 1990s (Davenport 2005, 1993; Davenport and Prusak 1998; Hammer and Champy 2003; Liker 2004). Few business activities escaped the attention of business process re-engineers, including functions related to sales, marketing, customer relations, accounting, personnel management and even medicine (Head 2003). Indeed, much ink has been spilled trying to recast scientific management in a modern light, especially with the rapid pace of technological development. For critical labor scholars this reinforces the importance of identifying the role of labor within information revolutions (Downey 2003, 2001).

It follows from these generalizations that possibilities for resistance, the transformation of work, and collective action are subordinate to functional, and highly sensationalized, categories of call center employment. In reality the conditions are far more complex. Even outside the discussion of resistance, workers still manage to salvage redeemable qualities of call center employment. After a lengthy conversation about the negative aspects of his job, one inbound customer service representative in Kingston, Ontario said to me, "There are times when I get a lot out of it, like when I use my brain . . . [I]f I could add a little comfort to a person's day, that's something I like doing" (interview with Paul 2008).

Personal identity, authenticity, and emotional labor are further characteristics that have been subject to the process of routinization and organizational management. In fact, emotion itself is a service commodity packaged and sold by the call center industry—a reminder that the standardization of human interactions extends economic rationality to an otherwise social space (Leidner 1993; Scharf 2003; Hochschild 1983). Customer service representatives act as creators of emotion and are not simply processing or transmitting information. The models of value-added customization have greater implications than just offering blanket suggestions for call center labor processes (Batt 2002). Emotional labor is intensely social, demanding skill and varying levels of depth. Ignoring this critical aspect of service employment generates overly simplistic and inaccurate accounts of call center work. Worker control over emotion as part of the labor process can also be an exercise in resistance when customer service agents are forced to confront abusive clients.

For call centers servicing foreign customers, managerial control over emotion is not only an additional layer of exploitation, but also an important contribution to how space and culture help to develop particular working conditions and labor processes. Despite the gendered nature of the industry, this identity and platform for inequality is "eclipsed" by racial hierarchies embedded in transnational call center work, to use Mirchandani's (2005) phrase. Control over emotive reactions contains additional significance when agents attempt to deal with racism by customers. Requiring workers to undergo "accent neutralization" and assume supposedly western identities and names is part of this hierarchy. A growing global division of knowledge work amplifies these problematic features of call center work. What this means is that Arjun Appadurai's (1996) *production fetishism* and *fetishism of the consumer* play instrumental roles in conforming possibilities of resistance as well as structure the labor processes. For customers, the fetishism of the consumer sustains the illusion that they constitute the most important social actor in business relationships, when in fact producers and other forces within the production process are equally significant seats of agency. Customers still play an active role in defining global social relations, as Mirchandani (2004a, 2004b, 2012) and others (Coyle 2010; Poster 2007) demonstrate, by sabotaging attempts by companies to shift services to low-wage regions, by abusing foreign workers or expressing dissatisfaction with the companies themselves, or both. Such are the cultural and social characteristics of the now globalized call center.

Labor scholars, like Ursula Huws (2009, 2003), correctly emphasize that call centers represent a microcosm of the post-industrial economy and knowledge production as a whole. What makes the labor process distinctive is how telecommunications technology is integrated with call distribution systems and interactive software (Taylor and Bain 1999). This complexity has created a challenge for scholars, unions, and businesses in their attempts to develop comprehensive theories, organize, and create lobbying strategies for these important workplaces. In Canada, the United States, and Mexico, the term "telephone call center" (56142) is defined by the North American Industry Classification System (NAICS) as an *industry*

> comprised of establishments primarily engaged in receiving and/or making telephone calls for others. These establishments are engaged in activities such as soliciting or providing information; promoting products or services; taking orders; and raising funds for clients. This industry also includes establishments primarily engaged in answering telephone calls and relaying messages to clients; and establishments primarily engaged in providing voice mailbox services (Statistics Canada n.d.a.)

Included in this definition is an eclectic mix of floral wire services, telemarketing bureaus, wake-up call services, and so on. And, as a subcategory of "business support services", call centers are accompanied by collection agencies, credit bureaus, business service centers, and document preparation. However, the gathering and tabulation of public opinion data, providing paging services, conducting a fund-raising campaign, and a handful of other services are officially *excluded* from the technical "telephone call center" designation. This is despite their similar, and in some cases identical, work processes and management systems. The NAICS also recognizes call centers as *third party* establishments providing services for other organizations, not in-house divisions or customer service departments.

In India, call centers are referred to as part of the broader business process outsourcing (BPO) designation, along with dozens of occupations and workplaces that constitute the information technology enabled services (ITES) sector. BPOs provide services such as data processing, product development, payroll and benefits administration, recruitment services, leave management, and a host of customer interaction services that are facilitated through call centers (see Nasscom 2004). Call centers, to be sure, continue to be the cornerstone of ITES-BPO mainly because they represent the human face of India's dynamic global business and IT services industry. In 2012, Nasscom urged for the rebranding of BPO to that of business process management (BPM), if only to reflect the higher value products and services that Indian companies have started to provide to international clients. And, whereas business process *outsourcing* is meant to denote the cost savings associated with this practice, business process *management* represents value-added knowledge-based products and services, like complex data analytics, financial and accounting processing, legal processes, patent filing, and so on—predominately the most skill-intensive segment of BPOs (BPO India 2012). The two terms are used synonymously throughout the book because the shift in terminology is a product of marketing and not a qualitative change in meaning for what Indian ITES companies produce. "ITES", meanwhile, includes any form of employment that is *enabled* through information technology, while "IT" is sometimes used as a moniker for anything ITES-BPO/BPM. As an industry, however, IT includes the advanced planning, design, and conception phases of knowledge production, as well as the design and manufacturing of information and communication technology (ICT). It is the difference between working at Infosys's world class Bangalore campus and taking calls from international clients in the city's BPO suburb of Electronic City. For the country's nascent trade unions and labor associations, UNITES, the YPC, and the ITPF, have identified the expanse of ITES and BPOs in particular, not just call centers, because of the overlapping policy, regulation, and business environment that govern these workplaces.

Throughout the book, however, the following typology of a call center will be used: it requires considerable technical knowledge to perform; it is dependent on rapidly evolving information and communication technology systems; it provides mostly immaterial services; it can be located virtually anywhere in the world, depending on the availability of infrastructure; it caters to the customized *and* mass production demands of clients and firms; it is subject to scientifically managed labor processes, with these processes conditioned by where the call center is situated in the industry (e.g., telemarketing versus customer care); the services provided can be conducted in-house or as a subcontracted third party; and finally, call center work is gendered, classed, and racialized, with the division of labor in the global industry determined by the nature of information handling and processing (Huws 2009; Martin 2002; Buchanan and Koch-Schulte 2000; Remesh and Neetha 2008; Belt 2002; Belt and Richardson 2000; Mirchandani 2005; Basi 2009). And, because call center work involves direct and immediate interaction with customers, work processes and conditions of employment develop unique characteristics that set the industry apart from other areas of knowledge production. For these reasons, business and industry groups in both Canada and India, like Contact Center Canada and the National Association for Services and Software Companies (Nasscom) respectively, have isolated call centers as a unique industry worthy of independent lobbying, research, and "best practices". It is the labor process and configuration of customer/client-employee interactions that define call centers as an industry.

POLITICAL ECONOMY AND POST-INDUSTRIALISM

Innovators in the field of political economy argue that the strength of this approach is its capacity to realize the power dynamics that bind the economic, political, and cultural/ideological moments of social life (Clement 1997). As political economist and communications scholar Vincent Mosco (2009, 25) maintains, political economy constructs a totality that includes the political, social, and cultural realms where the whole is irreducible to the sum of its parts and focuses on a "study of *the social relations, particularly the power relations, that mutually constitute the production, distribution, and consumption of resources*" (emphasis added). As such, political economy identifies interrelationships as the elements of a totality that possess tensions and contradictions that generate conditions for the emergence of struggles and resistance. A *critical* political economy, therefore, is concerned with how intellectual and practical resistance can inform a commitment to understanding and *transforming* the prevailing social order. Political economy is just as concerned with the study of the labor process as a political process that plays a part in reproducing social relations.

In the political economy discourse, interrelationships are described as mutual constitution, namely that social processes cannot be fully grasped without piecing together a comprehensive and emergent program of analysis. Research on work, economic development, offshoring, outsourcing, globalization, and neo-liberalism, for instance, is dependent upon the interrelated social relations that bind a given field of study. Political economy, then, is a piercing conceptual and methodological tool calibrated precisely for the task of addressing the power relations invested in economic management. As Scottish moralist Adam Smith (2003/1776, 537) described it, political economy is "considered as a branch of the science of a statement or legislation" concerned with the provision of subsistence and revenue for the state and its people. Foucault added to this explanation that political economy is also a process of "isolating the economy as a specific sector of reality" and a science of intervention by the government into that reality and wielded as a modern discourse of governing (cited in Birla 2010, 21–22). In both cases the political economy denotes sets of practices and ways of rendering intelligible the intersection of state structures, economic affairs, power, and social formations.

It is through this interpretation of political economy that a characterization of a global division of call center work is constructed. Following the work of political geographer David Harvey (2005a), I maintain that a re-articulated version of classical economics, generally understood as neo-liberalism, has become a leading force in the shaping of contemporary globalization and call center employment. Global economic development is determined by this definition of neo-liberal philosophy, which was embraced in the 1980s following the political interventions by leading banks, insurance companies, retail chains, automobile manufacturers, oil companies, aerospace firms, and other corporations located in Western nations, as well as Japan, which sought to reorganize the political and economic landscape in the interest of rapid profit accumulation and the fluidity of capital (Schiller 1999). This development was spurred in response to the economic crises of the 1970s, specifically the stagnant rates of profit that were illustrated by business and industry lobby groups as symptoms of Keynesian macroeconomic policies.

Neo-liberal economic models, which have evolved from classical economic theory, stress that the absence of barriers to trade and the flow of capital is inherently beneficial for both private enterprises and the citizenry in general, who benefit from increased wealth, lower prices, and expanded economic opportunities (Weeks 2001). For Harvey, neo-liberalism results in the "financialization of everything and the relocation of the power center of capital accumulation to owners and their financial institutions", marked by a de-centered and unstable evolutionary process (Harvey 2006a; 24–25, 41). Such a process of financialization has been empowered, and in fact made possible by intellectual traditions, economic actors, and policy-makers operating in a purposeful manner with the intent of configuring government policy making around the interests of capital accumulation (see Harvey 2005a, 2005b). The defining features of this system—namely an expansive regime of commercialization, liberalization, and privatization (Mosco 2009)—are brought upon by intensive state interventions on behalf of capital. It would not be inaccurate to define these accomplishments, from the viewpoint of multinational enterprises, as what Karl Polanyi (1944) feared to be the ultimate subordination of social institutions to economic interests and practices.

Within the broader overtures of global capitalism, neo-liberalism is established by intensive regulatory frameworks (governed by the market) that limit the power of labor, allow for rapid and relatively unfettered flows of capital and money, and further enforce the sanctity of private property over that of public services. This has meant subordinating social policy-making to economic interests that favor technical (but ideologically motivated) indicators of growth and development over democratic participation in political affairs, especially as it pertains to the generation and distribution of wealth. Business elites, along with their intellectual support system and political allies, actualize a neo-liberal model of governance through an entrenchment of possessive individualism in public policy, economic decision making, and cultural transformations. Neo-liberalism is ultimately a term used to describe profound assaults on existing forms of social solidarity, using the state to advance pro-business policies and to defend the interests of capital rather than investing in social programs and public goods. This is what defines the term as a *socio-political project*. But as with any project, neo-liberalism is not unilaterally imposed, nor has it been left unchallenged; there is tremendous confrontation and opposition that demands intensive state involvement. Adam Smith (2003/1776,

95) recognized that powerful classes bind together and "call aloud for the assistance of the civil magistrate, and the rigorous execution against the combinations of servants, laborers, and journeymen". Labor, on the other hand, has historically been prohibited from such combinations and subjected to persecution and repression, as Webb and Webb (1920) recount in their classic study of trade unionism.

Drawing from the work of Pearce and Tombs (1998), neo-liberalism is characterized throughout the book as a struggle for hegemony, albeit incomplete and nowhere established in a pure, unadulterated form. One example is the appeal neo-liberalism has for policy-makers who argue that business interests are best served by pro-market policies that revoke the interventionist role of the state in economic management. Such claims are evidenced by examples of state-supported policies that have functioned as catalysts for the development of IT and ITES industries, which I explore further in Chapter 2. In India, Five Year Plans since at least 1997 have been attentive to the significance of state and national government involvement in building the country's IT sector. Pro-business reforms in the country preceded liberalization and were brought about by political forces that channeled the support of certain sections of capital toward transforming the regulatory structure of the economy in the direction of market-driven competitiveness. The story is not so different in Canada. Government subsidies and changes to provincial legislation have helped entice foreign companies to establish call centers in the country. Foreign direct investment, policies aimed at reducing corporate taxes, and weakened labor market regulations continue to be integral dimensions of neo-liberal and post-industrial capitalism in both national cases.

What I argue is that the neo-liberal philosophy of economic management and relations has worked to frame and develop a particular form of post-industrialism, of which call centers are a part. The premise of post-industrialism is also based on the mythical ascendancy of knowledge production as the primary resource within advanced economies. Fiber optic networks, satellite communications systems, advances in microprocessor technology, and the growing use of computers in the workplace have indeed provided the physical infrastructure for post-industrial economic formations. Along with these marvelous innovations in technology, the technical features of post-industrialism have been shaped by telecommunications regimes, on which call centers and ITES, generally, depend. Political economist and communications scholar Robert McChesney (2007, xii) is astute with his observation that the communications revolution was not a consequence of "geniuses and free markets", but the result of structures and markets "created and shaped by policies and extraordinary public subsidies". Indeed, it has been the policies of governments and decisions of corporations that have decided the course of post-industrial economic development.

North America's dot-com boom of the early 1990s also produced the idea that the crises and contradictions of capitalism could be resolved through exciting advances in IT, notably personal computers and the spread of the Internet for peaceful, civilian purposes. The dot-com collapse, meanwhile, heralded a subsequent bubble, this time in real estate and complex financial instruments, which proved to be even more fragile. But the high-tech bust of the late 1990s showed that post-industrialism failed to provide a solution to inherent crises of capitalism. In the 1970s, Daniel Bell remarked in his landmark volume, *The Coming of Post-Industrial Society*, that the "idea of a post-industrial society, like that of industrial society, or capitalism, has meaning only as a *conceptual* scheme. It identifies a new axial principle of social organization and defines a common core of problems which societies that become more and more post-industrial have to confront" (Bell 1999/1973, 114, emphasis added). Post-industrialism, as a concept, has always signified a set of social and economic problems rather than a definitive era or resolution to economic contradictions.

The term post-industrialism actually goes back to the early 20th century and was coined by the English-trained Indian scholar, Ananda K. Coosmaraswamy. Coosmaraswamy suggested that industrial civilization would collapse and allow for the return of a decentralized society. He was not far off from the socialists and anarchists of the time and their vision that from the ashes of industrial society would come a new world order. A post-industrial society, Coosmaraswamy anticipated, would involve a rediscovery of cultural diversity, which was threatened by the centralized and standardized practices of industrialism (cited in Mattelart 2003). Mythologizing seems to be a handy tool for futurist and post-industrial prospectors alike. Before Friedman's "flat world" was Francis Fukuyama's (1992) infamous "end of history" thesis, wherein political and economic forms of organization had reached a zenith in this technologically-induced vision. Sensationalist claims such as this have been the subject of debate for decades. Futurists like Alvin Toffler (1980) acknowledged the social implications that should accompany technological predictions, while others have pointed to the interconnected realities of myth and social institutions invested in these processes (Mosco 2004).

Post-industrialism, as a conceptual tool *and* as a phase in the development of capitalism, has, as its circulatory system, communications networks that permit the flow of information and knowledge. The maintenance of post-industrial relations of production is conditioned by such systems. Dallas Smythe (1981, 1977) and Herbert Schiller, founding scholars of the political economy school of communications, took to task questions of power as they existed in the fields of mass media and, generally, mass communication. One of the guiding concerns that steered Schiller's (1973) work was the extent to which consciousness and political manipulation influenced the character of, and prospects for, new information technology. The question being asked was: *for whose benefit and whose control would such technologies be implemented*? In Canada, Rideout (2002), Babe (1975, 1990, 2000, 2008), Mosco and Schiller (2001), and a host of others (see

Kozolanka 2006; Mosco and McKercher 2006; Moll and Shade 2008) have wielded this question to understand the historical context leading to the development of the policy and physical infrastructure that is the foundation of Canada's telecommunications system. India's booming telecommunications market has also drawn significant scholarly and policy attention, as I explain in Chapters 5 and 6.

Where a political economy of post-industrialism and communications converge is in the field of work and labor. Bell (1999/1973) may have written one of the most recognized treatises on a coming post-industrial society, but earlier attempts at understanding the significance of economic transformations were evident in the work of Fritz Machlup (1962) and renowned management theorist, Peter Drucker (1959), as early as the late 1950s. What continues to make Machlup's work innovative is his positioning of labor and employment as a point of departure in the analysis of what was at the time an emerging knowledge economy. "The question", he asked, "is whether, how, and to what extent the occupational composition of the labor force and of employment has changed, and how this change is connected with the changing role of knowledge-production in the economy" (Machlup 1962, 377).

In the 21st century, policy-makers and academics have yet to resolve these concerns, lending credence to the claim that post-industrialism is indeed a term describing a transitory era. Take for example Richard Florida, spokesperson for the "creative class" and creative capitalism thesis (see Florida 2002), and his advising of the Ontario government in Canada. The province spent a lavish $2 million commissioning a report, *Ontario in the Creative Age*, by the Martin Prosperity Institute, which is headed by Florida (Martin Prosperity Institute 2009). The report illustrates the need for government investment to help develop a creative class of workers required for this new economy. India's premier IT-ITES industry group, Nasscom (National Association of Software and Services Companies) has since its founding in 1988 focused on how the knowledge society has impacted the country's economic terrain and progress on social development (see Nasscom 2008a). These are by no means hollow attempts at economic planning. Machlup and others indicated in their projections of economic development that the rise of service and knowledge production would herald new challenges not only for governments and industry, but also for labor. The transition, these scholars recognized, has constructed new inequalities in the labor market as well as maintained old ones, creating social and economic problems that needed to be managed politically. Call center employment, I maintain, is situated in this spectrum of *knowledge work and production*, as initially described by Machlup's classic study.

India and Canada have both benefited from this division of labor that characterizes post-industrial capitalism, particularly as it relates to the global call center industry. Certainly, the questions that social theorists and policy-makers raised about knowledge production throughout the second half of the 20th century have now taken on international dimensions, as Chapter 2 illustrates. In the early 1980s, Folker Fröbel, Jurgen Heinrichs, and Otto Kreye (1980) wrote of the emergence of a *new* international division of labor and charted the changes taking place in the world economy. While their thesis paid closest attention to the industrial sector, Fröbel and his collaborators observed that the emergence of a global economy throughout the 1970s created conditions in which the survival of major companies could only be assured through the transnational reorganization and relocation of production. This transformation brought about the development of an international division of labor through which commodity production was increasingly subdivided into fragments that could be assigned to different parts of the world, in turn providing the most profitable combination of capital and labor in the global networks of manufacturing (Fröbel, Heinrichs, and Kreye 1980).

Where the "old" international division of labor was based on the trade of raw materials by underdeveloped regions, the "new" division of labor is one dependent on the relocation of production, mainly of labor-intensive processes, to less developed countries where labor is more plentiful (Taylor and Thrift 1982). Southeast and South Asia are the leading recipients of FDI among the developing regions for the reasons Fröbel et al. outlined in their classic study, with India and China counted in the top five investment locations in the world (UNCTAD 2009). Limitations to the new international division of labor (NIDL) hypothesis, namely its silence on how labor forces and markets are developed, ultimately gave way to a global division of labor (GDL), as Chapter 2 elaborates.

Advocates for the liberalization of trade emphasize that a growing international division of labor has led to increases in standards of living, as measured through quantifiable economic metrics, such as GDP growth. Much of the intellectual and ideological support for "free trade" is built upon the arguments advanced by 19th century political economist David Ricardo, who maintained that an extension of foreign trade would "increase the mass of commodities, and therefore the sum of enjoyments" (Ricardo 1911, 77). But Ricardo's claim does not simply denote a division of labor premised on *absolute* advantage, as Smith (2003/1776) argued, but one of *comparative* advantage, in which economies would concentrate efforts on producing goods that they are the *least* poor at producing. Eli Heckscher and Bertil Ohlin (see Heckscher and Ohlin 1991), Paul Samuelson (1947, 2004), Albert Hirschman (1945), and other economists extend the Ricardian model of comparative cost differences, adding to the development of what is understood as classical political economy. Throughout the 1980s, critical political economists started to pay closer attention to knowledge production and the changing internationalized strategies of multinational firms (see Mytelka 1987; Caporaso 1987). The newest dimension of the global division of labor is one decidedly oriented around knowledge production, as the United Nation's chief organization responsible for analyzing trade and development, UNCTAD (2004, 2006), has recognized.

For knowledge workers, the global division of labor has extended the realm of economic turbulence that initially characterized the globalization of manufacturing. Offshoring and outsourcing, initially a practice adopted by multinational industrial firms, has become standard for leading IT and service companies from the wealthy *and* developing economies. By 2004, over 60 percent of total foreign direct investment (FDI) stock flowed to the service sector, compared to less than 25 percent in 1970 (UNCTAD 2004). The offshoring of work is a reflection of the liberalization of trade and part of the broader efforts to implement comparative advantage as the central support base for trade policies. These tendencies are supported by the fact that in 2009, 71 out of 102 new national policy measures affecting FDI favored a move toward further liberalization and promotion of foreign investment (UNCTAD 2010). What labor scholars have recognized for at least a decade is that the globalization of knowledge work has come to condition the prospects for labor organizations, namely trade unions, and their allies. How workers have begun to respond to the global division of service work is a leading concern in union literature and scholarly research (see Mosco and Stevens 2007; Huws 2003; Mosco and McKercher 2006; Sarikakis and Shade 2008; Frenkel, Korczynski, Shire, and Tam 1999; Young Professionals Collective and Focus on the Global South 2005; Van Jaarsveld 2004; Brophy 2006, 2009).

TOWARD A POST-INDUSTRIAL UNIONISM?

Bell (1999/1973) observed that a full-scale analysis of the problems facing labor in post-industrial society would have to include the nature of trade unionism. He was referring to the changing occupational structures that labor organizations represent. Unions would necessarily have to reconfigure their strategies to recruit workers from sectors that had traditionally fallen outside their scope and interest, particularly in professions dominated by women. Identity formation and status constitute an additional challenge. The neo-liberal forecast of post-industrialism described by Peter Drucker (1959) suggested that the knowledge society would be driven by entrepreneurialism and liberal individualism. Drucker added that this new generation of worker would be decidedly middle class and identify as "professional" in "outlook, expectations, rewards, opportunities and values"; class, he emphasized, would be outstripped by educational attainment as a material basis for inequality. Drucker's observations are strikingly relevant today and his conceptualization of "professionalized" workers has had real consequences for union organizers trying to make gains in IT-ITES.

Research on how labor organizations have been able to recruit supporters often invokes an engagement with Tilly's (1978, 7) description of *mobilization* as "the process by which a group acquires collective control over the resources needed for action". Industrial relations scholar John Kelly

(1998, 38) pushes further by emphasizing that consideration needs to be given to how individuals are transformed into collective actors "willing and able to create and sustain collective organization and engage in collective action against their employers". This concern is paramount when addressing the formation of unions and labor associations in industries that foster a sense of "professional" identities—an archetype for the individual, skilled, and mobile white-collar career person, who is reluctant to engage in collectivist practices traditionally associated with trade unions. As Strauss's (1964, 535) seminal treatment of engineering unions in the 1950s suggests, the professional "wants to expand the power, status, and freedom of his group", to be more successful at work, and to win greater job control and economic security. For Strauss, both professional aspirations and the demands of employment prompted the engineers in his study to identify as a collective. Similarly, the capacity of labor organizations to mobilize employees in IT and ITES is founded on their ability to appeal to the professional *and* employment-related needs of these workers.

Other pressures are generated in the global division of knowledge labor. Even public sector unions have had to contend with the displacement of employment as members are increasingly confronted with privatization and the contracting out, and sometimes offshoring, of government services. Austerity measures in the UK have prompted the government to employ Indian call center workers to service the country's National Health Service in efforts to slash costs and control deficits (*IBNLive* 2011). Incentives to cut the exploding cost of private health care delivery in the United States has also forced health sector companies to look to the subcontinent's back office providers as a relief to rising administrative costs at home (Barnes 2010; *The Economic Times* 2010). Canada's federal Conservative government has similarly targeted the public service labor force as ripe for austerity, pointing to privatization of service delivery as a means of rationalizing costs.

Labor unions representing workers employed in manufacturing have had a head start in this regard. The United Steelworkers (USW) and their allies in Europe and Oceania continue to build on the solidarity networks that have taken root in Latin America and South Africa, following the operations of major mining companies and steel manufacturers. Global union federations (GUFs), like the International Metalworkers Federation (IMF), the International Transportation Federation (ITF), and others, have acted as centers for developing union networks across borders, breathing some life into the possibility of union internationalism. But even these institutions are at a crossroads. GUFs reproduce the same inability to engage the rank and file and have failed to mobilize as social movements, in large part due to the even greater distance between the leadership and the members. For unions active in the knowledge sector, the ambition has been to avoid these pitfalls and develop cross-border strategies that draw directly from the conditions of employment—Union Network International (UNI), for example, is examined in Chapter 7 for this reason.

Knowledge workers certainly have a long and rich tradition of union activity, as the existence of media, print, engineering, and health sector unions indicate (McKercher 2002; Mosco and McKercher 2008; Lipset, Trow, and Coleman 1956; Strauss 1964). Workers affiliated with IT firms and business services, however, are mostly unrepresented. Only about 5 percent of workers in Canada's business support services are unionized, seven times lower than the service sector as a whole, according to the most recent figures (Akyeampong 2005). IT and ITES professionals who are unionized are often represented by labor organizations that cover entire industries, like the automotive and manufacturing sectors, but not specific to IT or ITES specifically. In India, call center workers, software engineers, and back office BPO workers have, since the dramatic growth of their ranks in the mid-1990s, mostly existed outside the scope of established unions. Interviews with the Union for ITES Professionals (UNITES) and the IT Professionals Forums (ITPF) reveal that it has been precisely *because of* the international character of the respective industries that IT and IT enabled services sectors have developed outside the existing regulatory environment and largely beyond the reach of unions. This has also meant that the emergence of these notable white-collar jobs has taken a trajectory away from the highly politicized and powerful trade unions and federations, which currently represent bank and state employees, themselves economically and socially privileged. UNITES, through the support of Union Network International (UNI), the world's leading service sector GUF, has worked to construct a union movement that avoids affiliation with traditions marked by long histories of militancy. Unfortunately the results, in terms of membership and activities, have been disappointing. Still, there is much to be gained from a study of UNI's direct involvement in India and the reasons for its limited successes in the region's high-tech workplaces.

REFLECTIONS ON THE STUDY

Using political economy as a methodology means developing critical interpretations of social phenomenon by accessing a range of sources with the purposes of exploring possibilities for resistance and change. The collection of information for research aimed at understanding the structural features of an international knowledge industry, and the attempts at unionizing workers in this sector, took several forms. Political economy offers a channel through which a range of literatures, primary sources, and interviews are compiled to establish a research design appropriate to a multinational comparative study. Such a method acknowledges the usefulness of drawing from extant texts like news publications and industry reports. Industry and union publications provide vital information on statistics, growth projections, strategies, and insights into the political aspirations of the organizations they represent. These are also significant sources for details on individual policy-makers and power brokers in respective institutions—this method was used to establish who should be interviewed and why. Media publications sometimes provide the most valuable sources as they can lead the researcher to uncover important individuals and organizations that define industries and national economic landscapes. Journalists and media sources also shed light on (and publish) facts about current events far quicker than peer-reviewed academic sources, making them significant and timely resources. Germane to this study is that debates between unions and industry representatives sometimes unfold in the press, as do public statements by politicians and industry leaders.

Interviews and field research for this study occurred primarily between May 2008 and October 2009; follow up interviews were conducted in 2012 and 2013. In total, over sixty semi-structured interviews were conducted with participants located in India, Canada, the UK, and Switzerland. From call center workplaces, to union offices, cafés, phone and Skype interviews, and even the monstrous ILO building in Geneva, I was introduced to the participants engaged with throughout the book. Most of my time in India was spent in the generous company of UNITES and other union activists that occupied the UNIDOC office in Bangalore where I conducted most of the interviews with union officials, rank-and-file activists, and staff. Union contacts were instrumental in helping me acquire interviews with local politicians, health and wellness consultants, and business people in the city. Nasscom also granted me an audience in their Delhi office to discuss the future of ITES-BPO in India, as well as to conduct a delicate conversation about unionism. In other cases, participants welcomed me into their homes to speak about life as call center workers and union activists. In an interesting turn of events, I ended up living for several weeks with graduate students in a southern suburb of New Delhi, where it turned out that one of my new roommates had worked for a brief time as a call center worker dealing with American customers. But it was in Bangalore that I became acquainted with the ubiquity of that city's exciting BPO nightlife. After losing my wallet and getting lost late at night amidst the maze of streets, a kind driver who ferried workers from the suburban workplaces of Electronic City back to their homes generously picked me up and helped me find my hotel. It was this immersion that provided me an appreciation for the social and cultural influences of call center development.

The USW (United Steelworkers) was used for the Canadian study because the union has over a decade's worth of experience in the call center industry, starting with the unionization of a financial services call center in Toronto in the 1990s. With a growing percentage of Steelworkers now employed in the service sector, the core competency of the trade union has been gradually shifting away from the manufacturing and commodities sectors in which it was founded. And, when, in 2007, the USW merged with Unite the Union (the largest trade union in the UK) and formed Workers Uniting, a third channel of research—international unionism—was incorporated into the study. USW researchers subsequently helped facilitate the recruitment of interview participants. After initial contacts were made, interviewees provided further contacts. With the exception of the one manager from Political Communications, a call center that performs polling and opinion surveys for left-of-center organizations and clients, none of the managers from the other unionized call centers agreed to participate in interviews. In fact, senior managers prohibited other supervisors from speaking with me about company business. To paraphrase one prosaic public relations officer from the company I call Visa Financial, who spoke to me briefly over the phone, "No one can speak for [the company] except for the CEO".

As for the Steelworkers, theirs is a tale of mixed success and regrettable losses, much like any number of unions facing de-industrialization, offshoring, and technology-induced redundancies. In 2009, two call centers located in the northern Ontario mining community of Sudbury forever closed their doors. At their peak, about 1,200 workers were employed by Omega Direct Response (OMDR) in the Sudbury operations. By winter of 2013, Visa Financial will have shut down its Vancouver call center and relocated these jobs to its Toronto facility. Over 120 call center workers were given notice before the USW local was forced to negotiate a closure agreement. Such is the fragile nature of call center employment, even in the relatively stable and profitable financial sector.

The Union for Information Technology Enabled Services Professionals (UNITES) was included in the study for one undeniable reason—it is the only trade union representing call center workers in India. Preceding the formation of UNITES in 2005, the Information Technology Professionals Forum (ITPF), a non-union association of managers and employees engaged in India's IT sector, was the only organization ostensibly seeking to represent the interests of various stakeholders in information technology workplaces. What connects both of these projects is Union Network International (UNI), a global union federation that was formed in 2000, which has provided seed money and support for a number of union projects in India. In fact, most of UNI's involvement in union organizing and bargaining takes place in India and other developing countries. The Young Professionals Collective (YPC) also began in the mid-2000s as Western companies were rushing into India to tap into the country's inexpensive human capital. This was an association centered around activists, most of whom functioned as legal professionals, who had an extensive history with social movements in India. Officials and members from each of these organizations were forthcoming about the strengths and limitations of their respective organizations, and their candidness provided exceptionally rich conversations and interviews. Research contacts often began as serendipitous discussions and progressed to a point of significance for the study. By 2009, the YPC ceased to function as an advocate for IT-ITES workers in India, as most of the membership from the country's BPOs had moved on to other careers. The most central activists, however, remain committed to social justice projects in Mumbai, as they continue to work as advocates for HIV/AIDS patients, sex workers, rag pickers and other hyper-exploited workers that populate the informal sector (personal communication with Rege 2013).

These interviews helped to construct a conceptual framework through which to understand the call center industry, its global expanse, as well as the nature of trade union activity. In both national case studies, over 400 media articles, government reports, organizational documents, industry publications, and personal correspondence were consulted in my effort to assemble a model that characterizes the political economic terrain on which call centers develop. Such texts are consistently deployed in research on call centers, unions, and labor studies (see Beirne, Riach, and Wilson 2004; Mulholland 2004; Norling 2001; Remesh 2004a, 2004b; Taylor and Bain 2008, 2005; Taylor et al. 2007; Buchanan and Koch-Schulte 2000). These sources also work to chronicle historically contextualized understandings of social phenomena, making it necessary to explain their production and material effects, as well as to interpret and render an understanding of their meaning. Political economy and media scholar Robert McChesney (1999) provides useful insights into the importance of delving into a broad spectrum of materials, especially those that come from business and government sources. An author, McChesney (1999, 8–9) writes, "must be immersed in trade and business literature to use it as the foundation for a scholarly argument".

The book is divided across six substantive chapters. Chapter 2 explores the nature of political economy research and the interrelationship between globalization, development, and the emergence of a global division of call center labor. The ambition of Chapter 3 is to provide a foundation for the examination of a political economy of call center employment through a review of existing research on call center work, starting in the late 1990s to the present. An analysis of a political economy of communications is established to engage with the question of how post-industrial workplaces and institutions are organized. Chapter 4 addresses the specific political economic condition that defines the internationalization of the call center industry, and the cases of Canada and India specifically. Here, government policies, corporate activities, and technological advances globally and nationally are accounted for in the broader regime of global telecommunications. Chapters 5 and 6 bring to the forefront the book's contribution to call center studies and union interventions in the industry. Finally, Chapter 7 draws attention to internationalist efforts by UNI, the global union federation at the cutting edge of mobilizing IT workers, Unite the Union, and the USW, in their attempts to build a transnational union movement.

2 The Globalization of Knowledge Work

Canada's largest financial institution, the Royal Bank of Canada, faced a firestorm of public anger in 2013. Gordon Nixon, RBC's CEO, was forced into damage control when news spread that the bank was subcontracting the work of some fifty in-house investor services employees based in Toronto to iGATE, an Indian ITES-BPM multinational company headquartered in Bangalore (Nixon 2013). Since 2005, iGATE has been working closely with the bank through the RBC Offshore Development Center in Bangalore (Tomlinson 2013a). Reports indicated that iGATE workers brought in from India were making less than $70,000 per year, compared to the $80,000 to $100,000 earned by existing employees. Five years earlier, the IT services company was forced to pay $45,000 to settle charges by the U.S. Department of Justice for discriminating against American citizens in its U.S. facilities. Media reports suggested that the soon-to-be redundant workers were forced to train their own replacements before being left in the cold, adding to the tragedy. Even among the foreign recruits, there was public discontent. A handful of temporary foreign workers complained that iGATE would threaten to send them back to India if they dared to speak of settling in Canada as permanent residents (Tomlinson 2013b).

When the British Columbia Federation of Labour had threatened to withdraw $4 billion in pension assets from RBC for the bank's cost-cutting transgressions, Nixon was on the phone with union president, Jim Sinclair, within a day (Nuttall 2013). Unlike most offshore outsourcing stories, RBC's relationship with iGATE represents a new phase in information technology services globalization in Canada. The Indian workers were brought to Canada through the federal Temporary Foreign Workers Program. Even though the TFWP was set up by the federal government to mitigate the alleged shortage of skilled workers in Canada, RBC was in the process of laying off employees and replacing their division with a company that was bringing in replacements from another continent. Offshore Indian labor was, in this case, literally being on-shored. Incidentally, Nasscom has been active in promoting business opportunities like this in Canada for India's ITES industries, of which iGATE is a part (Nasscom 2013). iGATE is one of Nasscom's 1,400 member organizations.

In 2012, the world was horrified by the grotesque sexual assault and murder of a 23-year-old woman in Delhi, who was heading home with her friend from a late night film. Police and politicians in India scrambled to prosecute the suspects as public, and indeed international, pressure mounted for the culprits to be brought to justice. The young woman, like so many other educated Indian youth, worked in a call center servicing foreign customers, in this case Canadians. Over a quarter million women work in the 2,200 BPO and ITES facilities that dot the National Capital Region (NCR) that surrounds Delhi. One survey discovered that the incident prompted a majority of women to leave work early and arrive home before sunset; a stunning 67 percent described the high-tech work environment as "bad" because of these safety fears (Basu 2013; Ha 2013). Sadly, this story is not unique. In 2005, Pratibah Srikanth, a young women who worked at Hewlett Packard's BPO division, GlobalSoft, was raped and murdered by her driver as she was ferried home after an evening shift. The Union for IT Enabled Services Professionals (UNITES) gained national press by holding rallies and offering a collective voice for the growing ranks of women and men staffing the country's flagship industry.

Chapter 2 addresses how post-industrial capitalism became a global phenomenon and how a parallel global division of knowledge labor took hold. What I argue is that technological, economic, and social demands by capital have mobilized for the purposes of transforming regulatory regimes that govern the operations of major corporations. These are the conditions that frame the development of global information technology (IT) and information technology enabled services (ITES) sectors, of which call centers are a part. Specific to the international call center industry, technical innovations *and* political economic conditions have mutually determined the existence of these workplaces. What I consider is the interrelationship between post-industrialism and the emergence of a global division of *knowledge* labor. Indeed, advances in technology and access to less expensive (yet skilled) pools of labor have made it possible for corporations to operate call centers as inexpensive cost centers. Such political economic developments have also made it possible for call centers to develop as profit centers and as industries in their own right. An important element of this account involves a transformation in how economies, labor markets, and the accumulation of capital are regulated through what is described as neo-liberalism.

What the story of RBC and the tragic death and assault of a call center worker in India illustrate are just some of the cultural and economic symptoms that constitute the global division of knowledge labor. From the gendered dimensions of work to the corporate-driven support for labor and trade policies that facilitate temporary employment practices at a time of record profits, such are the political economic conditions of post-industrial capitalism. But our story goes back to the 1990s, the heyday of globalization. Business leaders, futurists, and scholars were enamored with the possibilities of an integrated global market place, and the promises these hopes provided.

A 1998 *Business Week* article penned by Keith Hammond offers a representation of the times. Hammond made a bold case praising the promises offered by innovations in technology. Riding the IT boom that took off in the mid-1990s, Hammond reports, "Revolutionary technology and rapid globalization . . . will send productivity soaring, allowing faster growth with low inflation and modest unemployment. This dynamic could last for decades, bringing unimagined prosperity worldwide" (cited in Yates 2003, 25). Two years later the high-tech boom came to a crashing halt and a decade later the world economy slumped into its worse recession since the 1930s. Still, the legacy of this unbridled optimism for technology continued unconstrained. In India, the growth in access to mobile technology has been described as nothing less than a revolution in the way companies do business and interact with customers, offering opportunity to citizens and governments alike (Narasimhan 2011). Post-industrial and communications scholars have been grappling with the same sociological and economic questions for decades, but only some accounts looked at labor in this new terrain of information capitalism. For businesses, on the other hand, the possibilities associated with such transformations seemed limitless. Consider the example of IBM.

Throughout the 2000s, India was becoming an important fixture in IBM's global business services strategy. As part of the "globally integrated enterprise" vision promoted by the company's chief executive, Sam Palmisano, IBM's initiative in India stressed the importance of putting people and jobs anywhere in the world "based on the right costs, the right skills and the right business environment" (cited in *The Economist* 2007b).[1] A number of information technology firms were moving along a similar path, meaning that globalization was becoming a competitive necessity. Technology-outsourcing giant, Electronic Data Systems (EDS), also identified "low-cost" countries as part of its global expansion project. After shedding 12,000 employees in 2007, the company sought to hire 10,000 additional workers in emerging economies (Associated Press 2007). Advances in information technology and the development of a global division of information and knowledge labor have made these corporate strategies possible, and a changing economic terrain brought about by financial catastrophe in 2007 actually accelerated this trend.

Since the economic recession of 2008, business has been good despite the dire warnings of governments that talk of structural deficits and ballooning public debt. In 2011, a total of nineteen out of twenty-two Canadian industries reported higher profits than the previous year, with the non-financial sectors taking the lead (Statistics Canada 2011). Labor's share of GDP, meanwhile, has sunk to a 40-year low, from about 51 percent in 1976 to around 45 percent in 2012 (Shepherdson 2012, 14). Corporations in most industries were returning to their pre-recession levels of profitability not long after the recession officially ended. American companies were making even more remarkable gains. In 2010, U.S. corporations experienced record-setting profits amidst chronic unemployment (Rampell 2010).[2] The response from business groups on both sides of the border has been more of the same: domestic job creation and investment are contingent on the further deregulation of business and the loosening of rules governing the mobility of capital. But, as the case of IBM's India strategy illustrates, many of these new jobs are destined "offshore".

Evidence from the U.S. suggests that the new employment opportunities generated by American firms have largely emerged *outside* of the country. Over the past decade the quality of the global knowledge work force has reached a level that matches and even exceeds the basic skill and competency requirements of leading IT and higher value-added firms. Increasingly, in business and information services, knowledge-intensive jobs are being staffed by skilled and educated workers beyond the borders of Western economies. Columbia University economist Jeffery Sachs observes that U.S. firms are compelled to take advantage of foreign labor markets in order to remain competitive (Associated Press 2011). This is hardly a new phenomenon. These conditions were made possible by decades of transformation in the global operations of multinational firms and a changing division of labor.

WHAT'S NEW ABOUT NEO-LIBERALISM?

It was Italian Marxist Antonio Gramsci (1971) who initially described Fordism as a means of organizing the production and distribution of wealth. Subsequent analysis furthered Gramsci's theory by arguing that Fordism was more than a means of organizing production; it also functioned as an ideology premised on the development of consumption patterns manufactured through cultural industries and advertising (see Ewen 1976; Baran and Sweezy 1966). As its name suggests, *Ford*ism refers to the American industrialist and automobile manufacturer, Henry Ford, and his company's pioneering use of assembly line mass production. Emerging after World War Two, Fordism, as a concept, was used to articulate a dominant regime of capital accumulation, and what Lipietz (1987) described as a stabilization of the allocation of social production between consumption and accumulation, characterizing the wealthiest capitalist economies, namely the member states of the Organization for Economic Cooperation and Development, or OECD.

Around the same period of Gramsci's writing, the economic ideas of British economist John Maynard Keynes were gaining prominence in the United States through the New Deal policies introduced during the Roosevelt administration. Keynes offered a prognosis that accounted for the Great Depression and offered demand side solutions to this global economic catastrophe. When economies sink into recession, businesses tend to become pessimistic about profitability and the prospects for investment spending, just as consumers become weary of consumer spending. No matter how low interest rates fall, the propensity to spend remains curtailed. Businesses stop hiring even though wages are stagnant or sinking and consumers remain skeptical about spending their income even as prices decrease. Without an increase in either investment or consumer spending, the economy is prohibited from recovering and stays in a slump. Governments are then required to invest in economic development through short-term deficit spending as a means of spurring business activity and employment growth (Yates 2003). Keynesian*ism*, therefore, involves a broad set of macroeconomic policies governing the state's regulation of the economy.

Keynes's model was not immune to crisis. Along with Fordism, Keynesian economic regulation depends upon international and domestic expansion. For decades, the United States benefited from a dominant market share in global manufacturing, especially in the automobile industry. To illustrate, in 1974 U.S. auto manufacturers held an 85 percent global market share of domestic consumption, which dropped significantly to 56 percent by 1991 (Carmel and Tjia 2005). The long boom years following World War Two were a consequence of American economic and military hegemony over Western Europe and Japan, emphasizing the wider geopolitical dimensions that helped to support Fordist relations of production. But with the virtual monopoly over international markets there developed a susceptibility to innovative foreign competition. By the end of the 1960s, the crises that Keynesian economic policy and Fordist regulation had successfully managed began to resurface. Intensive international competition among a longer list of newly industrializing countries jeopardized American hegemony *within* Fordism. Standardized mass consumption came under attack for its basic lineup of consumer goods and services. The growth in demand for non-standardized, higher quality and short shelf-life goods, in conjunction with the development of non-specialist and highly flexible manufacturing technologies and flexible work practices, contributed to the crises of Fordism (Amin 1995; Piore and Sabel 1984).

It was not only the macroeconomic policies of Keynesianism (i.e., debt financing, progressive taxation, extensive provision of welfare programs, etc.) that led to the destabilization of decade long booms, but also the inadequacy of existing models of industrial organization accustomed to a particular market share that contributed to Fordism's unraveling. Falling rates of profit and declining productive output were among the chief symptoms of this economic malaise. Between 1961 and 1973 average world output growth averaged 5.5 percent, sinking dramatically to 1.8 percent by 1992 (Veltmeyer and Sacouman 1998, 121). Another example is the drop in pre-tax rates of profit for American companies which fell to roughly 6.5 percent in 1982, down from 14 percent in 1964 (McNally 2009, 50). In Canada these rates have been steadily increasing since the late 1980s, from a low of around 4 percent to a post-War high of 14 percent in 2007, before dropping slightly during the recession (Shepherdson 2012, 14). Economic conditions of the late 1960s brought about what is described by David Harvey

(1990, 147) as *flexible accumulation*, marked by deregulated, adaptable, and diverse forms of labor processes, labor markets, products, patterns of consumption, new financial services, expanding markets, and generally intensified rates of commercial, technological, and organizational innovation. As far as labor is concerned, this shift was structured in the interest of capital accumulation and against the gains made by the unionized working classes with regard to wages and benefits between 1945 and 1970, when the Keynesian compromise was more or less still in effect.

When the pattern of debt-financed state spending failed to maintain sustainable economic growth, neo-classical liberal economic theory re-emerged to address the crises that confronted these mutually dependent regimes. The *neo* prefix is important. Other than the focus on moral arguments in support of individual freedoms, it is unlikely that Adam Smith would have recognized—never mind agreed with—economic theories that have invoked his name. Neo-liberalization of social and economic policy-making is a process of achieving hegemony, and not a fixed or clearly established economic program. And it is less a consensus than a new common sense through which economic and social policy decisions are made. This is why I define neo-liberalism *as a struggle for ideological and political dominance that involves an ontological and material shift in how the world and its leading economic and political institutions are understood and ordered.* Even among visionaries of a pro-business globalization—whether economists, journalists, business leaders, or those belonging to think tanks or government policy circles—there exists tension and debate. And where neo-liberalism is implemented, it is done so through coercive political forces, social institutions, and ideologies, all of which are indeterminately produced, transformed, and renewed by class struggle (see Peet 1989).

Historically the building of this new common sense was fraught with conflict, not only in Anglo democracies but also in developing economies that were subsequently forced to accept structural adjustment as a condition for loans and foreign aid. The turmoil produced within these transitory periods of the 1970s led influential coalitions of policy-makers, like those occupying ranks of the Trilateral Commission, a coalition of scholars and policy makers oriented around a pro-business agenda, to pronounce a "crisis of democracy". Inflation, labor strife, and a general economic malaise had precipitated a challenge to the legitimate authority of democratic governments to govern effectively. The result, one report by the Commission concluded, was that as developed capitalist democracies became more "anomic", democratic politics became more an "arena for the assertion of conflicting interests than a process for the building of common purposes" (Crozier, Huntington, and Watanuki 1975, 161). In other words, the hegemony of a particular consensus had been compromised, opening up spaces for alternative programs, both radical and conservative, to work toward the construction of a new social contract. Neo-liberalism is *one* such alternative, despite being portrayed by business groups as the *only* solution to economic malaise.

As a "science" of making economic choices, neo-classical economics is premised on intellectual traditions that were present for much of the 20th century (Yates 2003). Not until the general economic crises of the 1970s would the neo-classical school experience somewhat of a renaissance. Intellectuals like Friedrich von Hayek, Ludvig von Mises, Milton Friedman, and Karl Popper had for decades criticized state intervention in economic affairs, but were dismissed as irrelevant and even scoffed at by mainstream economists. It was through their assembling of funds from sympathetic corporations and economic elites throughout the 1960s and 1970s that they and their followers were able to found think tanks and construct a movement that produced a steady stream of analyses, writings, polemics, and political position statements (Harvey 2005b). The state's role, they argued, in contrast to the social democratic projects implemented since the end of World War Two, is to guarantee individual entrepreneurial freedoms within the framework of private property rights, free markets, and free trade (Harvey 2005a).

The transition toward the "free market" school has implications that extend beyond state intervention. Jessop (1993) defines this process as a move away from Keynes's model toward an idea of economic management derived from the work of Austrian economist Joseph Schumpeter. Schumpeter's economics, argues Jessop, provides the framework for a fragmented and geographically dispersed labor market, intellectual property regimes, changing patterns of work organization, and internationalized production chains and financial markets. Foremost is the changing role of the state in acting as the midwife of this new regulatory model. The "creative destruction" aspect of Schumpeter's work takes center stage. Schumpeter (1972, 83) himself characterized creative destruction as "the opening up of new markets, foreign or domestic, and the organizational development from the craft shop and factory . . . [which] illustrate the same process of industrial mutation . . . that incessantly revolutionizes the economic structure *from within*, incessantly destroying the old one, incessantly creating a new one" (emphasis added).

Constant innovation, expansion, and internal reinvention are all characteristics of capitalism generally, but these ideas have taken new ideological significance with the ascendance of neo-liberalism. Internationalization and growing competitiveness between firms are examples of this transformation in how the state and market interact. The "hollowing out" of the state is less a removal of state involvement from economic affairs than a shifting of priorities toward regulating markets based primarily on instrumental objectives lobbied for by businesses and their political allies—essentially, enhancing the capacities for capital accumulation by removing barriers that inhibit innovation and competition. Both the internationalization of production and supply chains, precipitated by changes unfolding in the world of information technology, has worked to create conditions for a revolution in where work is done and how. Indeed, both Fordism and Keynesianism were reliant on a national regime of regulation, and were outstripped by a competitive, global division of labor.

FROM A *NEW* TO A *GLOBAL* DIVISION OF LABOR

Fröbel et al. (1980) argued in their seminal thesis that there were three underlying reasons for the development of a phenomenon they described as the *new* international division of labor. What propelled this theory was a change in the political economic contour of global capitalism. Western firms began to see the Third World as more than a source of raw, natural resources. First, a seemingly "inexhaustible" reservoir of cheap labor had been made available in developing countries. Second, the division and subdivision of production processes became ever more advanced, to the point where disparate and fragmented operations could be carried out with an ever-diminishing level of skill. Finally, advancements in transportation, telecommunications, and computerization made possible the production of goods anywhere in the world, since technical and organizational limitations no longer prohibited access to distant labor markets. An important catalyst for this shift toward production in the developing economies was that of foreign direct investment (FDI), which Fröbel and his collaborators suggested had been steadily increasing throughout the 1970s. Because a bulk of this new investment was directed toward export-oriented production, the newly created industrial enclaves had little connection to the local economy, save for the utilization of cheap labor. The theory also rested upon the conditions of the hegemonic international political economy of the time.

If there has been one important development since Fröbel et al. (1980) drafted their thesis, it's that the scale of the international division of labor has grown dramatically. As *The Economist* (2006) reports, with the embrace of market capitalism in China, India, and the former Soviet Union, the global labor force has effectively doubled and the combined output of emerging economies accounts for more than half of the total world GDP. By some estimates, the number of workers added to the international labor market throughout the 1990s and early 2000s exceeded 1.4 billion (Nathan 2007)! Advantages offered by conditions of trade, immigration, and social mobility, along with a growing labor market, have permitted capitalism further opportunity for expansion. Offshoring and outsourcing have been facilitated—and indeed made possible—by the opening up of these labor markets. These developments extend, rather than create, practices that have been traditionally deployed by corporations. In the 19th century, New England's eminent textile mills took off for Southward labor markets to reap greater profits and escape the new industrial regulations that sought to end sweatshop conditions that defined the industry (Mosco and Stevens 2007). Contemporary offshoring and outsourcing, however, rest on political economic developments that had been percolating since the late 1960s.

Much of the post-World War Two economic development strategy rested on debt financing through the World Bank and private financial institutions headquartered mostly in the United States and Europe. The political dynamics of the Cold War period also meant that alternative economic models of lending and industrialization were being financed through the Soviet bloc. It was the financial crisis of the 1970s, sparked by falling rates of profit, spikes in oil prices, and dramatic interest rate hikes, which pressured advanced and developing capitalist economies to restructure their macroeconomic policies. The debt crisis of 1982 further unraveled the existing intellectual foundation of predominant economic development theories. Academic and political traditions oriented toward industrialization policies favorable to national-developmental models were fractured by the unfolding economic crises, and the gradual downfall of state socialisms focused attention on the failure of mainstream (and often Marxist-inspired) theories of development (M. Taylor 2005). In the wake of this destabilization, neo-liberal perspectives on economic development gained prominence, resulting in a radical shift in policy prescriptions offered by leading economic institutions in the global capitalist system, namely the World Bank and the International Monetary Fund. This new agreement came to be known as the Washington Consensus due to the fact that the IMF and WB were based in Washington, D.C. and their policies were predominantly influenced by recommendations imposed by the leading power brokers in the United States.

Under this new "consensus", indebted nations were required to adopt severe financial austerity measures, known as structural adjustment, in order to qualify for financial assistance. Structural adjustment policies usually demanded the removal of import quotas, improvement of export incentives, reforms to a country's fiscal system, improvement to the financial performance of public enterprises, and revising agricultural incentives that favored improved marketing and reduced subsidies (Fine 2001). Approximately 70 percent of structural adjustment loans contained a privatization component, despite the associated cost to labor and local businesses (Bayliss and Cramer 2001). In the early 1990s, India confronted similar conditions when the country faced a balance of payments crisis as the foreign exchange rate plummeted. The financial catastrophe was followed by the disciplinary interventions of the IMF, the Asian Development Bank, and the WB, all of which demanded that the country downsize its state sector enterprises and abandon the prevailing import substitution policies (Chakrabarti and Cullenberg 2003). A pivotal moment arrived for Canada around the same time as well, when pressures mounted for the federal government to eliminate its deficit, lest its currency succumb to the pejorative forecast of being reduced to a "Northern peso", as the *Wall Street Journal* pronounced in the early 1990s.[3]

The Canada-U.S. free trade agreement in the 1980s, followed by the North American Free Trade Agreement (NAFTA) in 1994, produced conditions favorable to the unfettered flow of capital between the economies of Canada, the United States, and Mexico. National governments dismantled existing tariff and protectionist regimes and allowed businesses, namely multinational corporations (MNC), to self-govern the regulation of trade in goods and services. Indeed, the MNC has become the principal agent overseeing the conditions of investment and movement of wealth. The significance of these economic institutions can be evidenced by their growth in numbers over the past four decades. Between 1970 and 2000, the total number of multinational corporations increased from just 7,000 to over 60,000 at the turn of the century (Kiely 2007). By 2008, the number of MNCs surged to 82,000, 28 percent of which were based in developing and transition economies. These emerging economies now host a majority of foreign affiliates' labor force (UNCTAD 2010). While most world trade still takes place between the wealthiest economies represented in the OECD and the bulk of investment is channeled through firms headquartered in these countries, MNCs based in developing countries are making gains in the world economy (UNCTAD 2004, 2006, 2010). In 2009, developing economies were for the first time receiving almost half of all FDI inflows, mainly through the operations of major corporations that sought to take advantage of new labor and commercial markets in Asia (UNCTAD 2010). These are the conditions that have nurtured the offshoring and outsourcing of services as part of a supposedly revitalized and global capitalism.

One of the promises of free trade and neo-liberalization that continues to resonate is that the economic renaissance premised on free markets would inspire a return to a competitive, entrepreneurial capitalism. Instead of a handful of companies dominating a market or sector, a constellation of companies in a range of diversified markets would offer innovative products and services at competitive costs. In contrast, what has happened is the formation of a relatively small number of firms wielding disproportionate influence. Business outsourcing service companies like Accenture, IBM, Tata Consultancy Services, Infosys, Wipro Technologies, Aramark, and Convergys possess an overwhelming market share. Of the 100 leading outsourcing firms worldwide, two of the top three are Indian-based companies (IAOP 2009, 2010, 2012). Offshoring, or the globalization of production and supply chains in manufacturing and services, has nurtured corporations from developing economies, while providing rich opportunities for companies headquartered in the West.

Based on traditional comparative advantage theory, offshoring is described as beneficial for all parties because a more efficient allocation of resources supposedly enlarges economic growth on a global scale (Paus 2007). Proponents argue that this is a realization of the benefits emerging from a global division of labor and trade described centuries earlier by the classical economic theories of Adam Smith and David Ricardo. For this reason the practice of service offshoring is often seen as synonymous with poor nations that are able to offer their most precious non-natural commodity to international buyers—inexpensive and, now more commonly, skilled labor. Smith proposed in *The Wealth of Nations* that in "civilized society" the individual is "at all times in need of the co-operation and assistance of great multitudes", and the benefit of all is accomplished through the appeal of self-love and mutual interests (Smith 2003/1776, 23–24). The division of labor in production, as in the market, compounds the skills and abilities of fragmented producers to provide more plentiful outcomes through efficiency gains. The "invisible hand" that Smith spoke of is a metaphor for this process, through which the pursuit of rational self-interest—in production, the acquisition of goods, and in trade, both domestic and foreign—not benevolence, enriches the commonwealth (Smith 2003/1776, 572). Ricardo (1911, 77) advanced this theory further by adding that an extension of liberalized foreign trade would simultaneously increase the mass of commodities available to a given market and, thus, the "sum of enjoyments".

However, the political economic consequences of a global regime of trade premised on Smith and Ricardo's notion of comparative advantage is not without dispute. Upon the founding of the UN Conference of Trade and Development (UNCTAD) in 1964, Argentine economist Raul Prebisch stressed that asymmetries in economic structures would require a model of economic governance premised on reciprocity, not subservience to theoretical outcomes developed by economic models. He was not alone in observing that "free trade" would translate into the imperialism of Western capital if left unattended. Prebisch had argued that "free trade" could, in fact, maintain colonial divisions of labor and enforce dependency by poor countries on advanced economies. Global integration, he argued, was very much unequal (see Toye 2003). Most importantly, Prebisch's dependency theory diverged from the optimistic accounts of liberalized trade offered by economists and policy-makers of his day. His account also brought into question the emancipatory potential of trade for labor offered by the classical political economists.

Sinking rates of profit for major American corporations sparked political and economic pressures to control labor costs. Japanese and West German manufacturers were, after all, producing high-quality and competitive goods at lower labor costs compared to their U.S. counterparts (Brenner 2011). Firms that had performed their core and non-core functions internally turned to subcontracting to help control inflationary wage rates. The same held true for Japanese companies that looked to on-shore and, eventually, offshore sites to produce goods destined for final product assembling in their advanced domestic facilities. Mexico's maquiladoras emerged in the late 1960s to supply manufactured goods destined for U.S. corporations, which established a new international division of labor that effectively tamed wage demands. This was accomplished in two ways. First, competition from lower cost labor put pressure on unions and labor generally to make financial concessions in the interest of saving jobs. Second, import of lower cost consumer goods worked to maintain particular levels of consumption and standards of living while stalling demands for higher wages. Pressures to accelerate the rate of accumulation pushed corporations to look abroad.

Corporations certainly exercise a degree of agency in their search for profits and cheaper sources of labor in foreign markets. However, is this a quest for an inanimate resource waiting to be extracted and used? The new international division of labor (NIDL) hypothesis developed by Fröbel rested on the assumption that labor markets simply exist for companies to employ and exploit. In some respects the theory described labor as a natural resource like any other, stripping workers collectively of class and agency. Shortfalls in the NIDL framework became evident in the 1990s as economic and technological developments outstripped the theory's capacity to fully grasp the new global political economy. What also undermined earlier perspectives on labor's integration into the world economy was the NIDL's failure to meaningfully contend with the process through which labor is constituted and reproduced—in other words, the *social construction* of labor. Capital does not simply "circle the globe" in search of a natural and inexpensive source of disciplined labor, as development scholar and political economist Marcus Taylor (2009) recognizes; this human resource must be created. And as a social subject, labor is classed, raced, and gendered. Labor also possesses a range of identities that, at times, it resists as well as constructs.

Developments in the global political economy also meant that the NIDL model was less effective in making sense of the globalization of skill and knowledge-intensive employment. The fixation on cheap labor obfuscated the fact that capital requires more than low wages as a propellant for expansion. Indeed, the attractiveness of an economy is conditioned by the structure of connections between the state, local capital, and MNCs, as accounts of India's computer software industry suggest (Lakha 1994). Depending on the nature of their business, companies are required to consider a range of factors, such as regional and locational issues, as much as they must consider the inexpensiveness of labor. This helps explain why countries like Singapore have been highly competitive in the world market despite the fact that it possesses labor costs that exceed those of its neighbors (Mittelman 1995). Nor is it any longer sufficient to talk about developing nations simply as export enclaves for MNCs seeking to bolster their low-value-added industries. India's information technology industries, particularly computer software design, succeed because of a dynamic that involves a particular interplay between local and international forces, and the country's foresight to take advantage of Western capital's need for high-quality and low-cost services and service products (Lakha 1994).

What emerges in the wake of the NIDL's problems is an alternative *global* division of labor, which acknowledges the importance of interlocking commodity chains, fragmented production networks and systems, investments in human capital, indigenous modes of social reproduction, migratory flows, connections to and between markets, as well as cultural and historical forces that lend to the *construction and maintenance* of particular labor forces. The transition from a *new* to a *global* division of labor also shifts the narrative toward the growth of post-industrial industries like finance, marketing, health care, and information and communications services, as well as other knowledge-based sectors. To satisfy demands, capital cannot simply rest on cheap, low-wage labor but instead requires skilled, educated, and talented (albeit less expensive) knowledge workers. Here the question of capitalist development crosses paths with knowledge capitalism.

POST-INDUSTRIALISM AND THE GLOBAL DIVISION OF KNOWLEDGE LABOR

In the 1960s, communications theorists proposed that mass media could be used as an instrument for social and economic development. Development communication reflects the guiding ethos of development economics, in this sense, by stressing that value and cultural development proceed along with the development of material conditions. Such a process unfolds as communications technology provides spill-over effects for rural areas as infrastructure and knowledge of communications systems develop in the core, urban spaces rural spaces benefiting from developments initially restricted to advanced, urban areas (Prasad 2009a, 2009b; Lerner 1967). For international financial institutions like the World Bank, knowledge itself, as well as access to information technology, has been considered the basis for economic and social development in the 21st century (World Bank 1999). Knowledge gaps between wealthy and poor countries and between the technical literati and those deprived of technical knowledge and IT, the Bank reported, would be the true indicators of global inequality in post-industrial capitalism. The National Association of Software and Services Companies (Nasscom), India's premier IT-ITES industry association, has adopted this type of powerful transformative imagery as emblematic of information technology as a force for social and economic development (Nasscom 2008a). Part of this business-driven imagery includes the commodification of services and knowledge.

Throughout the 1980s and 1990s, information technology was believed to function as a palliative for Western capitalism by providing a solution to the chronic crisis of profit. This function has been described by Nigel Thrift (2006) as "stockmarket Keynesianism", which fueled the telecommunications, media, and information technology boom that spanned roughly from 1995 until the stock market bust of 2000–2001. In fact, the history of telecommunications and information technology suggests that governments are actively involved in supporting the development of communications industries. Political economists have long recognized the contradictions of the communication and information technology revolution considering that the process as a whole is a product of extraordinary public subsidies and social policies, not the "result of geniuses and free markets", as McChesney (2007, xii) points out. Global communications are instrumental as a support network for capitalism's international growth and specifically, a chief apparatus within the ideological and material roots of developmentalism and dependency (Mosco 1982). These technologies are even more important for the development of a global information society, one predicated on the promises of post-industrial capitalism and the principles of the division of *knowledge* labor, made evident by the growth of IT and ITES sectors in so-called peripheral economies like India.

Information technology companies are both producer and purveyor of the knowledge economy's goods, particularly the "flat world" dreams scribed by one of globalization's most eager supporters, Thomas Friedman. In India, one member of Infosys' board of directors remarked during an interview that advances in the globalization of services have contributed to the flattening of the world, creating a profound effect on demand and supply activities (Nilekani 2008). Such claims fuel a popular conception that cultural and economic borders are eroded by the march of technology, empowering both business and civil society in an emancipatory and utopian vision. Critical communications scholars and political economists, on the other hand, have long held contrary thoughts on the prospects of information technology. Political activist and scholar Herbert Schiller (1996, 46) wrote that the "production and sale of information have become major sites of profit making. What had been in large measure a social good has been transformed into a commodity for sale".

For Schiller, the development of information and communication technology was a political concern as much as it was a technical question. In other words, there is no separation between regimes of accumulation and technological innovation. And, as labor scholars like Mosco (2009, 1988) and Huws (2009, 2003) have argued, the internationalization of knowledge-based employment, notably the global circuits of IT-enabled industries like call centers, cannot be divorced from the hierarchical structures of production that are conditioned by power relations and technical forms of control at the site of production. Indeed, the propensity for particular types of employment to be outsourced and offshored is determined by the capacity to commodify services, a process that is itself conditioned by technical-political factors characteristic of post-industrialism. Such is the importance of a political economy of communication as a framework for analysis. What the political economy framework achieves is a rendering of relationships in production and in society and recognition that communications is a "social process of exchange" (Mosco 2009, 67).

Marx's definition of the commodity form entrenches the social element of production and provides a starting point for political economy. "A commodity", he (1967, 77) argues, "is a mysterious thing, simply because in it the social character of men's [*sic*] labor appears to them as an objective character stamped upon the product of that labor". Arjun Appadurai's (1996) conceptualization of *production fetishism* and *fetishism of the consumer* furthers Marx's original definition to encompass consumption as well as the process of production. Appadurai (1996, 41–42) explains production fetishism as an

> illusion created by contemporary transnational production loci that masks translocal capital, transnational earning flows, global management, and often faraway workers (engaged in various kinds of high-tech putting-out operations) in the idiom and spectacle of local (sometimes even worker) control, national productivity, and territorial sovereignty.

Equally important is *fetishism of the consumer*, which claims that the "consumer has been transformed through commodity flows (and the mediascapes, especially of advertising, that accompany them) into a sign . . . in the sense of a mask for the real seat of agency, which is not the consumer but the producer and the many forces that constitute production" (Appadurai 1996, 42). In the Indian call centers, clients and managers would construct this fetishism by requiring workers to progress through accent neutralization in an attempt to provide the illusion that customers were speaking with agents at home. In turn, knowledge producers would construct new, often American identities. As Winifred Poster (2007, 291) wonderfully demonstrates in her study of this practice, "By masking the real identity of the call center workers, these firms are able to hide how their products are actually produced, by whom, under what conditions, where, etc. In a broad sense, it enables them to conceal the neo-liberal project of exploiting workers in the Global South".

Space and locality, outside of the usual vernacular that associates work sites as domestic or offshore, can be deployed to understand the disruption of private (leisure) / public (work) separation. The use of these terms also invokes Henri Lefebvre's (1979, 287, emphasis added) assertion that space is social and a means of production, itself a product that "cannot be separated from the forces of production, techniques, and knowledge; *from the international division of social labor*; from nature; or from the state and other superstructures". Fetishism, then, includes space and consumption. Just as this model can be used to draw connections between the seemingly objective nature of production (the base) and the subjective contours of consumption (informed by the superstructural processes), fetishization operates on two interrelated planes—one masks the crystallization of social relations in the commodity, the other shrouds a capacity to observe the cultural and spatial components of commodity production. It is also a symptom of tying processes of production generally to material production specifically—in other words, there exists what Downey (2001) describes as a mystification of the division of labor associated with and within "brain work" and knowledge-based labor. Appadurai's taxonomy of fetishism is useful for making meaningful the mystification of this division of labor, which renders invisible structures of inequality within the terrain of post-industrial economic relations and types of work. Where and how work and consumption take place become all the more important when factoring in the growth of global production networks and post-industrial employment. Indeed, the *points of production and distribution of goods and services* remain crucial to an exploration of call centers and the place that this industry occupies in the broader context of business process outsourcing and the internationalized offshoring of IT services work.

Since at least the 1950s, scholars have charted the stunning technological and social developments that were leading the transformation of post-War economies, particularly that of the United States. Fritz Machlup's (1962) comprehensive survey in particular drew attention to the remarkable growth of knowledge industries and the relative decline of manufacturing.

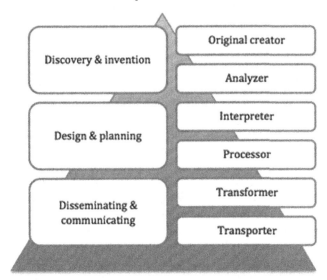

Figure 2.1 Machlup's typology of knowledge production.

Machlup's findings contributed to larger debates about commodity forms and the relations of production or, specifically, *knowledge* production. "Producing" knowledge, for Machlup, is described as "not only discovering, inventing, designing, and planning but also disseminating and communicating" (1962, 7). Not unlike the political economic scholars of communications of his time, he recognized that the production of knowledge is an economic activity, an industry. Machlup resolved that, while white-collar workers can be regarded as knowledge-producing workers, this identification could not be made without several qualifications. And, as an industry, important distinctions are to be made regarding the occupational or class characterization of "white-collar".

Knowledge producers, using Machlup's (1962, 33) morphology, are distinguished by their control over and relation to the production process ascribed to six interrelated categories: transporter, transformer, processor, interpreter, analyzer, and original creator. What makes the *transporter* qualitatively different from the *original creator* is the degree to which the original inputs are transformed or augmented by the knowledge worker (see figure 2.1). In other words, the value-added nature of their work. Marc Porat's (1977) subsequent investigation parallels the conclusions drawn earlier by Machlup, where huge disparities of labor and capital-intensity are shown to exist throughout the information sector (see Babe 1994). The questions of skill and education also apply to those workers employed by the knowledge industry, as Machlup described it, and what differentiates the transporters, transformers, processors, and creators of knowledge. Automation, which "displaces mental labor" and "saves the use of human judgment" (Machlup 1962, 379), addresses an additional problem when considering the capacity to replace, or at least supplement, the efforts of the least skill-demanding knowledge producers with computerization. Technical innovation in the knowledge industries, he added, constructs divisions of labor within sectors and configures systems of organization and control. Today we can understand this as features that prefigure types of work prone to subcontracting. What Machlup (1962, 380) argued is that automation would create the need for an ordered stratification of mental labor with "various degrees of analytical skill", but that this did not necessarily entail a reduction in the share of "brain workers" within an economy. The result could potentially *increase* demand for more highly skilled mental labor rather than precipitate a displacement of employment through automation alone. Recent business reports and critical labor scholars have supported these claims (Huws 2003; Hunt, Manyika, and Remes 2011). Machlup's framework also lends to an understanding of call centers and their place in the knowledge production chain, from IT to ITES-BPO, as illustrated in Figure 2.2.

Machlup's account of knowledge production acknowledges policy questions related to shifting labor and economic patterns. He shared the concern that changes would demand political intervention and sociological

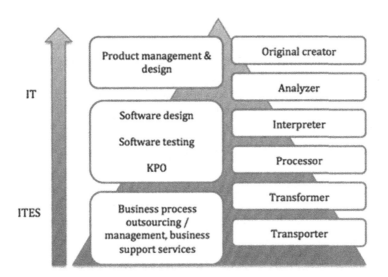

Figure 2.2   Knowledge production and the typology of the IT-ITES value spectrum.

reflection in order to mitigate the likely outcomes of such developments (Machlup 1980). Rather than a shapeless community of knowledge *producers*, his description is foremost a class structure of knowledge *workers*, subject to innovations in technology, labor processes, and organizational models; transformations such as these in turn alter the demands for particular skills in a rapidly evolving labor market. Finally, Machlup's prognosis does not declare a victory for knowledge work *over* manufacturing, but instead talks of both as overlapping sectors in the American economy.

Daniel Bell (1999/1973), acclaimed for his work on post-industrialism, developed similar conclusions about the post-industrial condition. For Bell, society is not a unified *system*, but a fractured entity constituted by social structure, the polity, and culture. Post-industrialism was, his account stressed, limited to changes in the techno-economic order, part of the wider social structure. In a darker follow up to his 1973 classic, Bell (1976) argued in *The Cultural Contradictions of Capitalism* that the ideas of modernity had become exhausted. Capitalist society in the United

States, he suggested, was pained by cultural styles that replaced a moral system rooted in the Protestant sanctification of work with a hedonism that embraced material ease and luxury. None of these problems are divorced from a material economic order. And, as Bell admitted, the transition to a post-industrial society is not without challenges. He optimistically forecast a society governed by ideas, merit, knowledge, and information, and welcomed the displacement of class and established privilege as the dominant political forces. But Bell (1976, 26) also envisioned new inequalities, namely a scarcity of information "which would arise from the growth of technical knowledge and the increasing need for popularization". The World Bank (1999) made similar claims in its report on knowledge and development two decades later.

Bell's principal flaw is that his forecast prematurely abandoned existing ideologies and class divisions. It is also the case that Bell's sophisticated concept of post-industrialism has been crassly usurped and brought to mean a general characterization of a particular social formation, i.e., the "information society". Post-industrialism, rather, marks a shift *within* capitalism, but has not fundamentally altered the nature of capitalist social structures (see Lash and Urry 1987). Furthermore, the global experience of post-industrialism has been decidedly uneven, due in part to the internationalization of production processes, the division of labor, and the relocation of industry. At the same time, the significance of industrial and resource sectors has not been displaced, despite the falling number of individuals employed in these industries in advanced economies. If post-industrialism is to remain a moniker of contemporary economic change, the term must be amenable to the realities of uneven regional development, as well as inconsistencies in the emergence and decline of particular sectors. In the workplace and for organized labor, post-industrialism is hardly an escape from capitalist relations of production. Bell was keenly aware that the changes he predicted in the 1970s would be brought to bear on trade unions that would have to reconsider their place in an ever-changing political and economic terrain.

3 The Political Economy of Offshoring

Ashok Desai (2007), an economist and former advisor to the Government of India on economic reforms, described the state of India's telecommunications sector as a "placid backwater" until the 1990s. It was only when the government started to relax policies on the import of technology and capital during the reforms of 1991 that economic interest started to stream toward telecommunications. Until this point, state-owned and highly regulated monopolies governed national economic policy making. Railways, electricity, fuel, and telecommunications were held by a restrictive licensing raj, which restricted private investment. The lack of competition and powerful, politicized trade unions, Desai emphasized, was responsible for retarding the growth of telephone connectivity since market pressures were not permitted to enhance service or allow for technological innovation.

Combined with the neo-liberal policy of deregulation and liberalization, the offshoring and outsourcing of call center employment—and indeed the formation of a global division of knowledge labor—is premised on the telecommunications revolutions of the 1970s onwards. As Robert Horowitz (1989) suggests, the telecommunications industry functions as an anchor for post-industrial society. Chapter 3 commences by examining how the offshoring and outsourcing of knowledge work followed from the development of a global telecommunications network and the growing trend in the commodification of services. Without advances in technology and changes to regulatory frameworks, an international call center industry would not have been possible. Second, a political economy of offshoring is established through a survey of government and industry data as well as media reports. What I maintain is that the globalization of IT and call center employment is contingent on political and social historical forces that characterize the demise of Fordism, as Chapter 2 established.

GLOBAL TELECOMMUNICATIONS

Since the mid-1980s, the telecommunications industry has undergone a process of transnationalization, brought about by mergers and acquisitions

(M&A), foreign direct investment (FDI), and changing patterns of regulation and ownership. Neo-liberalism, particularly its emphasis on revoking government regulation of economic affairs, has been a guiding philosophy directing this change. Privatization has also been a key strategy prompting the rapid commercialization of information and systems of communications. The corollary to this pro-business agenda has been to undermine labor's ability to bargain collectively on a sector-wide basis in what eventually developed into a fragmented ownership structure. Communications and labor scholar Harry Katz (1997) has pointed out that the "re-engineering" of former telecommunications monopolies has meant adjustments in how employees work because of changing management systems. Corporate restructuring has certainly been a global phenomenon, albeit one dominated by companies headquartered in a handful of wealthy economies. Between the early 1980s and the mid-2000s, there were over 10,000 mergers and acquisitions of telecommunications firms, of which 1,068 were acquired by Canadian-owned companies. Canada ranked a distant third, behind the U.S. and the UK, in acquisition of telecommunications companies (Jin 2008). In the 1990s, telecommunications was the second largest industry by dollar value at $524.3 billion, and the communications sector as a whole constituted the largest industry in the M&A market (Jin 2007). After the financial collapse of 2007–2008, telecommunications was one of only a handful of industries that attracted *more* FDI in 2009 than the year prior (UNCTAD 2010).

As a conduit of cultural transmission and communication, the communications sector has been instrumental in setting the terms for globalization. Mergers and acquisitions were allowed to accelerate by national regulators who softened foreign ownership regulations and limited the government management of pricing. What these policies enabled was an astronomical growth in the telecommunications industry in terms of profit and private (transnational) ownership. Such are the developments that facilitated the expansion of a global division of knowledge work. Canada boasts several world-class telecommunications companies that have been innovators in the development of new technologies, for example RIM (Research in Motion), and of course Nortel before it entered bankruptcy protection in 2009. India has only recently entered the scene, but has already gained acclaim for its highly skilled information technology workers, making it essential to the global call center and IT market. Offshoring and outsourcing in this sector on the scale witnessed today would not be possible if it were not for the regional and national policies allowing for inexpensive and reliable international communications (see Carmel and Tjia 2005). It was pressure from major telecommunications users and new telecommunications service providers that made the inexpensive flow of information a centerpiece in continental and world trade agreements.

The free trade agreement signed between Canada and the United States in 1989 heralded the North American continentalization of telecommunications, which furthered the regulatory reforms that commenced several years earlier. The Canada-U.S. Free Trade Agreement, and later the North American Free Trade Agreement (NAFTA) which included Mexico, determined to create an economic space through which telecommunications companies, as well as other major industries, could flourish under a unified trade agreement with minimal social policy oversight. American corporate telecommunications giants were especially keen on gaining uninhibited access to the lucrative Canadian and Mexican markets. Only four years after the signing of NAFTA, total FDI heading to the U.S. from Canada reached $74.8 billion, compared to the $103.9 billion invested in the Canadian economy by American sources. Canadian companies also benefited from the ability to expand their already sizable access to the U.S. market. Continental integration amounted to a substantial part of the larger process of building a new order in the global political economy (Mosco and Schiller 2001).

Because wire-line systems are dependent on a capital- and labor-intensive infrastructure, wireless transmission is appealing to India's densely populated urban geographies and vast rural population. Mobile providers had the advantage of being able to bypass what some have labeled the cumbersome and inefficient connectivity methods offered by the Department of Telecommunications (McMillin 2006). After China, India boasts the largest telephone network among the emerging economies. The number of wireless subscribers surpassed a combined annual growth rate (CAGR) of 90 percent between 2002 and 2007, increasing from 6.68 million to 166 million connections (ASSOCHAM 2009). Private entrants to the telecommunications market have contributed to the expansion of the industry, specifically the rate of connectivity, but the state-owned BSNL has taken up the bulk of investment in rural telecommunications, indicating that government involvement in the sector is still significant. The Eleventh Five Year Plan (2007–2012) set ambitious targets for telecommunications growth, with the government planners aiming to expand the telephone subscriber base to 600 million, including 200 million rural connections (Government of India 2008, 423–425). Expanding the telecommunications base, both wireless and wired, is instrumental in facilitating the growth of a domestic call center industry in India.

In the midst of a changing policy environment, the Telecom Regulatory Authority of India (TRAI) was encouraged to draw increasingly from the examples of Anglophone economies and their allegiance to pro-business policies. Voice over Internet Protocol (VoIP), global satellite networks, and expansive broadband access have been vital to the growth of India's information technology (IT) and information technology enabled services (ITES) sectors. A rapid decline in telecommunications costs effectively made India's global IT brand possible. The offshoring to India of ITES work that relies upon real-time communication with foreign customers was made possible by the introduction of these technologies. International integration was facilitated by the business-led effort to enhance the privatization of telecommunications, providing greater opportunities for the commercialization of information, knowledge, and services (see Paus 2007). But despite the rosy characterizations of deregulation, the phenomenal growth of telecommunications in India has been mired by scandal and corruption from the start.

As the *New York Times* reported, "[t]he telecom[munications] industry in India was essentially born in the mud pit of corruption" (Yardley and Timmons 2010). Poor regulatory oversights, a consequence of liberalization, meant that deliberate manipulation of policies favored particular corporate entities over others. The spectrum auctioning scandal that erupted in 2010 shed light on years of corrupt practices within government and corporate elite circles (Paranjoy and Kaushal 2010; Yardley and Timmons 2010). Indeed, information technology revolutions are not removed from the reproduction of inequalities and maintenance of corporate dominance that define a political economy of post-industrial capitalism.

THE POLITICAL ECONOMY OF OFFSHORING

A definition for a political economy of offshoring draws from Machlup's (1962, 1980) claims about the taxonomy of knowledge production, in particular the capacity to automate knowledge work within his hierarchy. Machlup's framework also transcends national boundaries and applies to global division of knowledge labor, even though this was not explicitly discussed in his work. As technologies and business practices develop, the implications for a company's potential to profit from the fragmentation of production channels means that regional and employment market advantages are dependent on where work is done and by whom. While major economies such as the UK, Japan, the Netherlands, and the U.S. constitute the leading importers of business and IT-related services, they are also major exporters of these same services, the U.S. and the UK especially.[1] In fact, both of these advanced economies have historically experienced the *largest* surpluses in the business and information services, which include IT and ITES employment.[2]

Of the countries in the OECD, which is populated by the world's wealthiest economies, Canada registered modest trade surpluses in business services between 1995 and 2003, but these categories still accounted for less than one percent of total GDP—in 2002 this surplus totaled approximately US$1 billion (OECD 2006a; Amiti and Wei 2004a; 2004b).[3] India and China, considered by many as major exporters and leading sources of offshore services, are themselves net importers of business services, ranking 11th (US$11 billion) and 18th (US$8 billion), respectively, in 2002 (Amiti and Wei 2004a). Between 1995 and 2005, India's export of these services increased by approximately 27 percent while imports grew by over 15 percent; business and computer-related imports to the U.S., by comparison, grew by just over 12 percent (OECD 2006a). India continues to import most of its state-of-the-art telecommunications equipment, which provides the physical infrastructure for the IT and call center offshoring sector (Government of India 2008). By some estimates, India's total information technology imports will exceed $400 billion by 2020, more than the country spends on oil. This is largely due to India's lagging IT manufacturing base (IANS 2013). These figures indicate that most of the developing world must turn to the wealthy countries to supply their business, computer, and information service needs. High-end and value-added services, perhaps the most valued commodities produced within knowledge economies, are still primarily designed and produced in the West. India remains somewhat of an anomaly, although in terms of computer and high-tech hardware it is heavily reliant on imports (Government of India 2008).

Until 2009, wealthy economies had been receiving an overwhelming majority of foreign direct investment in information services. This represents a change in the global flow of capital. In 2005, Canada was ranked the fifth largest host economy for FDI, with developed economies absorbing almost 60 percent of total FDI inflows (UNCTAD 2006). Advanced economies like the United States and the UK were still listed as the leading FDI destinations. However, between 2003 and 2009, developing and transition economies experienced six years of unprecedented growth in FDI. These same economies attracted almost 50 percent of all FDI by 2009, and are set to overtake the wealthiest countries. Half of the six top destinations for FDI flows are now developing economies (UNCTAD 2010). Foreign direct investment to India reached $35 billion in 2009, or 15 percent of all FDI to the East and Southeast Asia region (UNCTAD 2010). Between 2000 and 2008, services (financial and non-financial), computer software and hardware, and telecommunications sectors together attracted approximately 40 percent of all foreign investment (ASSOCHAM 2009, 24, 25). What UNCTAD's (2004) report emphasizes is that the structure of FDI has begun to shift towards services, with over 60 percent of total foreign direct investment stock now flowing to this sector. Contrast this with the 1970s when services accounted for only one quarter of all FDI, rising to one half by the 1990s. This is partly due to the liberalization of investment regulations in most of the world's economies, the development of global production networks, and the commodification of services. With the global expansion of service-oriented FDI flows, the market for offshore outsourcing has similarly grown.

Despite this growth, the service sector remains less transnationalized than manufacturing. It is only in the past decade that the prospects for offshoring service work, especially call center work and other back office operations, have become feasible and part of what critical labor scholars have labeled "new patterns of organization" (Norling 2001). Consultancy firms such as McKinsey, Forrester, and A.T. Kearney continue to project that millions of jobs in wealthy economies are at stake as a consequence of these technical and economic developments. But the realities of global business operations are not so simple. Companies seek access to foreign markets and build stronger networks with a global client base, enforcing the fact that physical location and contact with customers remains an important part of corporate strategies. A global division of knowledge work has also produced well-founded public fears over the disappearance of vast numbers of white-collar jobs, notably those at the lower skill end of the sector. However, reports of widespread unemployment have been fueled by media representations that are, in some cases, exaggerated. Nevertheless, the tradability of services is predicated on the feasibility of work being performed on a global platform. The example of RBC's use of iGATE, a subcontractor that recruited foreign workers for its Canadian operations, illustrates this point. The availability of telecommunications infrastructure and human capital are prerequisites for the development of a global division of labor that makes offshoring possible. Defined as "offshorability", the requirements also include outputs that could be traded and transmitted by ICTs, a highly codified knowledge content, and limited necessity for face-to-face contact (OECD 2006). But there is one caveat: a distinction must be made between *potential offshoring* and *actual offshoring*.

In 2002, Forrester Research published one of the most highly cited reports on the scale of outsourcing and offshoring. Forrester calculated the total number of U.S. jobs that could be outsourced by 2015 to be 3.4 million, an annual outflow of about 300,000 jobs per year (McCarthy 2002). Workers in the United States had much to be worried about, considering that between 1995 and 2003, the American economy lost some 2.6 million jobs in the manufacturing sector. However a 2007 OECD report showed that total employment in the services sector had *increased* by over 14 million jobs during that period. In Canada, the percentage of jobs that were susceptible to offshoring in the economy actually *decreased* from 19.5 percent in 1995 to 18.6 percent in 2002. This was at a time when total employment in services increased by over 1.8 million jobs in Canada. A similar decline was present in the U.S. as well (OECD 2006a).

For Canada, studies have isolated seventy-five occupational classifications prone to offshore outsourcing, eighteen of which are considered "clerical" (van Welsum and Vickery 2005). This does not mean that offshoring is the only trade- and industry-related practice lending to the erosion of jobs fitting this classification. Overall the list includes a range of employment categories from engineer and computer analyst, to journalist, word processing operator, and executive assistant. As the share of services increases in a given economy, the demand for ICT-using occupations grows. An expanding post-industrial economy intensifies the need for knowledge workers, thereby furthering pressure on domestic labor markets and accelerating the drive for offshoring as a means of meeting labor demands and stabilizing wages. Again, the *potential* for the offshoring of services is recognized in these models. Claims made by Forrester Research and others are, to be sure, based on intuitive assumptions regarding the occupational classifications prone to outsourcing and offshoring, and not necessarily based on actually existing practices or labor market realities (Kirkegaard 2004). For instance, between 1987 and 2006, the number of clerical occupations in the economy dropped by approximately 138,000, a majority of which were lost between 1987 and 2004, before service offshoring became a common practice (Morisette and Johnson 2007, 15). A high proportion of these occupations were situated outside of the commercial sector, such as in public service, where, for the time being, the offshoring of work remains negligible. Corporate takeovers, public sector redundancies, technology-related redundancies, and plant closures all made a larger contribution than offshoring to the reduction of employment in clerical occupations. The lack of systematic and reliable data sets further complicates the process of tracking offshoring, and since one method asks employers to self-identify their use of the practice, firms are reluctant to admit they are offshoring work because of possible public backlash.

Prior to the popular conception of offshoring understood today, which is tied to back office processes and call centers, common usage of the term *offshore* initially referred to foreign tax and financial havens sought after by corporations and wealthy individuals. More recently the concept is seen as the shifting of tasks to low-cost nations, rather than to any destinations outside the country (Carmel and Tjia 2005). A companion practice is *outsourcing*, which encompasses the contracting out of business operations to an outside provider. This process can entail a range of corporate activities from the use of staffing agencies to employing the services of outside expertise or other firms to perform non-core functions. The process, also called "externalization", reflects an increasing division of labor linked to technological innovation and changing patterns of business operations (Majluf 2007). Both practices go hand in hand, but in many cases the offshoring of work involves in-house operations—meaning owned and controlled by a single firm, and not subcontracted to a third party—established in a different location and possibly through the use of subsidiaries, which take the form of intra-firm trade.

Debates surrounding free trade agreements emphasize the extent to which developing economies should be linked to their wealthy counterparts, which provided the basis for the Doha round of World Trade Organization negotiations. Finding new sources of inexpensive labor is germane to the development of a global division of knowledge labor. Critics suggest that the richest countries have the most to gain when developing regions engage in these types of agreements (Jomo and von Arnim 2008). Even when the positive spillover effects of offshoring are included—such as the transfer of technology, skills, management structures, increased tax revenues, investment, foreign exchange, and new employment opportunities—the problem of uneven development remains prevalent.

Economic development, enabled through offshoring and FDI, is conditional on the prospects for an economy to move up the value chain and provide higher value-added goods and services. Without a broader expansion of skill-demanding industries, productivity growth and employment remain isolated to particular sectors and a relatively small percentage of the labor market (Paus and Shapiro 2007). Evidence from leading developing economies shows that productivity has far outpaced employment growth, meaning that the expansion of new technologies and capital has not generated economy-wide benefits (Conference Board 2008). Despite the obvious inequities, scholars and industry leaders maintain that in high-tech industries, the fortunes of firms in the wealthy economies are dependent upon the labor and knowledge of workforces in developing countries. This is evidenced by the fact that over half of Fortune 500 companies are now customers of the Indian IT industry, several of which have established subsidiaries on the subcontinent (Sahay, Nicholson, and Krishna 2003).[4]

For proponents of offshore outsourcing, the globalization of work enhances a sector's or country's competitiveness by increasing productivity, creating the basis for wage increases, and improving standards of living (Houseman 2007). These supposed improvements are due to the increase of efficiency with which inputs are used, namely by utilizing the services offered by expert providers that exercise their comparative advantage in a given industry.[5] Because of lower operating costs, companies in turn increase profits and expand investment and employment opportunities domestically into higher value-added services and operations. Leading business research firms like the Conference Board (2008) emphasize that the competitive pressures from developing economies, as they evolve from a dominant agricultural sector to manufacturing and services, push the need for growing productivity in the wealthy countries. These trends add to the business argument that general economic growth is supported by the entry of developing economies into the global market. Such an emphasis on the possibilities of growing economic integration, technology advances, and productivity growth led *The Economist* (2007a) to remark in 2007, less than a year before the sub-prime financial crisis, that "[t]hese are the glory days of global capitalism".

In their report to the National Bureau of Economic Research in the United States, Amiti and Wei (2006), two researchers most cited in the offshoring literature, suggest that service offshoring accounted for a 10 percent labor productivity growth in the United States between 1992 and 2000. Like most of the publications that chart the real economic impact of offshoring, results are based on scant empirical evidence given the limited availability of national economic data.[6] It is only in the last ten years that meaningful economic information on the effects of offshoring service work has become available. Even then, the data remains spurious. Tracking service sector production faces similar methodological flaws. In the case of Canada, this has resulted in a distorted image of the country's growing and increasingly important service sector (Goldfarb and Theriault 2008). Yet, the emphasis remains fixated on the case that even if outsourcing and offshoring results in an immediate shedding of labor, increased efficiency *should* lead to high productivity and an expansion of employment in other occupations (Amiti and Wei 2004a, 2004b). The rationale is that increased productivity leads to lower prices and higher rates of profit, as well as building potential for employment expansion in new, higher value-added sectors. There is also the promise of positive trends that follow from an expansion of offshoring, namely an increase in consumer purchasing power, export growth, structural inflation controls, and better returns on capital (OECD 2007, 7).

Conclusions drawn by the steadfast proponents of offshoring deserve to be held in question. There exists limited official data measuring the extent of offshoring and its impact at either national or international levels. Indirect measures such as data on trade in services, employment, input-output tables, and evidence from company surveys are used in the place of systematic information (OECD 2006a, 2006b). Inferences about the globalization of services are speculative and premised on research that focuses on the offshoring of manufacturing. What these claims ignore is that the figures tracking the offshoring of manufacturing jobs fail to account for the types of new positions acquired by workers displaced by the reduction of industrial employment. It is interesting, however, to recognize the class bias associated with the types of production being sent abroad and that globalization has been historically supported by senior managers and other privileged sectors of the white-collar economy. Indicative of the changing mood surrounding a broadening of offshoring to include services, an OECD (2007) report noted, "[s]killed jobs are no longer safe from being sent offshore . . . [and the practice is] increasingly spreading to technology-intensive industries". Consequently, there is reason to believe that these developments have meant a backslide in support for free trade policies, or more broadly, globalization, amongst the middle and upper-middle classes (Rajan and Wei 2004).

Not all economists share the same optimistic perspective on free trade globalization. Paul Samuelson (2004), eminent economist and recipient of the Bank of Sweden's prize honoring Alfred Nobel, recognized that the gains of the winners from free trade exceed the losses of the losers. He went on to emphasize, however, that the least skilled and least educated workers suffer the most, even in advanced economies, which contributes to deepening social inequalities and sinking incomes. Mainstream economists, Samuelson claimed, have paid scant attention to these developments and largely ignore drastic changes in mean U.S. incomes and social inequalities. Political economists have leveled a similar charge against classical economists in Canada who failed to acknowledge the income polarization developing in the economy throughout the 1990s (Veltmeyer and Sacouman 1998). This adds to the symptoms that follow from the expansion of the globalization of production, such as falling real wages in certain sectors, especially in sectors that employ unskilled and semi-skilled labor. Deterioration in terms of trade, declining capacity for innovation, loss of tax revenues, and variable regional effects are other notable potential consequences accompanying the use of foreign labor (OECD 2007).

What is lacking in the business case for policies supporting the globalization of work is recognition that the benefits of free trade cannot be realized without concerted political efforts in the form of social and economic programs that help offset the potential damaging consequences of offshoring (Freeman 2007). In this regard, policies inspired by the neo-liberal philosophy fail to address the symptoms of offshoring and outsourcing, opting instead to focus on the hypothetical benefits of economic liberalization while neglecting the social dimension of change. Even *The Economist* (2007a) has acknowledged that real wages for American workers have grown less than half as fast as productivity, while in contrast the top pay for leading managers has increased from roughly forty times the average to 110 times the average in the past twenty years. In Canada, the country's top CEOs now pocket 235 times more than the average worker. Accompanying the optimistic accounts offered by much of the business press there is still recognition that global capitalism has indeed marginalized vast segments of the labor force. For instance, *The Economist* notes that the objective for governments should be to help establish a transition to jobs in emerging sectors that offset the economic hardships of unemployment caused by trade policies and offshoring. Not surprisingly, the publication is silent on the details of how to remedy the problem.

An absence of official national accounts and the complexity of how offshoring is calculated suggest that the results of studies might actually underestimate the positive as well as the negative impacts of the phenomenon. Similar conclusions can be drawn about the global restructuring of MNCs when relocation results in the expansion of production in one region and the scaling back in another. In the 1960s, Indian economist Jagdish Bhagwati (1968) drew attention to the "immiserating effects of trade", when economies continue to grow while becoming relatively poorer because of the drop of export prices and deteriorating terms of trade caused, in part, by low wages. Similarly, as the OECD (2006a) reminds us, there will be both winners and losers as a result of the globalization of services. For policy makers it becomes a question of how those who prosper from offshoring can compensate those who do not. Preventing adjustment would only serve as a short-term palliative solution to an otherwise long-term structural problem, according to the OECD's prescriptions. Less is said, of course, of the potentially devastating consequences of laissez-faire liberalization. Positive accounts of offshoring are constructed on the premise that the ramifications of *not* pursuing a liberal trade regime in services could be more economically consequential. For example, a failure to offshore could mean that bankruptcies or closures, and subsequent unemployment, might well be linked to a company not taking advantage of global production networks and foreign sources of labor (OECD 2007).

It is important to consider, however, that the practice of offshoring can-not be divorced from other developments in global capitalism, notably a deterioration of employment standards and the growth of temporary and part-time work. Even during the current recessionary period in the U.S., the alleged threat of skilled labor shortages continues to prompt support among employers to accelerate the use of offshore workers. Canada has done the same through its Temporary Foreign Worker Program, despite suspi-cion that the labor shortage argument has been exaggerated by the busi-ness lobby (see *Huffington Post* 2012; Weir 2012). A direct consequence of this shortfall is pressure on firms to increase wages and salaries to recruit top talent, labeled as an "artificial rise" since it inflates the wage rate that would otherwise exist under a full employment scenario. The result ham-pers economic growth by raising input labor costs and therefore increasing the prices of goods and services produced by U.S. companies (Evalueserve 2003).[7] Firms become less competitive in the domestic and global market when they do not take advantage of lower cost operations, which implies a further loss of employment. Plants shut down, firms are incapable of consol-idating their financial positions, and companies are prevented from accumu-lating necessary resources to invest in new technologies or upgrade products and services. Citing the example of New Jersey, the National Foundation for American Policy (2007) indicated that efforts to prevent the outsourcing of call center contracts by the state in 2002 meant that returning the opera-tions to the United States ended up costing the public coffers an additional $886,000 for just twelve jobs. Policy responses that invoke the language of protectionism draw criticism from the business community for this reason.

Appeasing public outcries against job losses through protectionist mea-sures often involves excluding firms that shift operations offshore from government contracts, taxing offshore-related imports, and canceling gov-ernment aid to firms that shift operations offshore. In 2009, an Australian MP drafted an a bill entitled *Keeping jobs from Going Offshore* in an attempt to prevent call center jobs from being sent to India and the Philip-pines (Callcenters.net 2009b). Despite the rhetoric of free trade, the United States has been at the forefront of anti-offshoring legislation amongst OECD countries. In 2004, five U.S. states enacted anti-outsourcing leg-islation and by 2005 thirty-six states have brought forward at least 100 bills to limit the offshoring of service activities, many of which sought to restrict the use of foreign call center operations specifically (Le Goff 2005). Ironically some of these states outsourced their unemployment and taxation processes to a new division of India's Tata Consultancy Services (TCS) in the U.S. (Mazurkewich 2008). Canadian call center industry groups in turn predicted that state-level and national legislation could result in the loss of thousands of jobs if companies were prevented from establishing facilities in Canada. Most recently, lawmakers in the United States introduced the *Call Center Worker and Consumer Protection Act*, which would require the Secretary of Labor to make available a list of employers that relocate a call center overseas and to make these companies ineligible for Federal grants.

The sentiment against offshoring grew during the 2008 U.S. Presidential election when opposition to outsourcing was seen as a popular policy at a time of economic downturn. Obama's "Buy American" policy strengthened this sentiment. Part of the President's election policies involved canceling tax incentives for companies that took advantage of less expensive offshore services (Callcenters.net 2009c; UNIAPRO 2009). While India's premier IT and ITES lobby group, Nasscom, did not feel as though these anti-offshoring threats could compromise the country's IT-ITES industry, the state and national policy proposals were rational responses to the quarter million call center jobs lost in the United States between 2001 and 2003 (*The Economic Times* 2010). Just as the economic crisis started to hit the American working classes and unemployment increased to double-digit figures, Indian IT-ITES leaders were anticipating an *expansion* of service offshoring. HCL Technology's chief officer, Ranjit Narsimhan, stated in 2008, "BPOs in India are going to benefit from the global credit crunch as companies will resort to more offshoring to minimize impact on falling margins" (cited in Monga and Singh 2007). There is conflicting evidence on the effects, but to some extent Narsimhan's prediction came true as the public service and private sector sought to control costs in a sinking economy.

What think tanks such as the OECD (2007) suggest is that offshoring is inevitable. Academics like Richard Florida (2002; Martin Prosperity Institute 2009) have, for years, made similar claims about the need to accept this reality and brace for the future. Obstacles to this unfolding reality, such as protectionism, are suggested to be counterproductive in the long term and could be found in violation of a country's international trade agreements. But these fatalist responses ignore the historical dimension that precipitated the very existence of global service industries. It goes largely unstated that offshoring is considered by the OECD to be a form of structural adjustment in which the central policy challenge is to create conditions that facilitate the transfer of resources from declining to expanding activities and regions. But as a form of economic adjustment, the real political challenge is to offset the social cost of transition. This includes the organization of retraining, effective social policies that help those displaced by offshoring, as well as encouraging MNCs to comply with labor standards and discuss offshoring plans with employees, expand research and development efforts, and improve cost/benefit assessments of offshoring, as the OECD (2007) proposes. Whether or not business groups and their political allies have the interest or resolve to introduce such planning measures is another question. In the next chapter, I look at how the political economy of offshoring has shaped the respective call center industries in Canada and India.

4 The Global Division of Call Center Work

Call centers have become one of the most visible and recognized symbols of information technology service offshoring. They are also the cornerstone of the broader business process outsourcing (BPO) and business process management (BPM) industries to which India's success as a hub for outsourced and offshored IT employment is attributed. In 2002–2003, call centers represented a majority of export-oriented FDI projects in services (UNCTAD 2004). Call centers also reflect a pivotal step in the human-organization interface, one that has gradually evolved over the past thirty years. Governments, political parties, charities, and corporations from a number of industries have turned to these operations as a cost-effective means of interacting with citizens, potential supporters, donors, clients, and customers. Even unions are experimenting with call centers in their attempts at improving their responsiveness to members' needs (Early 2011). Initially utilized by airlines and financial institutions, the use of call centers has expanded vigorously to become a fixture for complex organizations in Canada. For economies situated in the Global North and the Global South, utilizing call centers has been recognized as an effective strategy to build a competitive and reliable information technology infrastructure, foster regional and national economic growth, and allow local firms and workers to integrate into the global division of knowledge labor.

Global expansion of the call center industry has for the past decade drawn attention to the advantage offered by low-cost markets like India. It has only been in the last five years, however, that developing economies have outpaced wealthier nations as leading destinations of call center FDI and ITES trade. In 2002, Canada held 11 percent (56) of all FDI call center projects. The UK, Israel, and Ireland, along with Canada, maintained the dominant share of call center foreign investment—of the 500 FDI call center projects recorded in 2002 and 2003, more than half went to developed countries. But the rapid growth of Asian economies has started to shift the balance, led by India, China, Malaysia, and Singapore. India received 12 percent (sixty projects) of total export-oriented FDI call center projects in 2002, besting Canada, one of its central competitors, for the first time (UNCTAD 2004, 163). By 2003, foreign companies were outsourcing work to 800 call centers in India, up from sixty just three years earlier (Mirchandani 2004a, 356). What this chapter uncovers is the political economic dimensions of how call centers developed in the Canadian and Indian national context. Through a corresponding change in government policy-making, technological development, the internationalization of human resource management practices, and the facilitation of foreign investment through liberalization and commercialization, the call center has become a global industry in its own right. I begin with the case of Canada.

CANADA'S CALL CENTERS: AMERICA'S "OFFSHORE" OF CHOICE

The neo-liberal model of telecommunications policy in Canada has been oriented since the late 1970s towards continentalism, which describes the convergence of technological and corporate integration on a continental scale in North America. Part of this transformation includes a regime of neo-liberal regulation, or the re-orientation of policies that favor the lifting of foreign-investment restrictions, the centralization of telecommunication jurisdiction within the federal government, and the privileging of business-led market forces. Canada's federal communications regulator, the Canadian Radio-television and Telecommunications Commission (CRTC), has in the last fifteen years deepened its subordination to the federal cabinet, the Ministry of Industry, the Department of Foreign Affairs and International Trade, and the Competition Bureau (Rideout 2002). In 2006, the federal Conservative government issued a Policy Directive to the CRTC stating that it was to regulate telecommunications in a "manner that interferes to the minimum extent necessary with competitive market forces" (Government of Canada 2008). One of the conclusions drawn from Industry Canada's *Compete to Win* policy report was that competitiveness within the telecommunications sector can and should be strengthened through the liberalization of foreign investment regulations.

Continentalization, as political economists have long recognized, involves more than a simple integration of industry in North America (Rideout 2002; Mosco and Schiller 2001). Through trade agreements such as NAFTA, the ability of federal and provincial authorities to determine telecommunications policy is superseded by the legal provisions contained within neo-liberal treaties. In a broader sense, the sociopolitical regime has prefigured attempts to build social consent for market-oriented changes by using the argument that increased competition leads to lower prices, enhanced customer service, and generally a higher level of economic well-being. The underlying motives, however, are driven by the interests of capital to commodify largely public services. This trend began in the 1980s when the Royal Commission on the Economic Union and Development Prospects for Canada, or Macdonald Commission, emphasized the need for Canada to move toward an "open-market society" (Rideout 2002, 54). Current trends in telecommunications policy represent a conscious unraveling of industrial and national policies that date back as far as the late 19th century, when the new country of Canada introduced the First National Policy based on a platform of economic nationalism and the nurturing of so-called natural monopolies. Natural monopolies, like the massive telecommunications giants, are premised on three main assumptions: "*efficiency* through economies of scale, *systemic integrity* through end-to-end control, [and] *service universality* through cost-averaging and cross-subsidization" (Babe 1990, 239). Cross-subsidization was pivotal in achieving telephone universality in Canada by allowing local usage rates to be subsidized by more profitable operations, namely business subscribers and long distance charges.

When the federal government entertained the possibility of a liberalized telecommunications policy, a seemingly mismatched coalition of opponents emerged. Unions, public interest advocates, consumer groups, provincial governments, and even established Canadian telephone carriers, like Bell, fiercely resisted the free-market telecommunications policy changes. As in the United States—where major corporate *users* of telecommunications services made up of leading manufacturers, financial companies, banks, broadcasting corporations, and transportation companies combined their lobbying strength under the umbrellas of the Telecommunications Users Committee and Committee of Corporate Telephone Users—it was Canada's corporate community that pushed for a transformation of telecommunications policy through liberalization. Multinational firms were critical in pushing for these reforms that would allow for expanded entry and low-cost access for their goods and services in other national economies (Rideout 2002, 72–73).

Industry leaders recognized that the cross-subsidization model affiliated with telecommunications universality was a direct hindrance to their pursuit of expanding their global market opportunities because local rates were allowed to stabilize by charging more for the services used by business. Liberalized markets offered new investment opportunities, particularly for major financial institutions, in the event that the telecommunications sector was opened to further competition. Prospects for international trade in services and offshoring were made possible by the subordination of social policy to market-led forces. Competing interests within the ranks of large businesses and their political allies also characterized this trend, although the major telecommunications companies did eventually benefit from the liberalized market place. Governments continue to be instrumental in facilitating this exchange among major firms, and can hardly be considered innocent bystanders in what was part of a global information revolution. Indeed, the political architecture was in great part designed and implemented by governments themselves. But the legacy of monopoly carriers and universality meant that the country has one of the most advanced and extensive telecommunication infrastructures in the world. This is what contributed to Canada's appeal as a leading destination for the call center industry.

While India has been ranked as the "star performer" in the offshoring industry, countries like Singapore, New Zealand, Canada, and Ireland have historically been at the center of the offshoring interest despite their relatively high costs (A.T. Kearney 2004). In the same index, Canada was ranked second as the most attractive offshore location and business environment. Canada's position as a popular "nearshore" destination for U.S. firms was identified by the *New York Times* nearly a decade ago, when the country's cultural similarity to the United States made it a top destination for high-value, sophisticated service work (Austen 2004). Because of Canada's then-favorable low dollar exchange rate at the time, the cost of a Canadian call center agent was approximately 85 percent of their U.S. counterpart (Datamonitor 2006). Business costs were also less in Canada and the use of Canadian ITES saved U.S. providers between 20 and 30 percent of operating costs by moving operations "nearshore" (Scott, Garner, and Ticoll 2004). It is a far cry from the 50 to 70 percent savings offered by the Indian advantage, but the cultural and national familiarity made the Canadian option more appealing in some cases.

Because Canada has been identified as a destination for offshoring, opposition to the practice has been, for the most part, less intense than in the U.S. This does not mean that the Canadian economy is immune to the negative effects of service offshoring or that the public at large has accepted the practice. In 2008, TD Bank, one of the country's largest financial institutions, employed the services of a call center vendor in India. Consumer and public backlash ensued following the bank's foreign pilot project (Roseman 2008).[1] Even though Canada ranks as a desirable offshore location, between 1961 and 2003 the share of imports in service inputs almost tripled from 2.6 percent to 7.6 percent, led by business and financial services. As industries increased investment in information and communication technologies (ICTs)—which include computers, telecommunications equipment, and software—they increased their service offshoring activities as well. The increasing use of ICTs has contributed to the reduction of distance barriers associated with trade in services, thereby creating the possibility of further growth in the range of occupations prone to offshoring in Canada (Statistics Canada 2008). Although no consensus exists with regard to the effects offshoring has on employment and wages, Canadian studies suggest that trade leads to *lower* demand for labor in industries and sectors affected by *increased imports*; on the other hand it leads to a *greater* demand in sectors where exports are increasing (Baldwin and Gu 2008). According to Statistics Canada (2008), service offshoring has had a *negative* effect, albeit a negligible one, on wages in the service-producing sector. So far, however, Canada's service-producing industries have been sheltered from the consequences of large-scale imports.

The appeal of India as a reliable offshore destination has drawn the attention of Canadian corporate leaders over the last decade. A corporate executive based in Canada remarked that, after his trip to India, he believed that his firm could potentially keep only 30 percent of its existing IT staff, notably for high-value creative work and management projects, and send the remaining jobs offshore. "I used to say we should consider the risks of offshoring", he said. "Now I believe we should consider the risks of not offshoring . . . *we could easily become a brand-name company, with most of the work done overseas*" (Scott, Garner, and Ticoll 2004, 34, emphasis added). But there is still reason to question the prevalence of offshoring by Canadian firms. Of the $1 billion of business service imports from the non-OECD region, some estimates indicate that less than 1 percent of the 13.5 million Canadians employed in 2004 would have been affected by this type of offshoring (Morisette and Johnson 2007, 10–12). What has provoked significant attention and public backlash in Canada is the recruitment of temporary foreign workers to Canadian soil, rather than the use of offshore foreign workers to provide information services. Still, public relations and political factors rank high on the list of obstacles for companies that are considering the offshore option, as well as the readiness and experience on the part of buyers to interact with foreign vendors and the ability to manage distant operations (Scott, Garner, and Ticoll 2004; Conference Board of Canada 2005). However, as industries and sectors grow their experience with offshoring, best practices and industry standards will make the use of offshore vendors routine and subsequently accelerate the practice. This is partly what has made Canada an appealing destination for call center work destined from the United States.

Estimates indicate that there are in excess of 14,000 call centers in Canada, employing over half a million full and part-time staff, or 3.4 percent of the total employed Canadian population, according to the most recent data. Ten years ago, the industry was estimated to contribute between CAN$36 and $38 billion to the country's GDP (Canadian Customer Contact Center Industry 2002).[2] These estimates are premised on the North American Industry Classification System (NAICS) definition of a call center which includes no less than eleven industry categories (see Statistics Canada n.d.a., n.d.b.). A majority of centers in Canada are inbound (approximately 77 percent) and many of these (40 percent) handle customer service activities. Most of Canada's centers service the finance, telecommunications, retail, hospitality, and public service sectors (Van Jaarsveld, Frost, and Walker 2007, 10). Growth in all of these areas has been substantial. Between 2000 and 2004, 166 call centers were established in Canada, creating about 50,000 jobs (EDC 2005). By comparison, Canada's entire information and communication technology (ICT) sub-sector, which includes manufacturing, software services, and wholesaling, generated $155 billion in revenues in 2011 and employed some 521,000 workers in 33,000 companies. Average annual income is approximately $68,000 (Industry Canada 2013).

There are, however, widely varying figures on the economic and employment impact of call centers on the Canadian economy. Some research suggests that industry revenues were far more modest, climbing from $424 million in 1998 to $2.76 billion in 2006, representing an average annual increase of 27.7 percent (Vincent and McKeown 2008). By contrast the overall economy grew at an average annual rate of 5.9 percent in the same period. Alternative employment figures show that in the broader category of business support services, of which telephone call centers are a part, the number of jobs grew from 20,000 to 112,000 between 1987 and 2004, an increase of 447 percent (Akyeampong 2005). Employment figures and the economic impact of call centers are difficult to categorize because they tend to service a number of industries and sectors, from manufacturing and the public services to telecommunications and retail. No matter the source, the evidence is clear that the Canadian call center industry has witnessed tremendous expansion over the past decade.

Employment growth in the call center industry was prompted by a variety of factors, but it has been Canada's multilingual capabilities, a highly skilled and proficient workforce, historically low exchange rate with American currency, and an advanced telecommunications network that facilitated the rise of call centers as a chief export-based industry. Canada's economic and labor market openness to U.S. companies is what defines Canada's position in the global division of knowledge work. However, it was the shifting pattern of how companies interface with customers that prompted the rise of tele-mediated services. Tendencies to increase profits by cutting costs meant that centralized and dedicated customer interaction centers were ideal ways of commodifying services. Economic crises and falling rates of profit accelerated this process. As the services offered by call centers became lucrative commodities, major outsourcing firms reached the status of multibillion dollar enterprises. Marketing strategies and public relations efforts by businesses and governments also helped to normalize non-personal encounters. Telephone banking, which expanded by 50 percent between 1994 and 1995, became a prominent service offered by financial institutions for these reasons. Handling customer complaints, conducting pre/post sales customer service, giving technical advice, entering orders and reservations, establishing help lines, and providing warranty and repair services contributed to this trend (Steedman 2003, 4). By 2007, 35 percent of Canada's call centers were serving international customers, the third highest after India (73 percent) and Ireland (37 percent), which far exceeds the global average of 14 percent (Holman, Batt, and Holtgrewe 2007). Canadian companies still dominate the domestic call center industry, despite their export-oriented status. Early estimates reveal that 82 percent of all call centers are Canadian owned (Canadian Customer Contact Center Industry 2002, 86).

Political and economic factors have played a decided role in building Canada's position in the global call center marketplace. With a universal public health care system, Canadian firms are less burdened with expensive health benefit packages in terms of attracting talented employees. Because of cuts to corporate taxes at the federal and provincial levels throughout the 1990s, Canada is at least comparable to the U.S. in terms of business and personal tax rates (Contact Center Canada 2006a). Metropolitan areas such as Montreal, Toronto, and Vancouver offered vast multicultural and multilingual talent to both foreign and domestic companies seeking to establish call center operations—by some accounts companies could draw from as many as seventy languages (Canadian Customer Contact Center Industry 2002). The province of New Brunswick is particularly lucrative because of its bilingual English- and French-speaking population, which offers an advantage over regions in the United States as well as other parts of Canada. But it was the economic recession that hit Canada in the early 1990s that contributed to the growth of a burgeoning industry. This was especially true for Canada's Eastern Atlantic provinces, which list the highest percentage of call centers per number of business establishments (Statistics Canada 2006). Indeed, the Eastern Canada case is of particular significance since a higher than average number of call centers in these provinces (58.7 percent) serve the international market, compared with Central (26.6 percent) and Western Canada (29.7 percent) (Van Jaarsveld, Frost, and Walker 2007). Incidentally, Atlantic Canada has the lowest percentage of Canadian ownership (at 60 percent) and a high percentage of U.S. multinational ownership (35 percent) (Carroll and Wagar 2007).

New Brunswick's dramatic entry into the post-industrial economy accelerated Canada's role as a leading call center offshore destination. Approximately 21,000 people in over 100 facilities are employed in call centers in a province with less than a million residents. Like other economies in Atlantic Canada, New Brunswick was traditionally dependent on the lumber and fisheries industries as a major source of GDP and employment. Upon the decline of these staple industries, the province, under the leadership of then-Premier Frank McKenna, turned to the promises offered by a liberalized and globally integrated post-industrial economy. McKenna's efforts relied on the extensive telecommunications infrastructure available in the region. However, despite the reference to a liberalized market, the transformation of New Brunswick's economy involved an intensive program of government intervention that deployed the policies and practices resembling the "development state" of Southeast Asian economies (Larner 2002a, 2002b). The draw of the province was the attention its government paid to providing financial assistance to company training expenses, removing taxes on 1–800 numbers, and the gradual reduction of payroll and corporate taxes. Research and development incentives, loan guarantees, reforming workers compensation regulations, and start-up capital were other enticements offered to firms willing to establish themselves in New Brunswick. Regional development agencies, industry groups, and the government were quick to add that the province boasted a bilingual workforce capable of servicing English- and French-speaking customers domestically and abroad. Economic recession and a low unionization rate, which deteriorated further after the decline of primary commodity industries, made the province especially attractive to American companies. Some of the leading candidates for the call center industry were staff members previously employed by the provincial government and those who had worked for the public telephone company before it was privatized.

New Brunswick's public relations strategy reproduced the myths associated with post-industrial capitalism, especially the argument that the jobs being created were knowledge-intensive and on the leading end of value-added performance. The basic requirement for many of these jobs, however, was a high school degree, along with basic computer and keyboarding skills. McKenna pointed out that the development strategy was actually one that sought to create employment across the spectrum of pay and skill. "[Y]ou need jobs for every skill set, and every socio-economic group". He went on to add, "An outbound center that pays $8.50 an hour doesn't sound great unless you compare it to a fish plant job at $5.25 an hour". As one study revealed, annual pay for workers ranged from $15,000 to $25,000 in the early years of the boom (McFarland 2002). At the high end of the pay scale, call center workers in the province were making approximately $16 an hour in 2000 (cited in Buchanan and Koch-Schulte 2000, 11, 19). The downside to this growth was that Eastern Canadian facilities witnessed some of the highest turnover rates and are home to the highest proportion of outsourced centers, not unlike their counterparts in India. Because of the export-driven nature of the industry being established in New Brunswick, McFarland (2002) labeled the sector as "maquiladoras of the North", drawing a comparison to the manufacturing export region skirting the border between Mexico and the United States. Benefits reside with the multinational firms that are able to take advantage of the low-cost workforce, propped by government subsidies, tax holidays, and pro-business reforms to labor legislation and health and safety requirements (see EDC 2005).

Nova Scotia and New Brunswick were not the only provinces attempting to make a transition to the post-industrial economy by using call centers as a launch pad. Manitoba pursued similar strategies by promoting its job-ready workforce, unemployment rate, and subsidized telecommunications and hydroelectric costs. Because wages in the Western province, like those of Eastern Canada, were lower than the national average at the time, the cost advantage was greater than that offered in the country's major urban centers (Guard 2003).[3] Even the province's New Democratic Party (NDP) government, traditionally a social democratic party with trade union support, was keen to protect the interests of business over that of workers.

A leading criticism of these "development state" strategies is that, like their counterparts in the Global South, export-dependent call centers are sensitive to overnight fluctuations in demand from a handful of foreign markets, and in Canada's case, just one. Sudden closures following a contract cancelation leaves workers unemployed without warning. Rapid technological innovations and declining international telecommunications rates have exacerbated the situation (see Buchanan and Koch-Schulte 2000). In 2007, call center employees in Fredericton and Bathurst, New Brunswick, were locked out of work when Connect North America shut down their facilities with no advanced warning (CBC News 2007a). Company CEO and president, Barry O'Donnell, stated that the appreciated exchange rate between Canada and the U.S. forced the closures. Despite the favorable conditions offered by the province, O'Donnell still chastised the government for not providing enough resources for job retention (CBC News 2007b). This story is not unlike dozens of other, almost identical, cases across Canada. Even after another firm, AOL, received a $1.2 million forgivable loan from the province to set up shop in Moncton, the company shed almost half of its workers by 2007 (CBC News 2007c). Corporate restructuring and the centralization of customer service call centers have also contributed to layoffs and reduced benefits even for those workers employed by regional monopoly telecommunication companies (CBC News 2008). Bell Aliant, one of North America's largest regional communications providers and part of the BCE empire, recently announced plans to close three of its five Atlantic call centers, which employ a total of 1,100 workers. Over 30,000 jobs in business support services, which includes call centers, disappeared between 2007 and 2012. Nearly all of these losses were experienced in New Brunswick and Ontario (Campbell 2012).

Higher value-added call centers, particularly those in the IT and financial services area, are more sustainable. It is the lower end telemarketing and customer service segments of the industry that are most likely to fall victim to international market pressures and overnight closures. Economists note that the transient and unstable nature of the industry, once seen as a savior of the province's economy, requires economic and employment diversification (Morris 2007). David Campbell, an independent economic consultant, emphasized that New Brunswick should put greater effort into attracting financial service and hedge fund centers, which offer more stability and higher wages. He went on to argue that these are the kinds of salaries the province needs if it wants to reap tax revenue windfalls required to become a "have province" by 2026 (CBC News 2008).[4] "Upper Tier" services (as defined by Contact Center Canada [2006b], the industry's leading national lobby group), which demand specialized knowledge of products, services, and technical skills and are rewarded with higher levels of discretion and wages, are required if the industry is to grow and generate domestic demand. This corroborates other indications that call center outsourcing to Canada is slowing because the country is becoming a more expensive destination for U.S. outsourcers, especially since the financial collapse of 2007. Since 2002, Canada's cost advantage over the United States declined from 23 percent to less than 4 percent in 2005 (Contact Center Canada 2006a, 127, 4). Low-end and highly routinized business process operations are likely to head abroad as a result. Foreign direct investment in new contact centers will consequently have ceased to be a major source for growth in the Canadian sector. Offshoring to less expensive foreign destinations, like India and the Philippines, will likely increase as Canadian-based third party service providers experience financial difficulties and struggle to maintain their share of the U.S. outsourced market. One estimate suggested that offshoring would affect between 7,000 and 9,000 call center positions in Canada annually, although these figures were never confirmed (Contact Center Canada 2006a).

Such forecasting is premised on a general theory of how the call center industry develops. As the export-focused segment of the Canadian call center industry develops, the number of workers employed in this type of facility will likely flatten out or experience a moderate decline, confirming the prognosis offered by Samuelson (2004). It is possible that prospects might improve for work that is closer to the top of the value-added scale, and that employment in the sector will lead to a growing demand for high-performance and knowledge-intensive processes.[5] Pressures for particular skill sets, training, and education will increase as lower skilled call center employment decreases in Canada. Meanwhile, economic growth and a declining unemployment rate are detrimental to call centers that depend on low-cost labor. Citing a lack of available employees, the Quebec-based firm, Atelka Inc., closed down its operations in Bathurst. This small New Brunswick community had over 1,000 people employed in call centers, up from about 300 just ten years prior (Shipley 2008). StarTek, a U.S.-based outsourcer, experienced a labor shortage in Saskatchewan's capital, Regina, following an unforeseen resource boom that propelled the province's economy. The company's site manager, Wendy Hofford, said that the corporation was now forced to compete for employees and could no longer rely on a stagnant economy to draw applicants (Schussler 2007). In fact, instances of closure for this reason are too numerous to cite.

Technology also factors into why Canadian centers come into competition with offshore destinations. Basic and highly routinized business process operations, which dominate the call center industry, are especially prone to global competition and, thus, a downward pressure on wages. With Voice over Internet Protocol (VoIP) moving into mainstream usage it has become a feasible practice to manage "virtual contact centers" that employ home-based customer service agents (Contact Center Canada 2006a). But while the "here today, outsourced tomorrow" perspective has some ground in reality, consideration needs to be given to the spatial and geographic significance embedded within regional labor markets and political economic conditions. *Threats* of relocation, and offshoring specifically, have nonetheless been used by low-ranking managers as a union-avoidance strategy (see Contact Center Canada 2006a). Indeed, the public image and myths surrounding the international division of work have an effect in themselves, despite the reality that place still does matter. Still, the costs associated with recruitment, hiring, and retention means that the "footloose" reputation of the industry has some challenges. Firms have a vested interest in fostering a stable workforce and avoiding, where possible, relocation (Contact Center Canada 2006a, 128). Attrition, most of all, has been one of the major problems with India's darling industry, in addition to the hurdle of moving past the simple, routinized task associated with much of the call center and ITES employment that is sent offshore.

INDIA AS A GLOBAL IT/ITES AND CALL CENTER HUB

India emerged among several developing nations as a leader in the offshore call center market shortly after the liberalization of its telecommunications sector. In 2007, the number of call center workers in India was estimated to be approximately 316,000, up from roughly 270,000 in 2006, representing a 16 percent increase (Holman, Batt, and Holtgrewe 2007; Callcenters.net 2007a; Nasscom 2006). Recent figures indicate there are about 350,000 call center workers populating the country's call center landscape, about 50,000 less than the Philippines (Bajaj 2011). India remains a key player in the global call center industry due to its population's high level of English proficiency, relatively inexpensive labor, a highly skilled and educated urban middle-class, as well as the government's commitment to expanding the IT-ITES sector. Indeed, both intensive state intervention and related development of India's human capital have worked to integrate the country into the global division of knowledge labor. These factors have contributed to the development of a multibillion dollar industry, with software and information services accounting for US$100 billion in revenue in 2012, and the entire IT-ITES industry constituting 8 percent of GDP, up from 1.2 percent in 1998 (Nasscom 2009; Nasscom 2013). Accordingly, services, particularly IT and business process management, will likely continue to drive India's export growth for the foreseeable future.

Almost a quarter of India's total exports are in IT-ITES and the country accounts for over half of the global outsourcing market. The fastest rate of growth for IT services, of which call centers are a part, has been experienced in the domestic sector with a compound annual growth rate of 40 percent between 2006 and 2007; the domestic market grew 14 percent in 2012 alone (Thanuja 2007; Nasscom 2013). This development in the domestic sector stems from the increased acceptance of information technology as a growth enabler and competitive tool for Indian corporations. Unlike the export markets for many Asian countries, India's advantage has been in skill-intensive tradable services, exemplified by software, ITES, biotechnology, and project engineering and design, rather than natural resources and labor-intensive manufacturing (Kapur and Ramamurity 2001). In fact, IT-ITES accounts for over a third of India's foreign exchange reserves and currently stands as the largest employer in the organized private sector

(Nasscom 2008a, 2013). Direct employment in the sector reached about 3 million in 2012, with an additional 6.5 million workers indirectly employed by information technology industries. In a country with over 1 billion citizens, these figures are just a fraction of the total working population.

Like their counterparts in Canada, India's call centers remain deeply involved in the business services *export* market, where 73 percent of the facilities serve foreign customers.[6] This is a dramatic inversion of global averages, in which 86 percent of centers serve local, regional, or national markets in their own country (Holman, Batt, Holtgrewe 2007, 5). Of the offshored centers, most are subcontracted (i.e., outsourced) and serve multinational companies based abroad. In India, there is a high likelihood that of the subcontracted vendors, most provide sales or service to the mass consumer market (Batt et al. 2005, 5, 7). Because call centers clustered in these market segments are likely to have lower profit margins and are more focused on cost, Indian call centers are subject to the most standardized work practices and highest levels of performance monitoring, and invest less in skills and training (Holman, Batt, and Holtgrewe 2007, 30; Batt 2002). Almost all of India's call center workers are full-time. Wages and benefits are kept low relative to international standards, but pay is on average 50 percent higher than alternatives offered to this same group of workers in other sectors (McKinsey Global Institute 2003, 508). Skilled labor has certainly benefited from the growth of the industry, since factor cost arbitrage has permitted companies to offer high wages to attract suitable employees.

The labor arbitrage advantage is a leading selling point for India's call center and broader ITES market, and was a deciding factor in the early phases of the sector's "offshore" development. Cost arbitrage involves exploiting differences in the cost of hiring labor across sectors within and across countries. This could involve a multinational company using a foreign subsidiary or subcontracted vendor to perform a variety of core and non-core services (Houseman 2007). As the global market for offshore services grows, so too does the opportunity for capital and skilled labor situated in India. Building on pre-existing business and technical strengths, several Indian firms, like Tata and Infosys, transformed from recipients of offshore contracts into world industry leaders—both companies now rank in the top ten among the world's leading service outsourcers. India's corporate giants have even established themselves internationally in countries like Canada and the United States. As early as 2006, Indian call center experts were being hired to train British and Irish workers. In just a few short years India went from periphery to marquee brand within the sector (*Times of India* 2006). Leading Indian firms like Wipro Ltd., TCS, Infosys, and TransWorks emerged as leading providers of complex business services, and eventually branched out to establish their own operations in wealthy economies. TransWorks, part of the greater Birla Group, now owns the Canadian business processing operation specialist, Minacs, and Silverline

Technologies Ltd. acquired another Canadian customer interaction specialist, OMDR Inc., which I examine in Chapter 6 (*BusinessLine* 2008).

In the context of India's dramatic entry into the global economy, many attribute the country's economic successes to the reforms that began in the early 1990s under the stewardship of then-finance minister and economist, Manmohan Singh, in the Congress-led Rao government. Prompted by a balance of payments crisis in 1991, India was forced to accept an International Monetary Fund (IMF) bailout package under the provision that it adopt deep-rooted neo-liberal reforms. The country's policy-makers put faith in Singh's turn toward liberalization, which involved the cutting of trade barriers, lifting caps on foreign investment and ownership, dismantling the licensing raj, slashing corporate income taxes, and privatizing state assets. Traditional development policies that followed the import substitution industrialization (ISI) model, the hallmark of post-Independence "Nehruvian socialism", were largely abandoned in favor of economic strategies stemming from the "Washington Consensus" (see Fine, Lapavitsas, Pincus 2001).

While this post-1991 shift is attributed to the end of constrained private economic activity, in reality it was the *pro-business* reforms of the 1980s, rather than the *pro-market* policies of the 1990s, that launched India's productivity growth in certain sectors, notably those industries dependent upon information technology (Rodrik and Subramanian 2001).[7] Rajiv Gandhi's tenure as Prime Minister marked an era when special attention was put on the software sector and the potential it held both for the domestic and export markets. This came after a shift within Congress ranks, spearheaded initially by Indira Gandhi, when the party became more supportive of private business. These incentives included a ten year tax holiday for IT, income tax exemption on export earnings in the software sector, export subsidies, as well as the free import of both the hardware and software requirements of these companies (Krishna 2005). In fact, as a sector classification, the term "ITES" was invented to allow BPO companies to dodge taxes, since information technology services were traditionally exempted from the country's existing tax regime. These benefits have further enhanced India's cost advantage (Mirchandani 2012). Bangalore emerged in the 1980s as a center for IT production as a result of the government's direct involvement in developing the city as a high-tech hub. Interventionist policies date back to the 1950s when Bangalore was the hub for publicly-funded research and development, made possible by the concentration of educational institutions that are still housed in the city. An interview with then-IT secretary of Karnataka in 2007 revealed that the State Government offered a range of incentives from assistance in acquiring land as well as direct subsidization in the form of exemption from commercial tariffs. For this reason it is hardly a coincidence that Karnataka, Bangalore's home state, generates 36 percent of India's IT revenue (Mayer-Ahuja and Feuerstein 2007; *The Economic Times* 2008b). Pro-business policies, in the case of IT development, were at the same time state interventionist policies.

During the parliamentary elections of 2004, "India Shining" was adopted by the Bharatiya Janata Party (BJP) as its central campaign platform. The BJP's seemingly radical and futurist vision departed from the imagery of India as home to poverty, illiteracy, and slow economic progress. India's Finance Minister at the time, Yashwant Sinha, promised to further the recognition that the country was moving towards major-power status as a nuclear-weapons state and highly developed in the areas of science and technology (Ramamurti 2001). As early as 1998, then-Prime Minister, Atal Bihari Vajpayee, declared that India should aspire for IT superpower status by 2008. The government proceeded to establish a National Task Force on Information Technology and Software Development that same year as a way of realizing the objective. By the end of 1998 the Task Force provided over 100 recommendations related to policies in the area of cyber laws, labor laws, fiscal incentives, promotion of IT in schools and rural areas, and increasing computer literacy in the country (Government of India 2001). In 2000, the government passed the Information Technology Act, which provided the basic regulatory framework for the domestic IT industry. An institutional framework for the convergence of services (i.e., telecommunications, IT, media, etc.) was provided that same year with the passage of the Communication Convergence Bill. Both of these policies set regulatory standards for the growing IT-ITES sectors.

Throughout the late 1990s and early 2000s, economic growth rates rose at a rapid and sustainable pace. In terms of GDP expansion, integration into the world economy was helping India secure a prosperous future. Liberalization was cited as a cornerstone for an emerging knowledge economy and facilitated near-double-digit growth rates. Despite efforts to build a high-tech India, the BJP's campaign failed to win over the Indian electorate, largely because a majority of the population had yet to witness any benefits from the knowledge economy. Worse still, job growth in booming IT sectors was outpaced by job losses in other, less sensational areas of the economy (Young Professionals Collective and Focus on the Global South 2005). Manmohan Singh's new Congress-led government ran on a platform, under the center-left United Progressive Alliance (UPA) coalition, which made political use of the fact that millions were left out from the "India Shining" proposal. The UPA has continued to govern from a position that on the one hand appeals to the interest of global capital, but simultaneously addresses the glaring inequalities that has accompanied a "high-tech" India (see Chakravartty and Zhao 2008; Government of India 2008). Singh's success, to be sure, stems from his ability to secure support from leaders of corporate India and their faith in the Prime Minister's ambition to speed up reforms in pension, insurance, and labor laws (*Sify. com* 2008b; M. Singh 2007).

Of the planning measures taken on by the central government, the implementation of the *Special Economic Zones Act 2005* has been the most radical. Underlying the theory of special economic zones (SEZ) is a neo-liberal ethos that these spaces carry with them a promise of economic prosperity for workers and investors because they facilitate an accelerated rate of economic growth in urban and rural areas. By December of 2007, the Indian Ministry of Commerce projected that these zones would be responsible for attracting $20–25 billion of FDI and create over half a million jobs (Aggarwal 2006). Both Indian and foreign multinational companies have cause to be optimistic about the promises offered by SEZs. Tax incentives, low rents, extended lease periods, government provision of infrastructure and utilities, simplified acquisition procedures, and exemptions from various regulations are the chief benefits available to domestic and multinational firms who invest in these zones. For corporations and investors, the real promises offered by SEZs is that they exist as geographic bubbles in which national labor regulations are essentially made void. For instance, as public utility services, SEZs offer additional exemptions from labor laws, the Minimum Wages Act, and the Contract Labor (Regulation and Abolition) Act. Strikes have also been made illegal in these economic enclaves, further evidence that economic liberalization in India is conducted at the expense of existing protections for workers and unions. Special economic zones essentially amplify already business-friendly reforms.

Successive Indian governments at the state and national level continue to applaud the benefits that these zones provide to businesses and their political allies. For these reasons the Eleventh Five Year Plan stressed that the Software Technology Parks of India (STPI) and SEZ schemes should continue "without constraints on where they may be located" (Government of India 2008, 255). However, even business groups have objected to the unapologetic displacement of peoples as disruptive and have advised governments to instead acquire the space by paying market rates for the land, if only to maintain public posterity (Pandit 2005). This is the platform on which the knowledge economy in India is built. Of the 366 SEZs that were formally approved in 2007, 257 have been established for IT-ITES. By 2008, there were in excess of 400 SEZs, most of which created space for the expansion of information technology service companies (Anthony 2007; Sampat 2008). Software Technology Parks of India (STPI), normally located on the periphery of major urban centers, provide similar spaces for high-tech firms, with 2,000 such facilities registered between 2001 and 2005. IT industry lobby groups anticipated that the government's decision to lift the tax-free status of STPIs will prompt more attention to focus on developing SEZs, given the financial and regulatory privileges they maintain (Nasscom 2008a, 2008b, 2008c). At a time when the government promotes an inclusive development strategy, the physical architecture of IT-ITES is founded on the displacement of peoples and the entrenchment of privileges already enjoyed by an urban elite.

What the Indian and international business community uses as a marker for this success is the country's astounding rate of economic growth. A steady acceleration of GDP began to unfold in the 1980s, when growth stood at a steady 5.6 percent up until the late 1990s. Domestic demand was financed in large part through rising levels of external and internal borrowing, which in 1990 led to a gross fiscal deficit of almost 13 percent of total GDP. Prior to this period the Indian economy was beset by what was coined as "Hindu growth", denoting a disappointing but not altogether disastrous outcome that reflected the ambivalence towards the present that the religion supposedly holds. In the years immediately following the 1991 reforms, GDP still did not exceed the levels attained in the decade earlier (ASSOCHAM 2009, 2). It was not until the first years of the new millennium that Indian economic activity reached the near-double digit levels that are seen today. Before the economic crisis of 2008, Indian planners estimated that by the end of the Eleventh Five Year Plan in 2012, the annual growth rate would reach an unprecedented 10 percent (Government of India 2008). These expectations ultimately fell flat. In 2012, India's economy grew by just 5 percent, the lowest rate in over a decade. Information technology industries have continued to exceed these aggregate growth rates, which is due in part to the relatively poor economic performance in agriculture, manufacturing, and other services.

Positive foreign attention toward the Indian economy took the form of FDI, which was instrumental to the creation of the business process outsourcing industry. While foreign investment certainly helped the BPO segment expand, for the software and other high-tech industries the effects have been negligible. A survey of multinational interventions in India emphasizes that an infusion of capital, training, and organizational management strategies by international companies facilitated the development of a back office operations industry (McKinsey 2003). Building upon existing human capital resources, leading firms such as General Electric, American Express, British Airways, and others have been able to construct a competent offshore business service infrastructure on which they continue to rely. This marked the beginning of an evolution within the IT-ITES market.[8]

Nasscom (2008a) has sensationally claimed that India's recent successes in building the brand of "New India" is a reflection of what can be achieved by "unleashing the power of middle class, first generation entrepreneurship". The narrative is not unlike the one that pervades the popular imagination about the creation of Microsoft, Apple, and other innovative start-ups emerging beyond the labs of IBM. One sensational story is that of Bangalore-based Infosys Technologies, founded in 1981 by Narayana Murthy and six other colleagues with $250 in start-up capital (Kumra and Sinha 2003). Such stories would be familiar to management scholar Peter Drucker (1959) and his characterization of the knowledge worker, who is enriched by merit and education, not inherited wealth. Without tremendous institutional support, however, it is unlikely that one of the world's poorest countries, in terms of per capita GDP, could have produced managers, scientists, engineers, and business leaders of the scale and caliber witnessed over the past three decades. For these reasons, India's premier educational institutions, like the Indian Institutes of Technology, Management, and

Science, are recognized as the most "consequential legacy" of Nehru, the country's founding political figure. "Today", *The Times of India* (2007) reported, "an IIT degree is held in the same reverence in the U.S. as one from MIT or Caltech". Even though access to these post-secondary institutions is restricted to India's privileged few, collectively they have been a deciding factor helping to distinguish India among other rising powers in the Brazil, Russia, India, and China (BRIC) group of nations (Pawar 2008). Still, only about 1 to 3 percent of the total graduate and engineering labor pool are considered suitable for employment in the export-oriented IT-ITES industry (Nasscom 2004).

Leading up to the 2007 financial crisis, IT-ITES firms complained about the availability of a technically skilled and English-language-proficient workforce required to staff the industry if India's information technology economy was to ascend the value-added ladder. These concerns were addressed at a time when the Western consumers of call center services and anti-offshoring advocates were suggesting that India possessed a limitless pool of knowledge workers. Skilled labor shortages worked to create upward pressure on wages, especially throughout the export-oriented call centers. This has forced foreign companies to look elsewhere for even less expensive, but equally skilled, labor (UNI 2006c). Some of this was a symptom of India's most talented workers seeking opportunities overseas (Farrell, Kaka, Sturze 2005). Recent studies suggest, however, that this trend might be coming to a close. Between a fifth to a third of the million and a half engineers graduating from over 1,500 accredited institutions now run the risk of being unemployed, according to a report by the *Economic Times* (Chaturvedi and Sachitanand 2013). It appears that the establishment of technical colleges designed to feed the IT-ITES industries has created a glut of skilled engineers now dealing with increased economic competition and shrinking employment opportunities.

What this focus on education has created is a narrative that the IT industry is principally merit-based, driven by educated entrepreneurs and not inherited privileges, which is at once capable of undoing what Chakravartty (2008) defines as India's "premodern inequalities". Nasscom (2008b) has worked to the imagery of an entrepreneurial middle class as the core of India's economic renaissance. The effect of liberalization, and the IT boom in particular, has been to *empower* the middle classes, especially those who were marginalized economically and politically during the post-Independence period of Indian capitalism. Some studies even suggest that globalization is making India "more Hindu" through a state-temple-corporation complex orchestrated by Hindu nationalism (Nanda 2011). Indeed, India's successes in information technology can be attributed to the reproduction of existing class and caste privileges, which continue to be maintained, in part, through the cultural capital obtained through educational attainment and a "westernized social orientation", according to anthropologist Carol Upadhya (2007b, 1866).

Education policies, labor law reforms, and the introduction of SEZs and STPIs have all added to India's comparative advantage in the global knowledge economy. Most of these developments are recent. Less than a decade ago India was still considered within the IT industry as a capricious venture. It was not until the mid-1990s, when the country's IT workers were being used to help resolve a looming Y2K crisis, that Indian companies were taken seriously by Western counterparts. Recently, however, India's reputation has experienced some turbulence as the theft of credit card and personal client information by a back office employee at HSBC's data processing center in Bangalore called into question the trustworthiness of India's IT-ITES workers (*The Tribune* 2006; Walsh 2006; *IBNLive* 2006). Governments and industry leaders have worked in tandem to establish India as a brand in order to allay the fears among prospective clients. Infosys founder Narayana Murthy recalls that Indian IT-ITES service providers helped to create awareness among Western companies that Indian enterprises could actually build the application that clients needed (see Kumra and Sinha 2003). Less than a decade later, IT service firms like Accenture, EDS, Convergys and IBM Business Services were establishing subsidiaries in India and competing for top talent. It was the Millennium Bug crisis of the late 1990s that propelled the country's talent reservoir onto the global IT scene, shedding light on the opportunities awaiting multinational firms capable of integrating foreign services into their international operations. The services, software, and technologies that were designed by Indian companies contributed to what some have labeled India's "tech renaissance" (Kanellos 2005).

India's industry groups recognized that in the years immediately following the dot.com bust at the end of the millennium, the country's ITES sector would continue to compete for a market share with other leading vendors such as Canada, Ireland, and the Philippines. Canada, for its access to the U.S., and Ireland, for its share of the UK market, were both seen as the first wave of offshore call center destinations, while India and the Philippines constituted the second stage. Competition from emerging destinations accelerated as the demand for customer interaction services matured, and firms started to seek access to skills, particularly non-English-language abilities, that India lacked. The nearshore promise offered by Canada, despite its higher wage bill and operating costs compared to India, was not lost on industry analysts (see Nasscom 2006). And like Canada, intensified competition in the offshore market has forced industry groups to focus on developing India's capacity to offer more value to the global service provision chain. Nasscom has also recognized the importance of strengthening the presence of Indian IT-ITES firms in competitor countries, like Canada, where the industry body now has a chapter with about seventeen member organizations that include Canadian, Indian, and global companies.

Another trend in the Indian ITES sector has been the growth of domestic call centers that are owned by Indian companies and service local customers.

Software and BPO spending growth in the domestic market, an important transition that will allow Indian high-tech industries to weather cyclical demands for exports, grew between 31 and 43 percent in 2006 (Government of India 2008). India's domestic IT-BPM market continues to outperform exports and is now considered the fastest growing IT market in the world (Nasscom 2013). An ability to boost domestic demand could further enhance India's attractiveness for FDI and improve the economy's rate of growth (Pandit 2005). One of the major stumbling blocks to the growth of this segment of the industry is the challenge of recruiting local talent. This is due, in part, to the question of wages. For example, the first rural call center opened as recently as 2008 as part of an initiative called Fostera (Fostering Technologies in Rural Areas). Wages are much lower than the national average, at Rs3,500 per month (B. Mishra 2008; *The Hindu* 2006). Customer service agents earned an average Rs114,380 per year in 2004, or about US$2,539. Pay levels were 30 percent higher in international centers (Rs121,444 or US$2,687) than in the domestic facilities (Rs94,861 or US$2,108) (Batt et al 2005, 19). More recent studies indicate a substantial increase to Rs149,191, with a median of Rs134,000 (Callcenters.net 2007a, 39). The distribution of these incomes throughout the BPO sector is hardly even. Over 37 percent fall below Rs70,000, 32 percent between Rs70,000 and Rs100,000, and 24.5 percent between Rs100,000 and Rs125,000 (Rajeev and Vani 2007). Regional call centers demand workers with knowledge of local languages but have been hit with high levels of attrition as labor moves to the international centers (Thakkar and Bhatt 2006; Remesh and Neetha 2008). With almost $2 billion in revenue for domestic call centers in 2007, the market has grown in importance. This figure is likely to increase as domestic demand for retail, telecommunications, and financial services expand among the lower and middle classes (see *Business Standard* 2008). Convergys has joined other outsourcers such as MphasiS Ltd. and Firstsource Solutions Ltd. in looking at expanding its penetration of the domestic market and enhancing revenues from India. This business strategy functions as a hedge against currency fluctuations between the American dollar and Indian rupee (Kulkarni 2008).[9] Public sector employers and government agencies in India have similarly sought to benefit from the evolving IT-ITES services offered by the country's information technology firms in recent years. One of the world's largest employers, Indian Railways, modernized its customer service interactions by establishing an inquiries call center, with large Indian and foreign multinational IT and telecommunications companies lining up for the contract (*Moneycontrol.com* 2006).[10]

Labor cost arbitrage further fragments the IT-ITES sector as call centers come to service more diverse market segments. Centers that aim for a regional customer base will require local language capabilities, and depending on the sophistication of services being offered, companies may be able to tap into less educated and less skilled labor markets. Evolution of the domestic market could also facilitate the entry of rural areas and small towns as prospective customer bases, adding to the advantage of indigenous IT-ITES firms that are more competent at addressing local needs than their foreign counterparts. Nasscom and governments also point to IT-ITES as a social development strategy. In the most sensational case, BPO initiatives have even been marked as strategies to counter the influence of Naxalites, India's Maoist movement, by offering well-paid employment in the troubled regions (Narasimhan 2008). Previously untapped pools of labor offer IT-ITES companies operating in India a chance to cut expenses by exploiting an even less costly labor market, stratifying employment in this sector even further. However, this will only be possible for a limited segment of the call center industry where particular skill sets are required.

Not unlike the challenges facing Canada's call center industry, new destinations beyond India's shores have been recognized as a possible threat to the country's share of the global market. Developing economies have borrowed from the Indian strategy by placing special attention on establishing a recognizable national brand by promoting local talent pools, capable technological infrastructure, and an inviting regulatory environment (i.e., liberalized and deregulated). But as the global division of labor theory suggests, workforces are not generated under ahistorical circumstances but must develop and offer an advantage to foreign firms and customers. Take for instance, China. One disadvantage for China, an otherwise serious competitor, is its lack of English-proficient graduates, which hinders the nation's capacity to venture into the (international) customer service interaction sector. Unless this resource is developed further, China's access to the business process operations industry will be restricted to back office services. India will likely maintain its dominance as an attractive destination for American and British voice-based contracts as a result.

The Philippines, on the other hand, does not face the same limitations, and is now the largest recipient of call center contracts in the Asia-Pacific region. The country's status as an ex-American colony and familiarity with American culture adds to the advantage. Canada's second largest telecommunications company, Telus, has steadily increased the number of customer service call center workers employed in the Philippines through Telus International, the corporation's BPO and outsourcing division. Incidentally, Telus International was launched in 2005 amidst a prolonged strike by the Telecommunications Workers Union (TWU), ostensibly one of Canada's most militant trade unions. Pramod Bhasin, president and CEO of Genpact, India's largest BPO company, has said, "India has lost tens of thousands of jobs to the Philippines" because the caliber of English is superior and companies face fewer infrastructure and technical problems (*The Economic Times* 2009). But even Indian firms are exploiting the Philippines advantage. In 2009, Tech Mahindra considered a new BPO operation in the Philippines, making it the third overseas operation for the company after it set up in Ireland and the UK. Indian firms know that the Philippines will grant it further access to clients in the Asia-Pacific economy and even North America. Wipro and Infosys have already opened contact centers in the country (*Callcenters.net* 2009a). Convergys is set to have over 20,000 employees in the Philippines, far surpassing the 12,000 currently employed in India (*The Economic Times* 2009). Other challengers include Egypt and Kenya, but it is likely that media reports have sensationalized the actual threat posed by these two countries. There are several examples of Kenya's companies winning contracts over their Indian competitors, but so far the sector has not developed into a serious competitor in terms of capability or recorded growth levels (Crilly 2007).[11] Nevertheless, what this has meant for the IT-ITES sector generally is that the India advantage can be secured only if it diversifies its capabilities and matures up the value chain. As wages in the sector increase, this *could* drive the low-value-added services to less expensive destinations, but without an adequate infrastructure, education and skills base, and an appropriate pro-business regulatory environment, the transition will not be as seamless as commentators suggest.

CONCLUSION

Uncertainty has come to define many aspects of the call center market. New entrants pose threats to the cost advantages already offered by an established Indian sector, and the structural dimensions to global capitalism can unseat industry leaders in one instant and lead to the development of others. Despite the air of precariousness that marks the liberalized marketplace for offshore services, government interventionist policies have provided foundations for the development of globally competitive call center industries in both Canada and India. The onset of the global financial crisis in 2007, prompted by unregulated financial and real estate frenzies in the U.S. and European housing markets, led to unease among information technology industries highly dependent on foreign demand, particularly those in offshore services.

Protectionist sentiments in the United States were a predictable, and certainly rational, response to the globalization of work defined by a global division of labor. But the financial crisis was hardly the first instance of mobilized responses to offshoring. In 2006, British energy giant, Powergen, scrapped its call centers in India and returned exclusively to the UK, largely due to customer complaints about service (Brignall 2006). This started speculations that a "homeshoring" movement was about to take off, although this trend has gained limited traction since. However, the British-based insurance giant, Norwich Union, followed Powergen by returning some of its Indian call center jobs back to the UK amidst similar pressures. As net suppliers of call center services to the U.S., Canadian and Indian vendors had something to fear from the economic backlash emerging from the world's leading consumer of goods and services. However, the corporate response to diminishing demand and fears of falling profit rates was to trim costs.

Companies operating in leading offshore and outsource destinations, like India, were fearful of what the recession would bring, but many were also expecting to gain from cost-cutting trends in the United States and the UK, as the main assumptions of liberalization and free trade propose. Som Mittal, President of Nasscom, defended the importance of the Indian BPO industry in light of these developments by claiming, "We are a part of the solution to get out of the recession. We are not part of the problem" (cited in Paul 2009). In Canada's Niagara region in Central Ontario, of the hundreds of call center workers that had lost their jobs with TRG Customer Solutions just one year earlier, over half were able to find work with global outsourcer, Sitel, in the same city. The recession, ironically, has allowed the company to pick up additional contracts since businesses were looking to outsource more of their services (Fraser 2009; *AsiaOne Business* 2008). Yet the industry has been struck by a degree of turbulence, and there does not appear to be a consensus that the ITES sector will weather the storm as well as business commentators propose. In 2009, after years of unprecedented growth, BPOs in India started to lay off workers, which was unheard of up until that time. Companies were deliberately citing the U.S. economic crisis as the reason for closures (see Sinha 2008). Canadian centers were beset by similar decisions after the cooling American economy and appreciating Canadian dollar started to undermine the country's previous advantages. Ironically, it was Canada's shaky economic circumstances following the recession of the early 1990s that had initially created conditions for the growth of the call center sector in the country.

From the vantage point of business, the uninhibited flow of capital, made possible by lifted restrictions on FDI, promised an open terrain for new "green field" initiatives and in making established ventures more promising. With the globalization of services and information capitalism this analysis has been expanded, since labor arbitrage has been applied to advanced capitalist economies as well. Canada's existing integration with the United States, long a target for critical political economists and left-nationalists, was an obvious first step in the externalization of sophisticated business service operations for American companies. Call centers are technological and organizational constructs that fulfill corporate demand for a centralized, predictable, and efficient provision of services. The newest global division of labor, to build on Fröbel and his collaborators, is one defined by knowledge production, the contours of which depend on the fragmentation of Machlup's taxonomy from the transporter to original creator in the production process. Each category is not reducible to a level of sophistication, but rather to its position within the firm, level of value, and technologically-enabled capacity to be done remotely. More importantly, each of the interrelated categories has a differential relationship to the process of commercialization. This means that processing and analyzing information, for example, is not an under-laborer for original creators, but in itself a commodity to be packaged and sold. To this model we can add knowledge process outsourcing and business process outsourcing as representing various positions on the spectrum of knowledge production. Leading outsourcers like Accenture, Convergys, IBM, Sitel, TCS, and HCL have constructed complex business models oriented to this very process.

Constructing a global labor force capable of turning customer interaction services into a commodity was an outcome of state policies, regulatory reforms, subsidies, and direct interventions by business. Canada and India have indeed followed radically different paths in this regard, but there is overlap. In India, the central government has enacted change through leading Ministries, Five Year Plans, and development agendas; educational institutions have been resourced, and infrastructure made a priority for the IT-ITES sector; land was usurped from common use and peoples were displaced. Canada's path, on the other hand, has been far less centralized and relies more heavily on provincial and local development initiatives that operate, to varying degrees, in competition with each other. Post-industrial planning has been overwhelmingly focused on constructing an inviting climate for *capital* but at the collective expense of labor. This is not to say that the projections offered by the proponents of offshoring, which are a realization of liberal free trade theorems, are fabricated. Rather, what has been argued is that many of the positive outcomes continue to be based on theoretical speculation and rely on limited empirical evidence; social costs are routinely marginalized or ignored altogether. Second, from labor's vantage point, there is a tremendous gap between what is being said regarding the shifting conditions and the opportunities for employment.

5 India
Labor Organizing Offshore

Veteran Indian labor organizer, Elvee Subramaniam, remarked during an interview that the economic downturn following the 2007 financial crisis might in fact precipitate labor mobilization in India's call centers and information technology workplaces. Subramaniam drew from his experience as a leader in the efforts to unionize the country's banks, a process that had a positive transformative effect on the conditions of work. It also propelled India's trade union movement by adding hundreds of thousands of new professional workers to the union movement. Thus far, his prediction has not materialized as anticipated. However, over 20,000 workers did join India's sole IT-ITES trade union, UNITES, between 2005 and 2010. But the story of UNITES, and other experiments at collective organizing in India's flagship sector, is one of a rise and ultimate decline. Chapter 5 examines the leading labor organizations that have made overtures at organizing employees in IT-ITES, namely the Union for ITES Professionals (UNITES), the IT Professionals Forum (ITPF), and the Young Professionals Collective (YPC).

This study constructs a narrative of labor organizing that weaves together the perspectives of founding figures in each respective association with that of primary and secondary accounts of professionalism, Indian industrial relations, and the political economy of information technology in India. Only a few years ago it seemed that UNITES offered at least some promise at forming a sustainable organizational model in an industry where unionization continues to be virtually non-existent. Now, its future is tenuous at best. In comparison to previous attempts at forming an association of professionals, like that of the ITPF, UNITES was building momentum in a highly competitive sector where employees are relatively privileged. While the associational framework offered by the ITPF was appealing to IT workers who identified as professionals and formed the most privileged ranks of the sector, the Forum's efficacy was hindered by an unwillingness to engage management as a representative body and its adoption of a volunteer-based perspective on membership recruitment. But what led to the development of these organizations and why did they fail to achieve widespread support among call center workers in particular and the ITES workforce generally? It should be made clear at the start that it is not possible to discuss efforts at organizing call center workers separate from labor interventions throughout the entire information technology enabled services spectrum. Because call centers are part of what is recognized in India as the business process outsourcing (BPO) / business process management (BPM) *industry*, all of the organizations that I discuss below cast a sector-wide approach to establishing professional and traditional trade union organizations. For this reason I use the hyphenated "IT-ITES" to talk of the general information technology sector. This is what makes the Indian example different from that of Canada, as subsequent chapters explain.

Information technology unionization has experienced numerous setbacks since first attempts began in the late 1990s. A leading challenge has been the ongoing apathy among the existing membership and the union's inability to organize workers outside of small- to medium-sized enterprises. As for the ITPF, it lacked an ability to solicit enough members to establish an autonomous financial footing, which is cited as a leading reason why its European trade union supporters revoked the organization's funding. By all accounts the ITPF has ceased to function, in part as a consequence of this financial development. While the "unionate" model that the Forum ascribed to proved successful in the case of WashTech (Washington Alliance of Technology Workers) and Alliance@IBM in the United States, the ITPF's reticence toward unionization undermined its capacity to effectively operate sustainably in the long term as a labor organization. Finally, the YPC example suggests that labor advocacy through public media campaigns, transnational research projects, and legal representation can effectively support the interests of workers in these industries. However, the YPC's main objective has not been to develop itself as a representative organization, like a trade union, but to facilitate worker dialogue and assist the efforts of labor to form their own association. And, unlike UNITES and the ITPF, the YPC was unique in that it was entirely Indian grown. From the start, UNITES and the ITPF were launched with support from UNI and other European trade unions, in addition to indigenous activists and rank-and-file workers.

Economic liberalization and the international nature of IT-ITES employment has conditioned the prospects for unionization and labor association formation. Even more so than the professionalized and individualistic nature of work in India's call centers, it has been the structural features of IT and ITES that shape the possibility for union interventions in a range of industries, from BPOs to software design. This does not discount the significance of workplace organization, or the effects human resource management has had on inhibiting prospects for collective action. Resistance by employers contributed to a union absence and early attempts to organize workers in call centers were met with managerial opposition (Upadhya and Vasavi 2006). Prospects for successful organizing initiatives are further conditioned by the social reproduction of anti-union attitudes as well as the philosophy of managerialism developed in the elite institutions and social networks that helped shape a large segment of corporate managers in decades past (Srinivasan 1989). Trade union history in India maintained the reputation that these organizations cater to vested interests, use disruptive tactics, neglect the concerns of members, adopt Leftist political support, and ignore the welfare of society at large (Noronha and D'Cruz 2009). Evidence from interviews and existing studies refutes assertions that sentiments towards unionization can be reduced to either ideological positions or to the institutionalization of professional identity formations. There is no simple predisposition to oppose trade unionism but a list of factors that include structural conditions, the particular features of a globally oriented conglomerate of industries dependent on exports and foreign investment, subordination to customer demands, and the limits of traditional strategies deployed by unions.

LABOR RELATIONS AND PROSPECTS FOR "WHITE-COLLAR" UNIONISM

As Strauss's (1964, 535) treatment of engineering unions in the 1950s suggests, as a professional and an employee, the professional "wants to expand the power, status, and freedom of his group", to be more successful at work, and to win greater job control and economic security. These aspirations, Strauss argued, prompted the engineer to identify with a group. Arlie Hochschild (1983, 103), recognized for her work on emotional labor, adds that workers don the moniker of professional "because they have mastered a body of knowledge and want respect for that". For companies, a "professional" employee is also a person who has accepted the rules of standardization accompanying the position. In Burawoy's (1979) terms, when workers embody a professional stature, they have accepted the legitimacy of managers to define the terms of professionalism and their relationship to the labor process. The capacity of labor organizations to mobilize employees in the IT-ITES sector is therefore founded on their ability to appeal to the professional and employment-related needs of these workers. Industry leaders, however, have denied the need for what they perceive as external intervention by working to maintain the enterprising imagery of IT-ITES, which is consistent with the principles of human resource management systems deployed in these organizations. Kiran Karnik, then-President of Nasscom, brokered this perception in the public sphere, stating these are "employees who think of themselves as the CEOs of the future" (cited in Iype 2005).

The three case studies examined in this chapter indicate that the conventional discourse of unionism—particularly references to job action, strikes, collectivism, and wage demands—have not been reproduced in any of the respective organizations. UNITES and the ITPF have instead focused on offering services to members and operating as agents of empowerment for professional, white-collar workers. The YPC, on the other hand, has engaged with workers in a consciousness raising exercise as a means to gauge the level of interest in collective resistance. Rather than acting against employers, these organizations have mobilized in favor of industry growth and expansion by building a recruitment platform based on the perceived professional and political interests of the workforces they seek to represent. Language and strategies, therefore, have been constructed with professional identities in mind. A balance can be struck between professional aspirations and labor rights, but the capacity to bargain collectively through a binding and legally recognized process is a privilege almost exclusively reserved for unions in the Indian industrial relations arena. A professional association can mobilize its membership based on the shared interests of a group and affect change within an industry, but the ability to negotiate conflict with management, in these instances, is restricted to the patronage offered by managers themselves.

Labor legislation in India developed under British rule, with the first laws enacted by the colonial government in late 1850s. Most of this legislation, like the Breach of Contract Act (1859) and the Employees and Workmen (Disputes) Act (1860), was directed against workers and meant to make punishable desertion or indolence of those under contract. Upon the insistence of British mill owners who feared competition from cheap Indian labor, the colonial government passed the Indian Factories Act of 1881, outlawing the employment of children under the age of seven. Trade unions gained legitimacy and collective bargaining rights in the early 20th century through a range of legislation, namely the Workmen's Compensation Act (1923), the Trade Unions Act (1926), and the Payment of Wages Act (1936). In the 1930s, industry-wide collective bargaining rights were secured through the Bombay Industrial Relations Act where the Congress Party held political influence. Special wartime ordinances were eventually formalized under the Industrial Disputes Act of 1947, arguably the most important piece of industrial relations legislation in the country. Under the Act, employees not defined as workmen, such as managers, engineers, and workers not employed in an "industry", were excluded from the right to raise an industrial dispute and prohibited from involvement in trade union activities. It is this exemption that IT-ITES companies in India exploit when assigning job titles.

What Hensman (2011) concludes in his comprehensive study of unions and globalization in India is that independence, and Congress-led rule in particular, did little to change the social practices, class relations, or even labor legislation in the country. The framework of India's industrial relations model has remained largely unchanged since the colonial period, with the state playing a leading role, at least formally. And, because of the significant influence communist parties and movements have had on the development of trade unions in the country, the Congress has also had an uneasy relationship with labor. Even when a former trade unionist, V.V. Giri, became labor minister in 1952, attempts to expand or strengthen the rights of workers and their unions were routinely curtailed by other factions and political interests in government. The legacy of industrial relations in India is such that the state is deeply interventionist if only to confine the influence of free collective bargaining and labor militancy through a paternalistic and pragmatic design. For these reasons, trade unionism and industrial relations in general have always been recognized as a politicized affair. Still, unionized workers in the organized sector have been provided with meaningful protections against unemployment and often enjoyed a standard of living and wage that would far exceed other elements of the working classes. In some cases, these protections are extended or withdrawn for political expediency. Less than 24 hours after Jet Airways laid off over 1,000 employees, the company's chairman, Naresh Goyal, directly intervened and reinstated the workers. Goyal said, in a carefully choreographed press conference, that his change of heart was due to the fact that he could not stand to see the tears in the eyes of his beloved employees. In all likelihood it was pressure from the Ministry of Labor, and perhaps even the Prime Minister's Office, that forced the chairman's hand (Koshy 2008). Such is the general characteristic of industrial relations in India. UNITES, the ITPF, and the YPC all tried to move from the shadow of this history to establish new methods and strategies for a fundamentally different business culture.

During the period of economic liberalization in the mid-1990s, the long-established practices of industrial relations, and more generally the regulation of capital and labor, were subdued by the influential forces of business-led globalization (Hill 2009). From the vantage point of organized labor in India, structural adjustment programs worked to erode even the basic standards of IR that had been won during the early years of national independence. State-led development strategies entrenched the government's interventionist role in the regulatory regime, but the character of this intervention gradually changed as policies favorable to free enterprise grew in prominence. The post-1991 reforms, global competitiveness, increased foreign direct investment, and the entry of private (often foreign) enterprises have, however, created problems for the static industrial relations legislation. This, Bhattacherjee (1999) proposes, constitutes the fourth and still incomplete phase of unionism in India. Structural adjustment programs, which led to demands for increased labor market and employment flexibility, outstripped the capacity of India's industrial relations system to cope with these economic changes. A centralized bargaining structure has been less responsive to market-led transformations. Coordinated industry-wide bargaining became increasingly difficult as the nature of commerce in certain key sectors was also decentralized and internationalized. For these reasons, industrial relations scholars accuse the country's trade unions of having failed to develop forward-looking strategies capable of responding to changes in the economy and work (Ackers 2006). The political relations certain unions enjoyed with India's leading parties also experienced difficulties as economic conditions changed. Most of the leading union federations, like the INTUC (Indian National Trade Union Congress), CITU (Congress of Indian Trade Unions), and the BMS (Bharatiya Mazdoor Sangh), are tightly aligned with the Congress, Communist (Leninist), and Bharatiya Janata Parties respectively. Political tensions among the parties and competing visions for development and labor policy are, consequently, fought in the administrative ranks of these massive federated bodies. India's newest trade union federation, the New Trade Union Initiative (NTUI), was formed in 2000 as an alternative to these politically aligned organizations. The related outcomes borne of this experience have meant that the affiliations trade unions make through their party-based federations and industrial relations practices have also allowed these organizations to neglect rank-and-file mobilization, leading to their failure in developing a grassroots constituency (see Hill 2009; Hensman 2011).[1] In effect, the established Indian labor movement has been unable to form a definitive challenge to the marketization process (Roychowdhury 2003), not unlike its counterparts elsewhere in the world. This is most evident in the information technology sector where the rapid pace of technological development and organizational change is leaving trade unions further behind. Labor scholars have gone even further, suggesting that the first unions had indeed been organizations *for* workers run by political leaders and not organizations *of* workers, controlled by an active rank-and-file (Ramaswamy 1977). Consequently, the effectiveness of critical statutes that structure industrial relations in India—the Industrial Disputes Act, 1947, the Trade Unions Act, 1926, and the Contract Labor (Regulation and Abolition) Act, 1970—have been eroded by business-led economic transformations and globalization. Both the structure of industrial relations in India and the turbulent history of trade unions have made IT workplaces particularly immune to labor organizing. More important, the introduction of Western human resource management practices has created ostensibly permanent barriers to union entry, especially if unions continue to resist the modernizing push of information technology in the workplace (Bhattacherjee 1999). It is hardly a coincidence that the notable examples of industrial conflict in the post-reform era have been in the banking and insurance sectors, where intensive drives to computerize technical operations have been led.

A pivotal moment in professional unionism arrived when the highly esteemed Indian civil servant became embedded in the union movement shortly after independence. Civil service employee organizations were traditionally interested in the advancement of professional interests and mutual benefit and welfare, more so than bargaining over pay and conditions of employment. It is worth considering that solidarity among the professional managerial classes was a feature of India's independence movement against the British (Srinivasan 1989). For those beholden to managerial posts, the aversion to trade union methods and collective action was sensible considering the desire to follow through with *individual* advancement. This is not unlike the philosophy guiding the IT Professionals Forum and IT-ITES workers as a whole. The contradiction lies in the social characteristics and the associated opposition to collective action and thus, trade unionism (Ramaswamy 1985). But, as this chapter maintains, the structure of the IT-ITES industry works to determine the propensity for employees to organize.

Both the individualization of work *and* the generous prospects of employment prohibit immediate interest in unionization, corroborating findings that job satisfaction in India is the most determinant cause of union voting intentions (Deshpande 1997). For labor advocates, patterns of social change brought about by employment in IT-ITES have had a profound effect on the prospects for association. Indeed, the cultural depths of socialization through work in the IT-ITES sector are compelling forces that create obstacles to collective identity formation and mobilization. For IT-ITES, unlike the civil service, the consequences of liberalization have involved both a government withdrawal from the regulation of labor *and* an active compliance with industry to restructure labor relations. *Withdrawal* has been used to denote that it is not the case that laws simply do not apply or that the state is no longer responsible for enforcing regulations. Instead, the state's ambivalence towards infractions in the IT-ITES sector is telling of its relationship with industry. Regulatory inefficacy has been interpreted by some to mean that existing laws simply to do not apply. As an activist and medical professional working with the ITPF explained to me, "Labor law does not apply to the IT industry. . . . You are considered management" (interview with Natarajan 2008). This legal ambiguity is held by a number of IT professionals who maintained designations like "associate" and "executive". But a young labor lawyer and activist who spoke with me at the YPC's Mumbai office clarified:

> The thing about existing laws is that it's not clear whether existing laws apply. . . . The lawmakers and the legislature and the policy people, as well as the industry, have kind of made this impression that there are no laws regulating this industry, and it's supposed to be a self-regulating industry. Which is not true, actually. All the labor laws, or all laws, are applicable to this industry. (interview with Rege 2008)

While certain exemptions for the IT-ITES industry have been made at the national and state levels, labor regulations still exist. Under the Industrial Employment (Standing Orders) Act, 1946, governments are empowered to impose penalties on employers who fail to submit or modify standing orders. The Act also provides guidelines for classifying workers, and establishes guidelines for hours of work, wages payable, and other employment standard provisions. In most cases industry has been successful at lobbying for reforms. A remark by the Head of HR at Infosys Technologies is telling: "We have antiquated labor regulations, which do not fit the requirement of the knowledge-based industry. This reform is necessary. We do not want inspector raj here, what we want is more such reforms across industries" (cited in Kumar 2009). This remark came as a response to the state of Karnataka's decision to exempt IT-ITES software establishments from the provisions of the Act for two years.

IT companies are widely recognized as subverting established labor laws and regulations, leading labor advocacy groups like the YPC to pursue grievances through the courts. This comes at tremendous time and cost to the employee, and in some cases the issue takes years to resolve. In 2005, the YPC took up a case where an employee at Spanco Telesystems and Solutions Ltd., which provides back office services for major Indian telecommunications firms and American-based companies, was given an exaggerated title of "Senior Customer Service Associate". YPC lawyers successfully made the case that this employee is defined as a "workman" under S.2 (s) of the Industrial Disputes Act, 1947. The purpose of this managerial interpellation was to deprive the employee of protection under existing labor laws. Since her tasks exclusively involved receiving calls from U.S.-based customers, there were no grounds for an elaborate executive title. After repeatedly being subjected to sexual harassment and denied a performance pay bonus, to which she was entitled, the worker was eventually terminated. While the YPC successfully convinced a court that this termination was indeed unfair, which subsequently ordered her reinstatement, the process took over two years and the employee in question had long since found employment elsewhere.

A handful of similar cases suggest that businesses in the industry perceive themselves as exempt from existing employment policies. For example, firms have asked workers to submit letters of resignation so as to avoid the administrative hurdles and financial burdens that accompany formal terminations (Tejaswi 2009b). A VP with Nasscom attempted to rationalize these practices accordingly. "The Constitution", he said, "provides all participants in any industry the right to try to assemble. However, the BPO and infotech industry is cost-sensitive. *There will be a huge burden in case the industry complies with the employment laws*" (cited in Verma 2004, emphasis added). State governments have worked to respond to these concerns by reforming legislation to benefit industry. Acting on this view, the Communist government of West Bengal has banned strikes throughout the state's IT-ITES sectors (*The Economist* 2004). Nasscom has played a leading role advocating for labor law reforms, since much of the existing regulations were developed with the manufacturing sector in mind. For instance, the industry association has insisted that the flexible nature of IT-ITES demanded that women be allowed to work at night and that the standard 48-hour working week be reviewed to accommodate the demands of the sector.

These efforts to reform India's labor laws have been taking place for over a decade. A report by the government's Working Group on Information Technology in 2001 recommended a series of labor law amendments targeted at ITES in particular. One of the most telling suggestions was for the establishment of a new "service category" to replace the existing Shops and Establishment Act, under which call centers are listed. Such is the political and economic significance of this industry in India. Allowing for longer hours of work per shift, rescinding limits on night work, and granting companies the right to lay off up to 10 percent of their total workforce without government permission, were additional recommendations. Flexibilization was formally instituted through the abolition of rules regarding the use of contract labor—currently governed by the Contract Labor Abolition Act—and through the extension of "temporary status" to employees who worked 720 days in the span of three years, up dramatically from 240 days worked out of one year (Government of India 2001, 55, 154). Based on the high turnover rates throughout India's call centers, an employee is likely to be considered "temporary" for the entire length of their tenure in the industry—or at least in a given workplace.

The State of Maharashtra, home to Mumbai's many booming IT-ITES districts, attempted to usher in the knowledge economy by granting resources to the establishment of a technological infrastructure and, just as importantly, a regulatory environment conducive to attracting information technology capital (Government of Maharashtra 2003, 9–11). Provisions under the Shops and Establishments Act were relaxed for working hours, women were granted the right to work night shifts, and a special police unit was established to ensure the safe transportation of employees to and from their places of work. Further amendments were made to Acts that regulate standards of employment and compensation. These include the Employees State Insurance Act, Factories Act, Payment of Wages Act, Minimum Wages Act, Contract Labor Act, Shops and Establishments Act, and Workmen's Compensation Act (Government of Maharashtra 2003, 10). Indeed, *all* existing laws apply to the IT-ITES sector, with some exceptions. However, for the central and state governments it became a matter of revising these regulations to suit the needs of high-tech industries.

Labor law reform also serves to induce foreign capital, so the proposed changes to existing regulations are not solely an appeal to IT-ITES. Business consultancies and free market advocates have long argued that India's legal framework regarding the rights of workers is in need of an overhaul (Das 2006; Nasscom 2004; Desai 2007). Distrust of organized labor by multinational firms has long been a point of contention. A general view does exist that the vision of India's entry into a global (IT-ITES) marketplace would be endangered by labor activism. As Dr. Ramani Natarajan, a founding ITPF organizer, clarified in a conversation:

Because unionization in the public sector, the white-collar sector and the banks, they have a totally different concept of unionization compared to the rest. Here, you don't get something, you go on strike . . . Things are going pretty well, but the thing you have to understand about the Indian system is that the IT professionals—I'm talking of hardware, software, not the enabled services—are not for unionization, including the government sector. Why? Because it is one sector that is so global . . . (interview 2008)

Conscious of this perception, strikes, militant labor action, and wage demands have been rejected as feasible strategies by both UNITES and the ITPF in their attempts to draw support from IT and ITES professionals.

ORGANIZATIONAL STRUCTURES AND EMERGING LABOR ORGANIZATIONS

Senior company managers started to wage a preemptive war of words against collective organizing well before UNITES took hold in 2005. As the CEO of WNS Global Services went on record as saying, "Unionization will drive away customers and kill the golden goose" (*Times of India* 2005; see also Verma 2004). Even rank-and-file employees had been documented as sharing this sentiment (Taylor et al. 2007). Indeed, many members of the middle class who benefit the most from information technology employment associate unions with blue-collar work and the pre-1991 era of slow economic growth and limited opportunities, as early studies on union formation suggest (Sandhu 2006). Raju Bhatnagar, who has spent decades working for various foreign and Indian-owned ITES companies and at the time was a senior member of Nasscom, elaborated on the divisive politics associated with trade unions in India in an interview. At Nasscom's headquarters in Delhi, Bhatnagar insisted that progressive human resource management practices, generous compensation, and favorable conditions of employment, mitigated any need for unions in India's hallmark industry. For such commentators, unions represent India's economic past; the future, in contrast, rests with the entrepreneurial and free market spirits of a highly educated youth, uncommitted to the traditional institutions of white-collar (unionized) employment, echoing Peter Drucker's (1959) prescription on the post-industrial society.

Yet industry perspectives offer only one account as to why a union movement was slow to grow, and more pressing still, why it has experienced only a gradual ascendance since being formally established. Following the work of Bain and Taylor (2002) and of Noronha and D'Cruz (2009), it is important to address how the neglect of unions rests in the general perception that these organizations have become marginal and ineffective. Part of this is due to the age demographic of the workers in this industry, with most call center professionals being between the ages of 20 to 35 years (Call-centers.net 2007a; Rajeev and Vani 2007; Batt et al. 2005; Holman, Batt, and Holtgrewe 2007; Kuruvilla and Ranganathan 2010). With relatively high levels of pay, the opportunity to interact with foreign customers, and other benefits, there is a real question of what unions or labor associations offer this new class of professional worker. Karthik Shekhar, the General Secretary of UNITES, was very clear that in his interaction with the predominantly young and well-compensated workers, unionization was not seen as a natural fit. Shekhar was a seasoned veteran of IT, having worked at IBM during the high-tech heyday of the 1990s. Despite the high regard that accompanies employment at a world-leading company like IBM, Shekhar explained that gradually, the rosy image of information technology changed. The pressure to make work a priority over his family led Shekhar away from IBM and IT altogether. However, it was some time before he looked to unionism as a avenue for changing the conditions of employment. Existing unions in India had flaws, he insisted, explaining that union reactions to technological innovation and the associated features of IT-ITES workplaces were additional reasons why workers have shunned organized labor. Existing unions, structurally and politically, proved unable to represent the employees in the sector if they maintained an allegiance to traditional ideologies and methods. Their dated and unsupportive approach to computerization in the workplace, Shekhar added, was especially poisonous (interview 2008).

Consideration of India's labor relations regime, and union attachment to this structure, is important. Indian labor scholar E.A. Ramaswamy (1977) commented that simple bread-and-butter unionism cannot but produce membership apathy; sustained participation by an identifiable group over a period of time cannot unfold if individuals are drawn only by isolated issues. Mobilizing the support of well-paid and educated young workers has required UNITES and the ITPF to pay close attention to non-wage concerns. The question becomes how this applies to unions dominated primarily by IT-ITES professionals, and what possibility there is for binding solidarity in the midst of economic hardship *and* prosperity. Slow rates of growth for both labor associations and unions can be attributed to ambivalence just as much as it is to ideological opposition. The words of an IT manager and UNITES activist I interviewed in Bangalore helps shed some light on the problem:

Yeah, why is a union required in IT? This is a place where people are paid enough and are not bothered about anybody else. So it is seriously a self-centered kind of an industry. Okay, I am getting my money and I'm safe. I'm doing my job, I'm doing my work—why should I be bothered about anybody else? (interview with Bhargava 2008)

Bhargava's depiction is consistent with Upadhya and Vasavi's (2006, 48) definition of individualization, which depends on "an orientation in which people center their planning and actions around themselves based on an ideology of self-interest, rather than around collectivities of various kinds". How this process takes root also depends on where labor is situated on the knowledge production spectrum, *vis-à-vis* Machlup's (1962) framework. The taxonomy of workers in this sector presents a set of challenges, since differences exist between call center agents, software engineers, medical transcriptionists, and so forth—or simply, between the back office processing and higher value-added employment.

Since prospects for collective organizing depends on occupation and industry, it is important to recognize the lack of a homogenous class of "professionals" occupying IT-ITES, especially when considering social inequalities that are reproduced within the sector (on the subject of gender see Remesh and Neetha 2008). Even what is commonly referred to as "IT" is representative of an assemblage of varying practices, with a multitude of structuring dimensions, with labor, capital, and technology reinforcing each other (Parthasarathi 2007). For labor associations, then, the myth of a "well-knit professional identity" (Srinivasan 1989) has to be addressed in the process of collective organizing. Transformations in work, identity, sociality, and culture brought about in the global information economy configure the experiences of India's IT and ITES professionals (Upadhya 2007a; 2007b; 2008a; 2008b). Unions, then, are obligated to shape their strategies around these socio-economic realities in order to be successful in their attempts at organizing. It also means that ITES unionism in India is a manifestation of top-down union initiatives, and not a wellspring of rank-and-file activism.

Despite the well-explored sociological significance of defining labor in IT as "professional" (d'Cruz and Noronha 2006; Remesh 2004a, 2004b), the successful history of unionism in white-collar workplaces in India is worth considering. As a founding member of the YPC, Vinod Shetty's remark points to the contradictory terrain on which IT-ITES labor organizing unfolds:

> I would say it's more of an identity issue. The average BPO employee and IT professional sees themselves as a "professional"; he doesn't see himself, or herself, as a working class group or even a white-collar employee. Even like a bank employee or insurance employee. Because, in our country even the pilots are unionized, so it's strange when you have a bunch of kids who don't believe that they are working class . . . (Shetty 2008)

But "individualism" and "professionalism" are just as much managerial constructions as they are functional identities. A joint research project conducted by Indian and U.S.-based trade unions and labor organizations found that the collective identity of call center workers was prevented from reaching a politically active threshold through a socialization process that fostered possessive individualism masked under the guise of teamwork, technologically-induced surveillance methods, and various management practices (CWA et al. 2006). In the BPO sector specifically this process of individualization is entrenched by creating the perception that work is fun and by constructing a human resource management (HRM) system that provides a seemingly effective outlet through which employees can air their grievances (Remesh 2004b). At the outset, the industry created a perception of call center employment as "fun", largely as a tool to recruit young college graduates, which became part of the socialization process embedded within the sector. "Initially", Shekhar explained, "call center work was known as . . . a place for fun, and the industry [had someone designated as] a Chief Fun Officer. These guys were promoting all this". UNITES made headlines by confronting the social policies embedded in IT-ITES company practices when an engineer with Nokia Siemens Networking died while participating in a pastry-eating contest in his office (personal correspondence with UNITES 2008).

Without an effective collective channel to empower workers, call center employees resort to other methods of subversion such as making fun of management style, disregarding the organization's scripted conversational rules, hanging up on offensive customers, and even exploiting weaknesses in the organizations' control systems so as to make free spaces for themselves (Remesh 2004a, 21). Work-to-rule initiatives, like the "Go Home on Time Day" initiative borrowed from financial sector workers in Australia, have also been tested, but individual forms of resistance have their limits without coordinated and sustained *collective* action (Shankar 2009; Shekhar 2009). Despite the significance of attempting to transform conditions of work, there remains cause for reservation about the efficacy of such actions in the long term. Such behavior is viewed as hazardous to an industry deeply concerned about its appearance in the eyes of foreign investors, particularly in light of security breaches that came to public attention in 2006 (*The Tribune* 2006; *IBNLive* 2006). Union representation provides an institutional outlet for addressing workplace grievances common throughout the industry, and offers the possibility of mitigating individual acts of subversion.

The appeal to professionalism, long advocated by Nasscom, is simultaneously a disciplinary mechanism through which labor is controlled by the construction of what constitutes "appropriate" work identities and conduct. Indeed, the logic of the enterprise, namely the ordered practices of production, is serviced by a diffusion of "professionalism" through to individual conduct, as Fournier (1999) ascribes. Not only does this include actions and behavior specifically designated as work related, but also the development of a professional ethos that supposedly separates IT-ITES workers from the rest of the private and public sector, and thus inoculates these employees from the lure of collective organizing. Ultimately, human resource management practices are established by firms as a means of resolving problems for *individual* workers, rather than a method of enabling *collective* responses. But the resolution of problems is what makes the HRM processes seemingly "progressive" and employee-oriented. Further, the structure of work in BPOs and the practices of hiring and compensation work to inhibit union efforts. While the IT-ITES sector is collectively represented by a handful of industry groups, labor, in contrast, has been without any form of representation until recently. For YPC activists, the refusal to identify as workers, a symptom of how the industry purposefully designates employees as professionals, means that employees are "conscious that an injustice is being done, but they are not able to take steps to remedy that", as one young YPC activist and lawyer, Ketaki Rege, remarked.

IT PROFESSIONALS FORUM

Writers who covered the early development of unionism in India's information technology discovered early on that the organizing techniques and methods adopted by labor associations need to reflect the characteristics of India's call center life if they are to prove successful in their efforts (Bibby 2000). FIET (International Federation of Commercial, Clerical, Professional and Technical Employees), now a constituent federation within Union Network International (UNI), tried organizing Indian IT workers in the 1990s, but without success. Gerhard Rohde, UNI's head of Industry, Business & Information Technology Services department (UNI IBITS) and longtime German trade unionist, declared in an interview that he had been involved in these early efforts. He explained that both management opposition and failed union tactics inhibited the formation of sustainable organizing campaigns in these early, and sadly undocumented, days of collective mobilization (interview with Rohde 2009). The IT Professionals Forum was one of the first projects that aspired to capture the professionally-minded interests of IT workers, some of whom were beginning to recognize the strengths of organizing. "Unity is strength", one Bangalore Forum member said, "and when capitalists get collectively organized, why shouldn't we?" (cited in Bibby 2002c). On November 19, 2000, the first forum was created in Bangalore and the launch event was attended by some 400 IT-ITES professionals, students, and trade union officials. By 2001, chapters had been established in Hyderabad, Visakhapatnam, Mysore, and Hubli. UNI and other supporters recognized that in order for the Forums to meet their basic financial requirements, the association would need around 3,000 members per state. Even though no conclusive figures exist on total national membership, it is estimated that the number never exceeded 4,300, including students (personal communication with Karthik Shekhar 2009).

H.R. Hegde, who in 2008 was the UNI Development Organization Center (UNIDOC) director in Bangalore, was involved with the establishment of the ITPF from the start. As an active member of the Federation of National Telecommunication Organizations, an Indian telecommunications union and member of Communications International (CI) before it became part of UNI, Hegde used his contacts to help recruit members to the nascent IT association after contact with UNIAPRO (UNI Asia-Pacific Regional Organization) Secretary, Christopher Ng. As Gerhard Rohde explained,

> It was an interesting adventure. Because it started [. . .] bottom up. It was essentially one person beginning with support from some activists from telecomm unions that existed in India, addressed young people in the IT industry. It was mainly their friends, neighbors, nephews and nieces. So it was started kind of [as a] grassroots initiative. Then these people approached others. (interview with Rohde 2009)

The Forums' earliest activists, drawn mostly from the higher value information technology workplaces and telecommunications, were concerned with social development causes such as bridging the digital divide, sharing wage information, providing a mechanism to address unfairness in the workplace, and advancing the professional interests of members. One of the ITPF's first interventions was arranging legal action against a dishonest training company that promised prospective workers a nonexistent e-commerce course and job placement service (Bibby 2002a; Hirschefeld 2005). Despite taking up popular causes, it remained a challenge holding the interests of young workers who demanded a different approach to organizing. "See, everywhere something new has started . . . the old is substituted by the new", Bangalore UNIDOC's Hegde pointed out. "[W]e want to organize the youngsters in a new forum. . . . People are not liking the unions, they are not attracted by the unions because of the old story, of past experience" (interview with Hegde 2008).

Addressing members of the Bangalore ITPF, Rohde argued that professionals need to find "new types of organization" and "should be trying to find new ways of expressing their needs and demands" (cited in Bibby 2002a). Using the financial support of UNI and several Western European unions—the Belgian Union of White-Collar, Technical and Executive Employees (BBTK), the Union of Technical and Clerical Employees (SIF) in Sweden, and the Union of Commercial and Clerical Employees (HK) in Denmark—as well as on-the-ground mobilization in India, support was mustered to formally launch Forums in India's major IT hubs. A memorandum of understanding was subsequently signed with the Association of Professional Engineers, Scientists and Managers, Australia (APESMA) in the interest of cooperation in research and education. Discussions were even under way regarding "reciprocal membership" between the two associations (ITPF n.d.). What this agreement actually accomplished on the ground in India is uncertain, other than an expression of solidarity between organizations. The ITPF purposefully distanced itself from political directions traditionally associated with the Indian labor movement, which provided a source for optimism in the innovative approaches and commitment to forming a professional association. The early activists considered the importance of forming a collective organization but, as Rohde emphasized, "it had always been a different type. It was not so much fed by the original idea of solidarity, it was more bringing professionals together, and that was the solidarity aspect, to achieve more than they could achieve as individuals".

Initially, even company owners were interested in affiliation, which projected the intention of employees and employers working together for mutual gain. As the CEO of a large building sector company suggested, employees "should feel good and can have a say: the company where I work is also my company" (cited in *Expatica* 2007). When rumors circulated that the ITPF would register as a trade union, Sangeeta Gupta, then a VP with Nasscom, responded, "trade unions are formed only when employees are unhappy. Today, employers are most concerned about the employees" (cited in Verma 2004). The ITPF organizer, Dr. Ramani Natarajan, echoed this sentiment in her explanation that there is "no basis for unionization. Pay as well as facilities [are good]. Unionization comes when there is a lot of discontent". Ultimately, the Forums elected to fall under the Societies Act and avoided the militant image they feared would hinder prospects at recruiting members if they registered as a trade union. Dr. Natarajan, a scientist who was charged with developing a women's wing called Women in the IT Sector (WITS), reinforced the importance of this approach: "We had made it very clear . . . that the question of unionization doesn't arise. In the sense of the white-collar jobs, this was an association or a forum".

The ambivalence and sometimes-public opposition to collective action reflects contradiction in the ITPF's mission and professional designation. Because these professional associations do not directly engage in collective bargaining, there are few if any guarantees for improvements in wages and working conditions (see Mosco, McKercher, and Stevens 2008). Nor would the government intervene into the business-led affairs of IT industries. The question of unionization versus professional association ultimately caused rifts among the groups that were part of the ITPF's initiation, as Noronha and D'Cruz (2009) discuss in their study on IT unionism. As a trade unionist, Hegde was part of a group that wanted to call the organization the IT Employees Association, or ITEA, and registered as per the Trade Union Act. But, he emphasized, "some people never wanted to call themselves unionists". Leading activists from trade union backgrounds, Rohde recounted, did not understand "that a non-antagonistic organization could also be beneficial".

As time passed, there was concern that many young members were losing interest due to what was perceived as a lack of action on the part of the ITPF. Since membership merely involved a loose affiliation based on the completion of forms, "there [were] to be no issues connected to the employees", as Hegde commiserated. From a trade unionist perspective, Hegde insisted during conversation that the ITPF's relationship with employers was "too soft", and that communications about the Forum's activities were going to employers, "whether they were members of ITPF or not". The ITPF's conciliatory strategy was embossed on its public image, as it was mandated to make itself "the voice of IT professionals, to enrich, empower and promote their interests and to contribute to the over-all growth of the ICT sector" (ITPF n.d.). Eventually, he maintained, the "ITPF started functioning [in] a different style . . . like a corporate office. . . . [A] lot of money was spent to buy a lot of things, very posh. . . . ITPF was neither a union, nor a company, nor a society". Shekhar drew attention to the ITPF's sponsoring of Nasscom activities, which illustrated the Forum's suspiciously tight relationship with industry groups and business leaders. At one point he claimed the Forum became a placement agency more than a representative worker association. It was, to use the vulgar term, a company union.

Discussion with early ITPF organizers revealed that the overwhelming focus for the Forums was on the most highly skilled IT sectors, which Natarajan insisted had different professional aspirations and problems compared to the ITES sector. Hegde went further, suggesting, "Whereas the ITPF was not touching the call center people, it was purely the software engineers who are in development or implementation". When meetings were held, attendance was composed largely of software personnel, medical transcriptionists, and other BPO employees, but few call center workers. The ambition to exclusively represent IT professionals as a skilled, craft-based association among certain circles was another source of controversy. Not everyone involved with the project agreed with this strategy, as earlier reports suggest (Bibby 2000, 2002a, 2002b, 2002c). Natarajan did, however, acknowledge that exploitation was taking place in the call centers, and that these BPO workers required some form of labor organization. "The people leaving [call centers] need to be looked after," she observed, "they do have a genuine problem". Forums, on the other hand, were commenced based on the lack of regulation and gaps in company HR policies, particularly with regard to sexual harassment and discrimination. Interest was also expressed in building stronger professional ties between prospective employees and companies looking to recruit talent. Inequality was widely acknowledged to exist in these privileged workspaces, but the argument held that problems could be addressed on an individual basis and without collective representation. In this sense, it was the intention that *individuals* could be empowered through Forums, which operated with the blessing of companies; discussion and consultation replaced collective bargaining as the mechanism for affecting change.

The stratification of the industry, noted by distinctions made between software engineers on one end and back office and call center professionals on the other, exposed further limits to what interests the ITPF could effectively represent. The conciliatory approach to addressing problems within the sector resulted in the failure to mobilize IT professionals and gain meaningful recognition by companies. Membership, from Hegde's vantage point as a trade unionist, had to be a meaningful commitment to the association. Only through the establishment of a community of individuals willing to confront companies with their concerns at a collective level could such an organization prove successful. It was also crucial that companies acknowledge the collective aspirations of such organizations. As Hegde said, "first registration then recognition . . . from the company. If they don't recognize you, how do you go in?"

In addition to the complex, yet seemingly problematic, relationship that had been formed between the ITPF and companies, which contributed to divisions within the Forum's support base, there was also the question of financial dependency on external networks. Dr. Natarajan expressed frustration toward the withdrawal of funds initially offered by the Belgian union, which was expected to last until 2011, according to her account. "We could have done it provided we had a little bit more time," she argued. "You can't expect financial sustainability in four years. We had to start from scratch, it was not possible in India". For Natarajan, the initial launch fell flat shortly after, when the funding dried up. "You can't start something in May of 2007 and kill it in March 2008, it's just not done". A similar sentiment was expressed by Hegde, who debated that a "union's existence cannot be dependent on the [individual] project. . . . In a true [labor-oriented] project you should train up your leadership and you should conduct meetings to encourage [members to join] and spread the concept and at the end of the day you must have some presence in the workforce. This is the normal style of union functioning". It was, as the discussions confirmed, the ITPF's inability to gather a sufficient membership base and make a noticeable presence in the IT-ITES sectors that resulted in the BBTK becoming disenfranchised with the initiative. Eventually the Forum simply ceased to operate and its initial members and organizers moved on, some to other UNI-sponsored projects.

YOUNG PROFESSIONALS COLLECTIVE

Whereas the ITPF offered an approach to organizing that operated through the development of a professional association, the Young Professionals Collective was an entirely Indian invention determined to address the concerns of workers outside of a union or societal formation. Commenced by labor activists, lawyers, and other professionals in 2005, the YPC started with the objective of eventually forming a trade union for IT-ITES professionals, specifically call center workers. By 2009, the YPC had wrapped up its advocacy for ITES-BPO workers as most of the activists from these workplaces moved on to other careers. At the beginning, YPC organizers aimed to build a movement of workers, not just a trade union. Sajjanshetty, an early YPC member and long-time social justice activist explained,

The idea was to organize them and make sure that if there is any kind of operation happening against them in the company, they can voice it and be a union. Like any other union, [the] objective would be to collectively bargain with the management for their own rights. (interview with Sajjanshetty 2008)

Like several of the founding members of the ITPF, the Collective had within its ranks trade union activists, several of whom worked with unions involved in the historic Bombay textile strike of the early 1980s and who are currently involved with the Textile Workers Struggle Committee. Roots in the trade union movement and a commitment to social justice prompted the formation of the YPC and a focus on the unionization of IT. For Ketaki, a young lawyer working with the YPC,

> Naturally, as trade unionists and labor lawyers, we were interested in finding out whether there is any, you know, what are the conditions of service, what are the employee-employer relationships, are there any rules, etc. A lot of people also came to us with inquiries [about their] rights. . . . If there is any injustice done to them, any unfair practice done to them, then we take the matters to the court. (interview with Rege 2008)

Like Rege, other leading activists in the YPC were either directly involved or had close friends or relatives employed in IT-ITES. But it was almost exclusively the call center industry that became the focus of attention of YPC organizers. The Professionals Collective took off shortly after the interaction began between groups of workers and activists. From this point, the idea was for YPC forums to emerge in call centers and, eventually, throughout the software industry as representative organizations. What prompted the formation of the YPC was a series of work-related concerns raised by call center workers with the labor activists. YPC organizers recognized that identity construction through the discourse of "professionalism" was instrumental in governing the limits of resistance and collective action, but they nevertheless saw that even at the managerial level, there is acknowledgment of exploitation within the workplace and that the self-regulatory model proposed by the industry falls short of addressing systemic problems. A young YPC member named Hussain Shaikh (interview with Shaikh 2008), who I spoke with in Mumbai, commented that there is an abysmal awareness of rights and regulations and that despite what the industry says publicly, management is concerned with productivity, not human or personal issues; only collective action, he resolved, could change the situation. Getting there, however, was going to be a challenge.

From the beginning, YPC activists realized that their organization would have to depart from the traditional union model that they were accustomed to. Vinod Shetty explained that although "there have been demands from employees that a trade union be set up, [my] feeling [was] that it would always work like a welfare association, or a forum, or a platform for employees to meet, and that organization would have to actively engage the government as well as the companies". Mobilization, activists suggested, would have to be built on employee networks sustained by an association such as the Young Professionals Collective. The purpose of the organization is, in Shetty's view, to provide a forum for dialogue and problem solving "amongst the employees themselves, [who] would discuss the issue and try and work out something. Then [members of the YPC] gave access to lawyers, psychiatrists, to financial consultants, to different fields, you know. Whatever problems [employees] had you could set them up, guide them" (interview with Shetty 2008). Instead of building a representative organization, the YPC established itself as a space through which experiences could be shared between workers, and chiefly as a platform to educate and empower call center employees by allowing them to "discuss their own issues and find solutions to their problems . . . where they can exchange ideas, form opinions, and maybe improve their service condition" (interview with Sajjanshetty 2008).

Organizers concluded that the tactic of union leaders meeting workers at factory gates would not be effective, so alternative methods were turned to instead. As Rege (interview 2008) reflected,

> We somehow found out, almost instinctively and from experience, that it would be difficult, in this industry, to have a union which is based on the traditional lines . . . *In this case we realized that since the workers never identify themselves as working class who need to have any kind of bargaining power, it was not happening . . .* (emphasis added)

Consciousness raising has been the chief objective of the Collective, a point of departure from which workers could go on to build the capacity to demand something from management. Activists recognized that the structure of the call center industry, and other workplaces with the wider IT-ITES sector, inhibited organizing activities. Work schedules, particularly arduous night shifts, as well as the fear of management's response to employee activism, made it difficult to for the YPC to organize these workers in one location. Shetty also addressed the additional challenge of confronting workers that come from distant parts of India, and how this obstructs the capacity of worker organizations to build a membership base.

> [W]e find that those who come from outside the state are very much apprehensive of any threat to their employment and to their salaries. They don't want to show to the organization that they are part of any such organizing, a union, which they think would cause the management to terminate them. (interview with Shetty 2008)

Factory gates, or more accurately the gates of special economic zones and software technology parks, certainly exist, but the potential to develop a collective identity is hindered by inconsistent work schedules, workplace hierarchies, and the spatial location of work. But how workers identified themselves and their relationship with colleagues was even more telling of the challenges for organizers. As Rege pointed out, "Our biggest hurdle is the *lack of class consciousness*. People just don't identify with having the need for any kind of association" (emphasis added). Competitiveness between IT-ITES professionals intensified the problem, as employees are instructed not to disclose their salaries to coworkers. "Automatically, this way the company discourages any kind of finding of common ground by the employees". Further, to assuage the fears of retribution by superiors, YPC members had to make clear that the prospective members would not be combating their managers. Sajjanshetty (interview 2008) pointed to the Collective's perspectives on job action, particularly the use of strikes, and considered this tactic a "double edged weapon" that can be used by workers to make demands, but could also result in the closure of facilities and harsh responses by the industry. Strikes were to be seen as a last resort, and even avoided in discussions altogether until the worker association reached a certain level of maturity and strength. Step one for call center workers and their organizations is to construct an ability to negotiate collectively. Strikes and militant action would not be an option, and even discussing this could damage organizing efforts.

In its publication with Focus on the Global South, a development policy research organization, the YPC made an important observation that "there are hardly any agencies representing the interests of BPO employees in India" and that the "interests of the sector are being solely represented by the owners/managements of the BPO sector" (Young Professionals Collective and Focus on the Global South 2005, 13). The Collective's activists came to realize that their organization "would be required to lobby the government and set up best practices. This would be [the YPC's] main work, [which] would be to provide information to society at large about this industry, work out best practices and codes for the industry so that they would self-regulate" (interview with Shetty 2008). Industry-wide regulation, then, was a chief objective.

Following the tragic rape and murder of Pratibha Srikanth, a female call center employee working for the BPO arm of Hewlett Packard (HP), women's advocacy groups and labor organizations mobilized to draw attention to what came to be seen as a structural issue with the BPO sector.[2] Like the fragmented service production chains that characterize the global information technology, the transportation network responsible for ferrying ITES employees from their homes to often-remote work locations is reliant on a complex subcontracting system. IT companies contract this service out to a transportation firm that in turn hires cars from another subcontractor, who then hires drivers to operate the vehicles. A lack of responsibility for the security of employees followed, and neither HP nor the taxi company were held accountable for the tragedy. The YPC responded that all drivers should have their names registered with the police and criminal record checks conducted, in addition to branding vehicles as BPO shuttles (*The Indian Express* 2005a, 2005b). To be even more effective, the YPC recommended that companies should employ their own drivers. But as the Collective and other labor organizations allege, structural problems such as these are not acknowledged by the industry. The rape and murder of Pratibha, Rege reflected, was treated "like an isolated [incident], it was her bad luck. [But], in Pune there were recently two cases where one women was raped and murdered and another girl was . . . raped". India's English press, in fact, routinely reports on such cases. Here the intersections of sexual inequality, the use of SEZs, a global division of knowledge labor, and hierarchies that construct the IT-ITES sector—from taxi driver to call center worker—are all made visible. For YPC activists, this tragedy is representative of the many problems embedded within the growth of IT-ITES in India.

The financial crisis further elevated ITES working conditions to public attention, and indeed served, however briefly, as a catalyst for labor organizing. Media reports indicated layoffs in the thousands and call center outsourcers were said to likely cut more than 25 percent of their staff following the economic meltdown. Even Infosys, one of India's flagship IT companies, reduced its workforce by about 3,000 employees (Nandy 2008; Ribeiro 2008). Despite assurances from the industry that the looming U.S. recession would not jeopardize the Indian IT-ITES market, public attention turned to reports of layoffs and restrained growth. When Lehman Brothers and Merrill Lynch, once star financial institutions and envied employers in India, were struck by financial problems, UNITES responded by taking up the concerns of employees who were no longer being paid the gratuity or provident funds they were owed. The union protested that even basic provisions covering retrenchment under existing labor laws were being flaunted by firms, some of which were widely recognized MNCs. Shetty's response to this unfolding of economic events was clear: "I feel that in the coming days organizations like YPC or UNITES or any other organization, trade unions, which are going to work for these employees, will have a large role in protecting the rights of the workers" (interview 2008). In many ways he was correct.

Unions and labor association emerged, according to activists with the YPC, in IT-ITES as nascent regulatory agents charged with confronting the deficiencies of government and industry oversight that, they claim, is ill equipped to effectively address labor-related problems. Not unlike the calls by trade unions in the United States and Canada for governments to help protect workers from the calamities of an economic crisis, the YPC recommended that a value equal to 2 percent of corporate profits, contributed by both the government and companies, be kept aside as a Contingency Provident Fund for retraining, education, and retrenchment compensation

(Young Professionals Collective and Focus on Global South 2005). "The worst case scenario," Shetty (2008) explained, is companies "leave or shutdown overnight, these BPO employees should be protected; they should have some kind of bridging of the gap between now and the next job". Lacking a meaningful industrial policy on IT-ITES employment, professional workers are consistently left without a buffer against turbulent business cycles, not uncommon in export-dependent industries.

UNION FOR IT ENABLED SERVICES PROFESSIONALS

When Amandeep Sandhu (2006) wrote about the newly-formed UNITES in 2006, the prospects for IT unionism were considered with restrained optimism. Since the publication of what was then one of the first articles focusing on the perceived failure of organizing workers in the IT-ITES industries, several key developments have led to increased interest in the sector's only established trade union. As of 2009, UNITES could boast of approximately 22,000 dues-paying members, over 1,300 of whom were covered by collective bargaining agreements. These figures need to be placed in the context of over two million IT-ITES employees, almost 700,000 of whom are part of the ITES and BPO sectors alone. UNITES continues to lack a substantial presence in major Indian and multinational firms, keeping it within the margins of Indian trade unionism. The vision of 42,000 dues-paying members by 2011—15,000 from call centers and BPO units—failed to measure up. Part of this was due to the failure of UNITES to organize workers in major multinationals operating in India such as ANZ, HCL, Tata Consultancy Service, and IBM.

Launched initially as the Center for Business Process Outsourcing Professionals (CBPOP) in 2004, the Bangalore and Hyderabad-based initiative involved organizers from UNI as well as individuals previously associated with the ITPF. As some studies suggest, CBPOP formed as a result of rifts that surfaced in the ITPF over an anti-union stance held by activists invested in being a professional association (Noronha and D'Cruz 2009). UNIAPRO, UNI's Asia Pacific Regional Organization, took a leading role in establishing what would officially become UNITES in 2005, the year it registered as a trade union. Karthik Shekhar, General Secretary since 2006, quickly surfaced as the public face of the union in India. Commencing his IT career with IBM, Shekhar observed the changes in how the company's employees were managed following economic liberalization. It was this transformation that prompted the programmer to investigate unionism at Big Blue. Eventually Shekhar encountered UNI's Hegde, who was at the time working on forming the ITPF, and got involved with the organization. After becoming disenchanted with the direction the Forum was heading, Shekhar started doing mobilization work with UNI's newest project, UNITES. From there he moved on to become the union's leading officer.

Shekhar's experience as a knowledge worker is worth some reflection. Despite lucrative opportunities in leading companies such as IBM, perceptions of injustice and unfair management practices opened the door to interest in unionization. As he was quoted in a major Indian daily, *The Telegraph* (2006), "There is exploitation in the BPO sector. A labor union is imperative". Shekhar's connection with IBM has an ongoing importance for UNITES. When Australian workers with IBM forced the company to negotiate a collective agreement after going on strike, Shekhar saw this as a significant breakthrough for organizing efforts in India.[3] The Australian context is important considering that the Association of Professional Engineers, Scientists and Managers, Australia (APESMA) serves as a model for UNITES. Years later UNITES joined IT workers, trade unionists, and labor activists from around the world in the landmark Second Life online strike against IBM in 2007, acting in solidarity with Rappresentanza Sindacale Unitaria IBM Vimercate (RSU), the union representing over 9,000 workers employed by IBM in Italy.

From its inception, UNITES has mobilized on complaints raised by IT-ITES workers about a range of perceived injustices in India's information technology industry. In 2006, nearly one hundred call center employees with Bangalore-based Bel-Air BPO fell victim to what has come to be known as the "fly-by-night" operations common in the industry. Workers discovered that the operation had been shut down and they were not going to be receiving pay entitled to them (Suresh 2006). For three years UNITES pursued the case at great expense. The case-by-case response to worker demands has raised the union's public profile, but it has also drawn attention to structural problems of IT-ITES organizing. "See, there have been trials, errors, there have been spontaneous workers coming together because there is an issue," the General Secretary recalled (interview with Shekhar 2008). But, as the Bel-Air example demonstrates, immediate demands by workers, not all of whom are members, does not amount to a sustainable membership base. This was an issue both with the ITPF and the YPC. As Shekhar continued, "once the problem gets solved, or the problem doesn't get solved, [the employees looking to UNITES for advice] just disappear . . .". This is an ongoing frustration, one that the trade union leader attributes to the pressures of ITES-BPO employment specifically. "So we have sort of become a safety net for people . . . where to come", Shekhar said. "But, they are not really active. They say, 'okay fine, you guys are doing a good job so please continue doing a good job, in case there's a problem I'll come to you.' That active involvement is not what we are seeing to a great extent".

Without a sustained membership base, particularly in flagship companies, UNITES was unable to bring a critical mass of information technology companies to the bargaining table. A few enterprises made it clear that they would only consent to a formal dialogue when UNITES achieves 30 percent membership in their call centers or BPO units. Lacking access to the workplace makes this objective a daunting task, and the experience in attempting to broker a dialogue has not been positive. As the General Secretary agonized, "in some cases they almost . . . threw us out. The problem", he continued, "is that the moment I speak to somebody he becomes a member, he maybe gets a promotion, he gets transferred, so it is like, they have never said no to us . . . but by some coincidence that person moves around" (interview with Shekhar 2008). These surprise promotions have led UNITES organizers to suspect that this is a direct result of an employee's interest in unionism. Gaining critical mass in a firm's BPO unit, some with over 10,000 members, is a monumental challenge. Because companies do not want the union network to become strong, a call center agent might be promoted to team leader, effectively relieving him or her of whatever complaint they initially had. It is for this reason that UNITES's current successes in negotiating six collective agreements have been limited to small to medium enterprises. But these successful agreements have also been accompanied by numerous failures to sign collective bargaining agreements with major MNCs such as HSBC, British Telecom, Barclays Bank, and Lloyd TSB.

High attrition and turnover rates are further obstacles to organizing. Because 60 percent of the existing call center workforce has a tenure of one year or less in any given facility, 50 percent in domestic operations, the constant turnover undermines the feasibility of a sustainable membership or organizing base (see Batt et al. 2005). Without the treatment of call center employment in particular as a career, the "worker in, worker out" mentality that supports rapid turnover contributes to a footloose and temporarily employed workforce. This in turn means that union contact with prospective members is fleeting. Collecting dues from the majority of UNITES members contributes to the union's uncertain fiscal situation. But this reality in the call center industry has led industry managers to support some elements of unionism so long as it controls attrition, a major stumbling block to the sector's growth (Sandhu 2006).

Managers at Excel Outsourcing Services in Chennai, a company that specializes in data entry processing, where UNITES scored its first CBA, recognized the union with hopes to control attrition. A collective agreement and union representation, it was thought, would assist in bridging the communication gap between management and employees by providing a voice mechanism that could enhance worker input and decision making (Pratap 2010). Recruitment and training consumes between 16 and 25 percent of gross annual earnings for a single worker, so the incentive of controlling turnover is clear (Holman, Batt, and Holtgrewe 2007; Batt et al. 2005). With Indian call centers possessing the highest global turnover rates of between 30 and 80 percent (Holman, Batt, and Holtgrewe 2007; Cohen and El-Sawad 2007), UNITES promoted the union advantage as working to regulate this aspect of call center and BPO employment.[4] Company attempts to fulfill the same objective have included using companies to carry out background checks to find out if prospective employees have a history of deserting firms. Forcing new employees to sign a bond is another method, but one that has resulted in bad press for the companies and provides an opportunity for UNITES to intervene on behalf of employees (Callcenters.net 2007b; Krishnan 2009). But this intervention normally takes the form of making a public case of the grievance and does not necessarily conclude with new members.

In its brief history, UNITES has made a name for itself in the public eye by bringing to light issues pertaining to inequality and exploitation in IT-ITES. One of the earliest initiatives involved holding a forum in response to the murder of Pratibha. Even after UNITES attempted to raise the issue of women's safety with IT-ITES companies, little was publicly said in response to this small Indian trade union. However, after this incident occurred, Shekhar explained to me, "that's when people actually started [. . .] started looking us up, and . . . [. . .] some of the things we were trying to talk . . . as a union, was something new to many of them" (interview with Shekhar 2008). An executive with HP, Som Mittal, who is now President of Nasscom, was reported as saying that women working at night was dangerous, confirming what the union had already been saying. While the responses to this incident were mixed—some in the labor movement were calling for a ban on women working at nights—UNITES was in support of women's rights and rejected recommendations for restricting women's access to the industry in a well-publicized campaign (*Deccan Herald* 2005). The promotion of gender equality and workplace safety became a major campaign issue for UNITES, and the memorial service held for Pratibha in UNITES's Bangalore office helped build positive press for the organization. It was shortly after this event that the President of INTUC (Indian National Trade Union Congress) and Governing Council member of the International Labor Organization (ILO), N.M. Adyanthaya, stated that the union federation would "support UNITES as it is a responsible new-generation union founded on trade union philosophy" (*The Hindu* 2005). Indeed, these early efforts attracted a significant number of members to the union.

In an interview with a UNITES activist and HR manager, sexual harassment and discrimination was identified as a leading form of injustice in IT-ITES workplaces. Because over half of the UNITES members covered by collective agreements are female the issue of sexism represents a leading concern for the union—it has also been a rallying point for worker support. In one instance, a prospective female employee was sexually harassed during a placement interview that the HR manager had arranged. This is a symptom, he insisted, of leading executives having little oversight, or concern, with regard to the actions of front-line managers. For Shekhar, the problem is more severe and related to the inherent corruption of middle management in IT-ITES firms. This was a leading concern at a joint UNITES and UNI press conference in Delhi in 2008. The ITPF's Dr. Ramani Natarajan (interview 2008) provided a similar response, saying,

"They [companies] all have these gender committees, but [what woman] is going to talk about sexual harassment when the whole thing is going to blow in the open?" Both organizations recognized the deficiencies in industry attempts to respond to sexism and structural inequality.

UNITES decided to respond to equity concerns by advocating for the establishment of a legal sexual harassment redress system in the BPO sector, with legal status under India's Trade Disputes Act (Acharya 2009). Another measure has been the Decisions for Life project, which aimed to raise awareness among young female workers about their employment opportunities and career possibilities, family building and the work-family balance. For UNITES, "[women's] choices are key to the demographic and workforce development of the nation" (UNITES 2009a). UNITES also took action against the assault of women in the South Indian city of Mangalore by helping to organize and participate in the March 8th Women's Day midnight rally (see Sengupta 2009; UNI 2009). Unions and professional associations are conscious of making meaningful interventions on behalf of workers, not through grievance procedures and the collective bargaining process, but through acts of social solidarity and public relations. But like many of the actions UNITES organizes, these rallies fail to transform into longterm projects and end as one-time events.

UNITES' role as a regulatory mechanism stresses how labor organizations serve to draw attention to poor managerial practices and structural problems in the industry. Major firms like HP, Shekhar explained, "know that it is very easy" to absolve themselves of responsibility for work-related problems (interview 2008). Legal routes take years and companies are in a better position to defend against allegations than a union with limited resources. One such concern is the widespread exploitation of unpaid overtime, which is a particularly difficult case to confront in salary-based workplaces (see Suresh 2006). After the economic slowdown in 2008, there were growing reports of global IT-ITES firms, like Accenture, having planned to increase working hours by almost an hour a day. Once claimed as the torchbearer of progressive human resource and labor relations practices, major IT-exporters such as Wipro have asked employees to strictly abide by the fixed nine-and-a-half hour working day. Of course, the reality is that IT professionals are working fourteen to sixteen hours a day, with performance and timing even more strictly monitored given the global economic climate (D. Mishra 2008). Without the basic provision offered by labor laws regulating work times, unpaid overtime is an expectation. Indeed, the economic crisis exposed problems within India's golden industry which was followed by negative changes to otherwise ideal conditions of employment.

Further scandals erupted shortly after the financial crisis began. Labeled as "India's Enron", in early 2009, Satyam Computer Services' Chairman, Ramalinga Raju, admitted to committing "financial irregularities", bringing down the reputation of the IT industry's corporate governance and management systems (see Timmons 2009a, 2009b, 2009c; *The Economist* 2009). UNITES responded publicly to the case of fraudulent accounting practices in one of the subcontinent's largest IT firms, and made inroads with employees as a result. "The horrendous act is the biggest in [Indian] corporate history", claimed a UNITES press release. "It appears corporations have taken advantage of economic liberalization and free market capitalism which is only a euphemism for casino capitalism" (UNITES 2009b). In response to this startling revelation, which ended with the resignation of Satyam's Chairman, the ITES union publicly announced that in October of 2008 it had written to what was then India's fourth-largest IT firm to take a stand on the World Bank allegations that account statements were being doctored, but received no response (*CIOL Network* 2009). In a major public relations breakthrough, India's major news sources were reporting that approximately 2,000 Satyam employees who feared for their jobs had approached UNITES; this was in addition to the 96,000 hits the union's website received in December and the estimated 270,000 it received in January of 2009 (Mishra 2009; Tejaswi 2009a). While website hits do not represent an accurate measure of prospective membership, nor a certainty of achieving recognition by a major IT firm, it is worth considering the changing public perception of a labor organization that emerged from obscurity just a few years earlier. And it has been the issue of layoffs and uncertainty facing India's IT-ITES sector that has drawn UNITES into a period of relevance, however briefly.

Employment security in IT-ITES was called into question following India's dramatic stock market plunge in late 2007 and what finally came to be recognized as a global recession. Considering that the finance sector is one of the major consumers of IT services and products, the concern raised by UNITES was warranted and eventually echoed by business leaders. Fears of widespread job losses, estimated to be around 10,000 according to UNITES, were quickly dismissed by Nasscom not long after the union began raising this issue in the media. Raju Bhatnagar, a senior officer with Nasscom, was clear in his statement that there would be "no large-scale layoffs. There are sporadic incidents here and there. The industry is growing and in fact, needs more people" (*The Economic Times* 2008a). Financial mogul George Soros bolstered these claims by singing the praises of India's economic renaissance under Prime Minister Singh, and expected that the Indian economy would perform well (*Sify.com* 2008a). Ultimately they were right, but speculation of a downturn nevertheless fueled a move toward downsizing, even if the market did not demand it.

In June 2009, a popular business publication, *Outlook Business,* estimated even higher figures than those initially projected by UNITES, with between 77,000 and 110,000, or 3.5 to 5 percent out of the total two million employed in the industry at the time, facing retrenchment (Mahalingam 2009). Nasscom's President, Som Mittal, remained steadfast in his claim that there would be no mass layoffs, but went on to note that the financial crisis meant that IT-ITES employees would have to understand the market realities, and "reset their growth and remuneration expectations" (cited in Tejaswi 2009b). The question of retrenchment continued to be a point of contention between UNITES and Nasscom, since officials with the industry group have repeatedly claimed that the IT-ITES sector continues to grow despite the global recession, in part due to expectations that the worldwide adoption of outsourcing will rise in the coming years (Nasscom 2009). By 2009, Infosys resumed hiring in the company's BPO units (Callcenters.net 2009a).

The situation inside leading Indian firms was not as optimistic as industry representatives suggested. For the first time giants such as Infosys Technologies and Wipro were cutting their usual annual pay increases of 12 to 14 percent down to 7 or 8 percent (Sayeed and Sekhar 2009). Even high-end designers and programmers were asked to sit on the bench, known as a "free pool", which functions as a disciplinary waiting area for IT workers with no work to do (Mahalingam 2009). There was little widespread sympathy for these privileged workers in a country mired in poverty and unemployment. With companies trying to rationalize expenditures, some call center employees were being asked to relocate to less expensive facilities in smaller cities, or risk losing their jobs. Small call centers were in a more precarious situation and susceptible to overnight closures, with estimates before the downturn indicating closure rates as high as 60 percent (Dash 2007). Admittedly, UNITES could do little to stave off unemployment, but the union did advise and advocate for workers on how to prolong the redundancy process and ensure that they receive everything to which they are legally entitled (Kazmin 2009). Advocacy on a case-by-case basis is a leading example of UNITES' attempts to make a breakthrough in the industry, such as assisting workers to receive their rightful compensation when companies close or when firms engage in unlawful terminations (Suresh 2006; Mohandas 2008). However, the effort to become "one big union" for any and all workers even remotely related to IT was costly and unsustainable.

UNITES has responded to the problems by engaging in a series of campaigns to raise awareness of industry developments. On May 1, 2009, the union launched a month-long "Stop the Pink Slip" initiative aimed at collecting 100,000 signatures from IT workers to force Nasscom to pressure the Indian IT industry to stop cutting jobs (Basu 2009). This was a response to an alien practice in India; a practice UNITES considers avoidable. "Instead of firing," Shekhar is quoted as saying, "companies should focus on staff training, skill enhancement or learning new languages . . . They should realize that bench sitters are live intellectual bodies and not perishable commodities. *And getting rid of jobs via the new-found, unscientific, biased performance evaluation is unfair*" (cited in Tejaswi 2009a, emphasis added). Other organizational changes are also possible, notably increasing lateral hiring as well as internal austerity measures, as Shekhar had proposed (interview 2008). Managers in large Indian firms have even resorted to verbally and physically harassing employees into quitting, which saves firms the effort of confronting labor laws (*SiliconIndia* 2009).

There was also reason to question the value of government incentives and subsidies directed at the IT-ITES sector, especially where labor is concerned. UNITES directed attention to how all of the tax-free revenues accumulated by the industry over the years have dried up, confirming that exemptions and indirect subsidies had outlived their usefulness (McKinsey Global Institute 2003). The YPC's proposal to introduce a tax and matching government funding for just such a scenario is all the more relevant considering what UNITES concluded. The recession, from this perspective, has been used to discipline the labor force and justify salary cuts and job losses. Lacking a long-term or sustainable policy, despite the targets set in Five Year Plans since at least the mid-1990s, the industry depended on the projected increases in offshoring from the United States and the UK to sustain growth. While Nasscom and other industry groups had called for further government attention to investments in education and technology-related infrastructure, the liberalized environment had abandoned the development of effective labor market regulations.

The ability of UNITES to operate as an information center and a publicly recognized advocate for IT-ITES employees granted the organization considerable promise of becoming a more influential player when negotiating with leading companies. However, there is the reality that a small percentage of workers, concentrated mostly in the BPO and call center workplaces constrained to the metropolitan hubs of Bangalore and Hyderabad, are actual members of this adolescent union in the constellation that is India's vast trade union movement. The critical mass achieved by white-collar unions in decades past has yet to be achieved, and without this important achievement the capacity to negotiate with multinational enterprises is restricted. As the union's leading activists have recognized, large foreign companies like HSBC and Barclays, both of which have negotiated collective agreements with unions in their home countries and have global framework agreements with UNI, have never opened the door for UNITES. After being ignored by these foreign multinationals, Shekhar realized "that these guys are not going to accept the same commitment that they have given to the European works councils or to the members there. That was an eye opener. Then we started focusing on concrete organizing at these firms" (interview with Shekhar 2008).

Despite setbacks, UNITES responded by working in solidarity with other employee groups associated with IT-ITES, building on UNI connections that have been established in India and throughout Asia. Unlike the ITPF, UNITES built an image of itself as "One Big IT Union", rather than appealing solely to the higher value software engineers and IT professionals. UNITES has adopted a pragmatic model that aims to conform to the needs of a highly skilled workforce, flexible employment, and temporary employment contracts. This also breaks with the strict division of labor and job protection strategy of white-collar unions in India, developing instead a broader "industrial" style approach that cuts across the sector to include IT, BPO, and even support workers such as drivers and security. The objective was to formalize wage rates through industry accepted minimum standards through a "living wage" campaign for different occupations within ITES. Security workers, drivers, and other support staff for the sector could benefit from a national or even state-level program aimed at regulating benefits and pay, as well as working conditions. For this reason UNITES created a Professional and Manager Services subgroup, drawing on a UNI initiative, so all ranks of information technology professionals could be members in a BPO-specific group.

Building an umbrella organization is essential for UNITES to become a representative IT union, and not just an organization for ITES employees. As UNI's Rohde warned:

> We should develop a kind of professional outlook, maybe also incorporation with professional organizations for engineers, computers societies [that] have these human resource managers' networks. So there are some considerations to make this organization more appealing to the higher educated professionals as well. That's the only way forward. You'll never succeed if you only organize support staff in those companies. (interview 2009)

Solidarity among the various economic and social classes embedded within IT-ITES—or, as Shekhar illustrated, the "workers' community at large"—is a worthwhile project, but mobilizing real activity throughout the UNITES membership base has its own set of challenges. Building on the interest of recognizing workers' rights, as we saw earlier, is one approach; women's rights, environmentalism, blood drives, and marathons are other approaches. Such strategies are premised on issue-based mobilization, as union activists commented. "It is a mixture of an NGO and a union that we are trying to make here", Shekhar insisted. One strategic advantage with this approach is a transformation of the union's image in the public eye and throughout the sector. For another UNITES activist, "This gives you an opportunity to help people: be organized, have a union. Not in the traditional sense of it, not go hardcore, go strike, or anything. Just be there. Give strength to your voice. If you have a problem, somebody's there to go to" (interview with Bhargava 2008).

Even though the relationship between UNITES and the IT companies assumes a confrontational tone in the media, the union's interests in modeling its activities on the ILO's tripartite governance structure—through which unions, industry leaders, and governments address issues of mutual concern *vis-à-vis* a dialogical process—is hardly antagonistic. In recognizing the importance of offshoring and the significance of this reality in the current stage of globalization, UNITES engages the global IT-ITES sector in such a way as to promote a means of regulating practices with the interests of workers and the industry's financial sustainability as primary concerns. This has been enshrined in the union's collective agreements, which state, "To work together to further the mutual success of both parties; positioning [the company] for continued competitive success in the marketplace while enabling UNITES to best represent and serve its members". The business union approach adopted by UNITES distinguishes the experiment from other, professional unions in India, to the extent that leading officials envisioned a close working relationship with companies and their interests.

Attempts at regulating one of the IT-ITES sector's most substantial industries, call centers, have been developed based on UNI's *Global Call Center Charter*. The "Stop the BOSS (Burn Out Stress Syndrome)" campaign showed that UNITES was initiating a movement that would draw attention to the conditions of work and not, in a traditional union fashion, by demanding wage concessions from employers. As Noronha and D'Cruz (2009, 229) observe, "UNITES aimed at becoming a forum that could reflect the professional aspirations of its key constituency". In this sense the union did not assume an altogether different course than that initially taken up by the ITPF. For reasons such as this, UNITES, as an organization, has taken the position that it will "strive towards creating a distinct and cogent link between employers and employees at all levels" and seeks to interface with the leading industry body, Nasscom (personal correspondence with Lekkad 2009).

In just a few years, UNITES had emerged from the wilderness to represent over 20,000 ITES workers throughout India. Yes, a mere fraction of the millions of information technology professionals, but still an important step in an industry that business groups insisted was immune to unionization. Much of its impact owed a great deal to widespread press coverage in India and even Europe. From organizing rallies, achieving recognition by a handful of companies, to addressing sexual harassment in the workplace, UNITES drew attention to the structural problems within India's global industry. By 2010, however, it appeared as though UNITES had exhausted much of its potential. Like the ITPF, UNITES relied on foreign financial support, particularly from SASK (*suomen ammattiliittojen solidaarisuuskeskus*), or Trade Union Solidarity Center, based in Finland. Starting in 2006, UNITES had been receiving between 50 and 60,000 Euros per year (personal correspondence with SASK official 2012). SASK worked closely with UNI and the global union federation's personnel and support structures operating in India. Otherwise, the Finnish organization has an arms-length relationship with the trade union projects in India, UNITES included. The intention was for UNITES to become financially sustainable through dues and membership. Of course, this objective has been frustrated by conditions largely beyond UNITES' control. Sources confirm that 2014 is the deadline for the Indian IT union to function on its own. UNI has also scaled back its support for UNITES in India, with the Bangalore UNIDOC office now closed.

CONCLUSION

The "New Generation Networks" (NGN), UNI's description of the latest union models, can with certainty be used to define the leading labor organizations in the Indian IT-ITES sectors. Trying to make headway into the sector and building on personal experiences with traditional manufacturing unions, activists and labor lawyers working with the YPC attempt to develop a forum through which IT-ITES professionals can engage in consciousness-raising initiatives as a starting point for identifying as *workers*. With a more professional image in mind, the ITPF approached IT as a forum for the industry's most privileged stratum and, through the knowledge of its most engaged activists, a response to perceived shortcomings in how workplaces are managed. Shrugging off the union image, subsequent tensions within the Forum helped clear a space for other UNI-supported projects, namely UNITES.

While industry leaders claim that the professional identity defining even the lowest ranking BPO employee inhibits a turn toward unionization, it is worth reflecting on Ramaswamy's (1985) conclusion that the ambivalence towards unionism is caused by a disillusionment with unions *as they exist* rather than with the principle of collective organizing itself. Undoubtedly, the radical heritage business leaders attribute to India's labor movement assists in sustaining a negative image of unions among India's most privileged workers. Yet it is worth recalling that the General Secretary of UNITES was drawn to unionization based on his experiences at IBM, perhaps the most lucrative information technology firm operating in India.

A range of success stories and limitations marks the history of these cases, with the ITPF a notable example of possessing more shortcomings than victories. As the first association formed in India determined to organize IT professionals, the Forum launched an initiative that gained public and industry attention for its efforts at building a *community* of professionals. Enthusiasm, however, was accompanied by setbacks and internal debates that eventually led to the suspension of external funding. The geographic dispersion of Forums also presented organizational challenges. Regional forums operated autonomously and there was never a coordinated communications strategy at the national level. There were also obstacles in forming a coherent strategy, as consensus did not form in the ITPF, or UNI, on whether the Forum should represent individual or collective demands. Another failure, according to some of the ITPF's founders, was the organization's failure to properly gather information about company practices and develop a strategic plan for organizing. This was a symptom of operating as a loose federation of members, rather than a union or representative association.

For UNITES, the transformation of the union image was important in order to appeal to IT-ITES workers. A militant and confrontational approach to negotiating with company management is replaced by strategies that work to enhance industry expansion *and* ensure that firms are respecting basic national and ILO standards of employment, as then-UNITES President Pritvri Lekkad described in correspondence (personal correspondence 2009). As countries like the Philippines and Kenya started to gain attention as emerging offshore destinations threatening India's dominance in the market, UNITES acknowledged the reality of offshoring and sought to support universal standards of employment rather than create an antagonistic and nationalist position of domestic versus foreign labor. Not surprisingly, the most vulnerable employees, namely those working in call centers and other segments of the BPO sector, have so far been the most receptive to unionization. Both UNITES and the ITPF developed a recruitment platform that emerged from the professional and political interests of their prospective membership; strategies determined to mobilize this constituency were ultimately based the social and economic characteristic of young, middle-class, Indians. For the trade unionists that had come from other industries, this was a serious compromise, but one founded on a pragmatic interest to see representative structures extended to IT and ITES.

Campaigns initiated by UNITES and the ITPF against sexual harassment in the workplace were matched with community organizing, leadership development, education and training, as well as working towards a sustainable and prosperous Indian IT industry. By making appeals that go beyond bread-and-butter issues and by focusing on regulating industry practices, both organizations, before the ITPF's dissolution, presented examples of how labor organizations can appeal to professionals in industries that some Nasscom officials had said are not in need of "intermediaries". It has also been the case that these two organizations made efforts to define what they are for rather than simply what they are against. By offering proactive recommendations, UNITES has attempted to shape the industry's engagement with employees rather than offer strategies that foster confrontation with companies. Meanwhile, the YPC represented a coalition of labor activists affiliated mostly with the legal profession, but ultimately concerned itself with the radical social and economic transformations that accompanied employment in India's booming call centers. If gains were to be made for workers, YPC members maintained, any attempts at collective action, or even the formation of collective identities, would have to be based on rank-and-file initiatives. Based on their first-hand experience representing these employees in courts, the YPC became aware that labor conditions were less optimistic than the industry reported.

Media and economic reports have indeed created awareness that not all is well for workers in India's call centers in particular, but business groups still maintain their reticence towards unionization. Even following successful efforts by UNITES to draw attention to structural flaws in how management has dealt with workplace harassment, Nasscom executives maintain that with responsive HR policies, few if any health and safety complaints, and good working conditions, employees have little need for unions. But a process of dialogue, however limited, did begin in 2008. Nasscom agreed to formally sit down with UNITES, but the industry association has not publicly stated that it recognizes trade unions in the sector, according to UNI's Deputy Secretary, Philip Bowyer. "It's very important for [UNITES and UNI] because," Bowyer said, it "would have been a great reinforcement to people in these difficult times, when people are worried about their future, when they are worried about their jobs, if Nasscom could have had the courage to say that it will come out and support what is a basic human right" (press conference with UNITES and UNI 2008). This ambiguity on the part of Nasscom maintains an important balance that on the one hand rejects the need for unionization without a clear statement of opposition, and at the same time undermines attempts by unions to gain legitimacy in the eyes of managers and their representatives at the industry level. Ultimately, Nasscom's ambivalent stance on trade unionism proved effective.

Threats of job losses and industry working conditions, experience has shown, are not in themselves catalysts for rapid union growth. To secure a significant membership base, UNITES is faced with the challenge of outreach and appealing to a workforce that is ambivalent towards collective organizing, as well as the dismal prospects of getting MNC recognition without a critical mass. So-called "new generation" methods of organizing have been complemented by traditional organizing strategies, particularly for UNITES. For instance, seminars and training programs at software parks were discussed as a means of getting the attention of thousands of IT-ITES workers. Second, the establishment of chapters at technical colleges and universities offer students career counseling and support services as well as strengthen the network of future BPO employees. Third, interfacing with industry associations has been acknowledged as a means of promoting common professional interests. The development of a strong communication network is an effective channel for providing online information about unionism and labor rights, job information, and support services. Activists with the YPC similarly acknowledged the need to engage with the media and operate on a social terrain that is unfamiliar to traditional trade unions. Such strategies represent attempts at breaking down the barriers between professional associations and professional trade unions, in the case of UNITES, just as Strauss (1964) suggested in his study. This could also represent a means of reconciling individual with collective demands, inspired by the formation of a professional community beholden to a situated set of aspirations and identities.

6 Centers of Steel

When the United Steelworkers organized Omega Direct Response's (OMDR) Sudbury call center, it marked an important new frontier for the union. For a time OMDR set a standard for successful organizing in this seemingly untouchable industry. But in a few short years this triumph would turn to defeat. The union failed to make inroads at OMDR's other call center located in Toronto, some three hours south of Sudbury, and by 2009, the company's northern Ontario facility shut its doors for good. This was one of a handful of call centers where the Steelworkers have had a presence since the late 1990s. But the unionization of these important post-industrial workplaces has an interesting history. Trade union representation in the country's call centers has traditionally followed the patterns of trade union density that correspond to the parent sector, like telecommunications, public services, and utilities. This is why a majority of call center workers employed within these industries possess a trade union density rate that far exceeds the national average. Conditions of work in the precursor to the wider IT enabled services (ITES) sector in Canada, then, has been shaped by the intervention of unions and the institution of collective bargaining. The emergence of call center employment as a relatively independent industry in Canada has only developed recently, which distinguishes the evolution of this workplace from its Indian counterparts. What's more, there is no definitive ITES or "call center" union in Canada. In fact, a constellation of trade unions now represent thousands of members in these important, post-industrial workplaces.

Despite the evidence supporting the claim that unionization provides net benefits to workers *and* managers in call centers, companies have a history of union avoidance in this flexible and just-in-time industry. Industry groups maintain their opposition to industrial relations reforms that might advantage labor, lest such initiatives reduce flexibility and increase the possibility of union involvement in the sector (Callcenters.net 2009d). Threats of globalization and facility closures illustrate how employers have countered the efforts of workers who have sought to organize with trade unions. Unionization in post-industrial workplaces is important for several reasons, not least of which is that call center organizing tests the trade union movement's capacity to respond to structural changes in the Canadian economy. The geographic fragmentation of employment, increasingly a "normal" feature of call center work shaping the industry, mapped by uneven economic development across Canada and the globe, means that unions are under growing pressure to focus their organizing efforts on outsourced, subcontracted, facilities.

Unionization in Canada's call centers has a relatively long history. This is perhaps the most distinguishable contrast with IT services union formation in India, where traditional labor organizations have been unable to take hold. Second, where Indian industry associations, state planning initiatives, and the sector development of IT-ITES are often governed by overlapping regulations and policies, call centers in Canada stand apart from other elements of IT, as per the North American Industry Classification System (NAICS). The development of the BPO industry in India, meanwhile has been the focus of national and state-level policies that have marshaled political and market-led forces to nurture and support the growth of call centers in the country. In Canada, the strategy is far less coordinated, with the exception of the few Atlantic provinces.

From the vantage point of trade union organizing and industry planning initiatives in Canada, call centers are similarly distinguished from other information technology workplaces. Post-industrialism has forced Canadian unions to step outside their principal areas of expertise and strength, much like counterparts in India. Labor organizations representing workers in manufacturing and the resource sector ventured into the service sector as technological innovation, de-industrialization, and globalization undermined their historic centers of influence. One of these unions, the United Steelworkers (USW), provides an excellent example of this form of new unionism. And, much like UNITES in India, the story of the USW is one of early successes and bitter losses. What follows is a story of call center unionism told from the perspective of organizers, shop stewards, union officials, and rank-and-file activists who are represented by, or members of, the United Steelworkers (USW). With one exception, managers refused to participate in the study.

The USW has been active in call centers since the 1990s, when the union first organized customer service representatives in a Visa Financial center in Toronto, Ontario. As a case study, the USW is as much an example of union transformation as it is about the unionization of call centers. As a conglomeration of steel, mill, chemical, and manufacturing workers, the USW's slow transformation into a post-industrial union presents a remarkable shift toward becoming a service sector labor organization. About 16 percent of the quarter million Steelworkers in Canada belong to various transportation, trade and service sectors. For the USW, call centers, as post-industrial workplaces, represent a challenge to traditional organizing methods, but they are also new and important frontiers for unionization. But even seasoned telecommunications unions have had to overcome their share of hurdles. The Telecommunications Workers Union (TWU), arguably one of Canada's most powerful unions until it faced major setbacks following five years of labor action against Telus, the country's second largest telecommunications firm, has for the first time in its history had to confront the reality of offshoring (see Shniad 2007; Stevens and Shi 2009). Outsourcing and offshoring present the most arduous challenge for trade unions in Canada today.

RINGING IN THE CHANGES

"In our business we have not the problem of the mill-owner or the steel manufacturer", remarked Bell System's chief officer, Henry B. Thayer, in 1922. "We have an exceptionally intelligent lot of people with more education than the average of working people. Among the men we have a large proportion with a considerable term of service and among the supervisory women", he continued (cited in Schacht 1985, 13). Thayer's comments would resonate in an HR document or industry publication describing the business perspective on call center employment today. In the 1920s, the growing telecommunications industry and its managers insisted that their privileged workers were without a need for union representation. In Canada, these firms worked tirelessly to construct an image of the operators' work as glamorous, professional, prestigious, and exciting in order to make it appealing to prospective employees (Bernard 1982). However, the almost exclusively female operators did eventually turn to union representation as a response to low pay, long hours, heavy supervision, the psychological strains of work, arbitrary management decisions, and a lack of appeal mechanisms. And why not? The skilled craft workers who built and maintained the early telephone and telegraph systems had a proud history of unionism. Since 1891, the International Brotherhood of Electrical Workers (IBEW) had been representing these and other workers throughout Canada and the United States. And where independent unions did emerge, companies fought them at every corner.

Being represented by a union in the handful of regulated telecommunication monopolies that defined the industry's landscape in Canada was almost a guarantee.[1] Operators, until recently the voice of service in the telephone industry, were cornerstones of the powerful telecommunications unions. When faced with deregulation, intensified competition, and radical changes in technology, the operator was eventually replaced with the multi-purposed call center worker, now tasked with customer service as well as sales. Selling customer service as a commodity and rationalizing the expense of call center facilities has put unions and workers again in a position to rethink their approaches to organizing. Today, unions face similar challenges in maintaining their foothold in Canada's call center sector as they do in other industries. The organization of employment, an internationally competitive environment, and pressures to rationalize expenses through the use of outsourcing and temporary workers add to the problems of gaining new ground.

The liberal market economy structure that defines Canada's call center terrain works to define working conditions, benefits, *and* the influence of unions in the sector (Holman, Batt, and Holtgrewe 2007). From a human resource management perspective, industry-wide studies have consistently published results illustrating that unionization produces positive results for labor *and* employers. Yet the union density rate for call centers, at 19.9 percent in 2007, remains below that of the national average of roughly 30 percent, but above the average rate for the broader information technology labor market, or 16.4 percent, during the same period (Van Jaarsveld, Frost, and Walker 2007, 4; Statistics Canada 2007; Software Human Resource Council 2007).[2] Unfortunately, no conclusive figures on call center union density rates exist past 2007, a symptom of the fragmented nature of the industry.

Union presence in the sector is dependent on four conditions: the position of call centers in the broader corporate structure, as either in-house or outsourced; a company's market base, international or domestic; the nature of services provided by the facility, in-bound or out-bound; and finally, the status of employees as full-time, part-time, or temporary. Working conditions, gender politics, state regulations, regional economic conditions, and union organizing strategies play a further role in conditioning the level of unionization. But as a report for Statistics Canada has concluded, compositional changes in the labor market are chief contributors to shifting rates of union density (Morisette, Schellenberg, and Johnson 2005).[3] Regional economic conditions, then, play a role in defining the union density rates evident in the area's call centers. Western Canadian call centers, for instance, are most likely to be operated in-house (33 percent), meaning the employees and facilities are managed and owned by the same company, compared to the national average (6 percent). These in-house call centers are also more likely to be unionized compared to their subcontracted or outsourced counterparts. Transportation and utilities possess the highest rates of call center unionization, at 50.7 percent and 70.4 percent, which reflects the overall density rates in these two sectors (Contact Center Canada 2006b). Centers located in Eastern Canada, on the other hand, where the prevalence of outsourced facilities catering to U.S. markets are above the national average, have one of the lowest rates of unionization, at 21 percent. Outsourced centers have a staggeringly low-density rate of 6 percent (Carroll and Wagar 2007, 2, 10). This fact can be attributed to the history of company and sector unionization, where trade unionism in the telecommunications, financial, and public services represents employees occupying a range of positions within the organization. Before the prevalence of subcontracting and offshoring, companies would usually perform these duties in-house, giving unions greater leverage in their efforts at organizing and in making industry or company-wide gains for workers. Strong collective agreements and an influential position in the labor market permitted an authoritative position at the bargaining table as well.

A variety of studies published since at least the early 2000s have concluded that unionization provides net economic benefits to both businesses and employees. For example, aggregate data suggests that union certification contributes to the stabilization of job tenure and operates as a regulatory mechanism securing both wages and employment conditions. Surveys of collective agreements in these workplaces have secured benefits like paid breaks, leave, seniority provisions, and scheduled vacation time that help to recruit new workers and stabilize turnover (Guard 2003). The combination of unionization and the nature of in-house and in-bound operations contributes to the longer tenure experienced by customer service representatives (11.3 years) compared to outbound operations (3.6 years) (Van Jaarsveld, Frost, and Walker 2007, 31). This reflects the general characteristics of the union advantage across Canada's labor market (Statistics Canada 2007). Lower turnover rates, measured by dismissals, quit rates, internal promotions, and retirements, reduce the costly expenditure of training and allow firms to retain highly skilled and experienced employees. Investments in human resource management practices directed at recruitment, job design, communication, and employee involvement also helped to increase employee satisfaction and lengthier tenures (Carroll and Wagar 2007, 3; Batt 2002; Batt and Moynihan 2002). Non-union centers, on the other hand, have twice the average turnover rates of unionized centers in comparable markets, at 33.6 percent compared to 16.1 percent; non-unionized centers have a quit rate that is three times the average of their unionized counterparts, 16.5 percent and 5 percent respectively (Van Jaarsveld, Frost, and Walker 2007, 3–4). Collective agreements also contribute to job security by providing workers with formalized responses to managerial authority and performance evaluation; just over half of unionized centers use performance information for discipline purposes compared to nearly three-quarters of non-union facilities (Van Jaarsveld, Frost, and Walker 2007, 28). Of course, much of these benefits can be attributed to the type of call center (telemarketing versus in-house customer service) throughout the industry.

Collective bargaining agreements also maintain the union wage premium across the Canadian labor market. Unionized call center workers earn 36 percent more than non-union employees, far exceeding the national average of 7.7 percent (Van Jaarsveld, Frost, and Walker 2007, 5; Statistics Canada 2007, 6). For unionized in-house agents this comes to $21.86 per hour compared to $17.82 for non-union workers; or $14.44 per hour over $12.53 for outsourced facilities (Carroll and Wagar 2007, 2).[4] Studies also demonstrate a startling differential base-pay rates, some as low as the provincial minimum wage and others as high as $125 per hour in the high-value financial sector (Guard 2003; 2006; Buchanan and Koch-Schulte 2000).

Tele-health centers, staffed mostly by unionized Registered Nurses, constitute the second highest paid call center market (Contact Center Canada 2006b). Women are especially advantaged by union representation, as they achieve 94 percent as much in hourly earnings as their male counterparts across industries (Statistics Canada 2007). Since over half of Canada's call center employees are women, union representation not only advantages workers generally, but women specifically in this gendered profession.[5] Wage benefits associated with collective agreements have also permitted gains for managers, who earn, on average, 21 percent more in annual pay than their counterparts in non-unionized call centers (Van Jaarsveld, Frost, and Walker 2007, 24). This fact has not prevented managers from actively opposing union organizing campaigns.

CALL CENTER UNIONISM

As research on Canada's call center landscape shows, workers employed in this industry are not inherently averse to unionization. In fact, as Buchanan and Koch-Schulte (2000) propose in their authoritative study of call center employment, unions are instrumental in shaping the industry as they actively pursue changes related to skill enhancement, worker participation in the labor process, minimizing burnout, and work to recognize the feminization of labor as an equity issue. Union intervention in call centers, therefore, has achieved a great deal for workers by transforming the process of work and provided a countermeasure to the arbitrary nature of management decision-making.

Responding to the fast-paced changes inherent to the post-industrial workplace has been a monumental challenge for organized labor. Technological innovations and, most importantly, the shift towards subcontracted and outsourced services have put labor organizations on the defensive. Automation through speech recognition software, for example, is a technical shift that has allowed companies in higher wage countries like the UK and Australia to use technology as a way of cutting costs by eliminating call center jobs altogether. In some cases this has led to the closure of well-paying and unionized call centers in Canada and elsewhere (Canadian Press 2006; *Sarnia Observer* 2006). Public sector unions have also had to contend with government cost cutting, evidenced by Canada Post's plan to outsource 300 call center jobs across Canada, fueling the commodification of public call center services (UNI 2010a). Indeed, the commodification of services has been particularly acute in the public sector, with privatization being an ongoing consideration for conservative, neo-liberal governments. Unfortunately for the union and its members, the postal service has not reversed its decision. This poses a threat not only to the workers who face immediate job losses because of government downsizing, but also to the national union movement which depends on the public sector as a membership stronghold.

Public and private sector call centers in Canada have been victims of this highly cost-sensitive industry. The worst-case scenario, workers being met at their places of employment with locked doors, is not uncommon. In New Brunswick, amidst a supposed boom in the province's flagship industry and after massive public investment, companies exercise little allegiance to their employees or region. Union intervention across the sector is subsequently hindered by company closures as workers become fearful that employers might be reticent to open new operations if union activity increases. Consolidation efforts by major telecommunications providers have further undermined economic development initiatives as well the strength of established unions. Bell Aliant's decision to close small regional call centers in 2009 resulted in the dismissal or relocation of about 100 unionized workers in five centers around the province of Nova Scotia (Power 2009). Large telecommunications companies, even where they hold near-monopoly status, have carried out corporate reorganization strategies that, in effect, undermine benefits and security achieved by unions and their members over decades of struggle.

Unions that attempt to organize call center workers have also had to face management opposition and unfair labor practices that include threatening individual employees for supporting a union or threatening to shut down a business. Employer resistance to union efforts is the norm in Canada, frustrating not only the certification outcomes but also the probability of establishing and sustaining a collective bargaining relationship (Bentham 2002). In 1999, the Canadian Union of Public Employees (CUPE), one of the country's largest and most influential unions, filed a complaint with the Nova Scotia labor relations board against a Connecticut-based call center operator after the union accused Ron Weber and Associates of firing two employees for helping with the certification drive (Canadian Press 1999). The powerful international union headquartered in the United States, the Service Employees International Union (SEIU), faced off against direcTel, a North Dakota-based company that operated an outbound call center in Saskatoon, claiming that the company tried to intimidate workers by dismissing several employees before a certification vote. Reports confirm that the mood among workers in the workplace changed during the union campaign, with one employee remarking, "We didn't want a union at first, but there's been so much crap going on". Multinational outsourcers like Convergys have been found guilty of unfair labor practices for similar reasons (BCLRB 2003). Sometimes, anti-union animus can be used in the union's favor, as the case of the USW at Omega Direct Response suggest.

CENTER OF STEEL

Much has changed within the ranks of the United Steelworkers in the last twenty years. Out of a total Canadian membership of 256,000, only 65,000 are employed in the steel and mining industries. The USW's second largest local, Local 1998, is composed of 5,000 administrative staff at the University of Toronto, most of whom are women. From factories to offices, hospitals, university campuses, hotels, warehouses, banks, and call centers, the USW has established a presence. Jorge Garcia-Orgales, Research Director for the Steelworkers' Canadian offices, helped to provide some historical depth to the USW's post-industrial unionism during an interview in 2008.

> We started in the 1980s. In Canada we started even ten years earlier than in the United States. At that point the union made a conscious decision that there was a new economy growing out there, and there was an opportunity for the union and a need for the workers to have unions in all these "new economies". We started there organizing health care sector, post-secondary education, security guards. (interview 2008)

The USW's development from an industrial union to one increasingly dependent on the service sector has proceeded through trial and error. Internal policy debates have also helped steer the USW into the post-industrial economy.

In 2002, the *Everybody's Union Everywhere* document developed from a Steelworkers National Policy Conference in Montreal. The document highlighted the remarkable challenges facing the union and focused on transforming the union's image and organizing strategy. The focus on women's empowerment in the union movement, a longstanding tradition within the Steelworkers, has been instrumental in identifying the potential of service sector employment and the current state of the gendered division of labor in the Canadian economy (see Fonow 2003). The report further emphasizes the need for organizing non-traditional sectors as a necessary response to the devastating decline of membership resulting from technological change and corporate-led globalization. There is also recognition of the growing "linguistic, racial, occupational, and gender diversity of the United Steelworkers" in Canada (USW 2002, 3). Such cross-constituency organizing, which stresses the intersectionality of social struggles and the significance of coalition-building inside unions, has been identified as crucial for revitalizing the Canadian labor movement (Briskin 2008; see also Yates 2006; Marshall and Garcia-Orgales 2006).[6] Since much of Canada's job growth has been taking place in the service sector, the USW has identified women and young people, those who occupy many of these part-time and low-paying sector industry workplaces, as a source of "new energy" in the union.

NEW UNIONISM IN THE NICKEL BELT

Compared to established telecommunications unions like the TWU, Communication Workers of America (CWA), and the Communication, Energy, and Paperworkers Union (CEP), the USW is a recent entrant to the call center business. Its first call center bargaining agreements were not signed until the 1990s, and still less than 1 percent of the total membership is employed in these workplaces. This development has been the focus of several influential articles on the USW's intervention at the Omega Direct Response (OMDR) facility in Sudbury, Ontario. Guard, Steedman, and Garcia-Orgales (2007) discuss the successful efforts of organizing the "electronic sweatshop", and how the OMDR campaign defied traditional strategies by relying heavily on inside rank-and-file workers as leaders in the unionization efforts. As these and other authors conclude, the "winning strategies at Omega were developed and implemented collaboratively by the organizer and the inside committee" (Guard et al. 2006, 283).

Experiences in the Sudbury facility helped prepare the USW for an engagement with the organizational features unique to outsourced call centers. Indeed, tactics were developed that reflected the situation at the Omega center specifically. This is what made the rank-and-file intensive efforts so instrumental. Denis Dallaire, the USW organizer in charge of the campaign, provided some insights to what was required to make the drive a success.

> If you're going to start any new campaign, you really got to have key people. You can't just stand outside and say sign your card and give it back. It doesn't work that way. You really have to inoculate the inside committee to prepare them for the management campaign. . . . We really need to build the inside committee and have natural leaders that are passionate about it. It's not always there, sometimes you have only one. (interview 2008)

Dallaire was no stranger to union organizing. In the mining town of Sudbury unions had a long and turbulent history, of which Dallaire was a part. He was even part of the efforts to unionize his workplace back in 1990–1991, the office and administrative wing of nickel giant Inco, now Vale Inco. For a time he was even president of his union.

Forming a sustainable group of supporters and transforming them into organizers was difficult. Employee turnover, emblematic of the call center industry, made it difficult to keep rank-and-file activists. Flexible shifts and inconsistent schedules prevented close relationships between employees from being formed, making the task of organizing even more difficult. For months, Dallaire was taking on the organizing by himself and, even as the campaign escalated, he was joined by only a small handful of staff. Intimidation by managers created further challenges. Several workers were nevertheless transformed into union activists as the campaign grew. A successful campaign, this case indicates, can be attributed not only to rank-and-file support, but also to the experience and support of veteran organizers who are sufficiently resourced by the union.

The case of OMDR's arrival in Sudbury is not unlike the story of other economically depressed regions of Canada that have been thrust into the post-industrial economy. Sudbury and its surrounding region is home to one of the world's largest reserves of nickel and for a century its population has existed on resource commodity capitalism, and the boom-and-bust crises that accompany such an economy. As historian and economist David Leadbeater (2008) explains, Sudbury's economic geography is defined by a chronic deterioration of living standards, persistent high unemployment, deepening poverty, deteriorating working conditions, declining job prospects, and the outflow of a younger generation. About a third of the region's private sector employers are foreign-based, the largest of which (outside the mining industry) is now a Delaware-based call center company, TeleTech. For these reasons, Omega Direct Response's arrival was looked to with envious eyes by employers and workers alike. And for OMDR, which required a low-cost, yet sufficiently skilled workforce, Sudbury's economic woes were the call center's gain.

Sudbury's local politicians had deployed an aggressive marketing campaign and even offered financial incentives to employers if they established call centers in the region. High unemployment rates, the availability of skilled workers, training opportunities in local post-secondary educational institutions, and property acquisition and leasing costs were all part of the city's appeal (St. Pierre 1999a). Attached to call center employment was the excitement of bringing high-tech, post-industrial workplaces to northern Ontario. OMDR was the first, and for a time the largest, call center to set up in Sudbury, with 1,500 employees at two sites, in 1999. Dallaire recalled, "there was excitement in the city, they were all very positive about the new employer coming in even though they're only paying $8.00 an hour [as a starting wage]". Unions had a substantial presence in the city already, notable the USW, with a density rate of almost 50 percent among the predominantly male, skilled, and semi-skilled workers employed in the mines and tertiary industries. The important public service presence in the city also added to union strength. Union halls and events were hubs for community life in this "labor town" (Guard, Steedman, and Garcia-Orgales 2007; Leadbeater 2008). But outside of the white-collar component of large firms like Inco (before it became Vale Inco), post-industrial unionization was limited to government workers in the city. Economic conditions created a favorable climate for call centers in the city, with an educated and largely female pool of workers making up the potential labor market. Omega was further advantaged by its ability to hire Ontario Works (a neo-liberal euphemism applied in the mid-1990s for welfare and social assistance) recipients as an inexpensive source of labor, contracting them for brief periods of time before letting them go. The company's decision to exploit this vulnerable group of workers provoked employees to recognize the injustices committed by the company and helped build support for the union (Guard, Steedman, and Garcia-Orgales 2007).

Conditions of employment, characteristics of call center work, and the behavior of management were leading catalysts for unionization. In fact, accounts by union leaders, shop stewards, and the USW organizer point to the arbitrary nature of managerial decisions and lack of respect by employers as the primary cause for union intervention. The company also reneged on its commitment to introduce a benefits package, even months after the facility opened. After the fanfare had settled in Sudbury, the reality of work at OMDR was known throughout the city. Dallaire told the story of an acquaintance working at the call center:

The first day I remember . . . she calls me says, wow, we got this big [policy and procedural] manual, and it looks positive, it's so up-beat. Then, two or three days later she says, I'm getting a funny feeling it won't be what is says in the book. And it went kind of downhill, [but] she was determined to make a go of it. . . . [She] calls me a week or so later and says, it's just not good at all. If there were any balloons involved, they've burst, and we need to bring in a union there. (interview 2008)

This prompted a discussion within the regional USW offices about whether or not the union should attempt to organize the facility. Not everyone thought the campaign would succeed. After the drive was formally approved by the USW leadership, Dallaire took leave from his job and began what would become a seven month organizing campaign.

Judy Searson, unit chairperson for the amalgamated local representing OMDR workers in Sudbury at the time of our interview, offered a powerful description of work at the call center. Trained as a human resource manager in the service and hospitality industry, Searson began working at Omega not long after the campaign had concluded. She took on the role of shop steward after six months with the company and moved on to become unit chairperson shortly after. "I would have never stayed there if it hadn't been for the union. I don't think I would have lasted two months", Searson recalled. "It had to be the worst job that I have ever worked at in my life" (interview 2008). Most accounts of the Omega managerial staff indicate a lack of professionalism in conduct and skill. "[T]hese people, they just, they figure, 'I'm management so I can say or do whatever I want to you and you just have to take it because you're this lowly worker'. . . . For some reason they think . . . in order to be a good manager you have to be hated. I had one of the supervisors tell me that one day". Even the selection process was described as unprofessional, confirming what studies have concluded about hiring requirements in outbound facilities (Carroll and Wagar 2007; Van Jaarsveld, Frost, and Walker 2007). As one shop steward named Wendy commented,

They were just hiring anybody by random when I got hired. There was like seventy people, there was three-day training, except Omega didn't know what they were going to do with seventy people. . . . They can't seem to keep people employed. The turnover in Sudbury, I would say about 17,000 people have been through that same call center. . . . Because it's not an easy job. (interview 2008)

In the end, a lack of professional and experienced management, as well as anti-union tactics used by the employer, contributed to the union's success.

As the union campaign gained traction with workers, OMDR brought in an operations director from another company tasked with the responsibility of keeping the union out. But, Dallaire said, "the project leaders were taking it upon themselves to do stupid things . . . and we took it to our advantage". The campaign helped to bring evidence of poor working conditions and alleged labor standards violations to the public's attention. After the union filed a charge with the Ontario Labor Relations Board (OLRB) over Omega's decision to fire an employee for being actively involved in the organizing campaign, support grew for the drive. The incident also gave the union an additional advantage, since the Board not only ordered the reinstatement of the employee, the company also agreed to mail all employees a package which included union cards and information about the USW. Whereas the campaign had previously been restricted to signing certification cards outside the workplace, management fumbling provided the union with a golden opportunity to communicate with all employees through the company database. Successful appeals by the union showed employees that the Steelworkers were an effective organization capable of representing the workers. OMDR President, Bharat Hansraj, however, was increasingly concerned about the public image his company had in Sudbury. Citing the jobs and other benefits Omega brought to the community, Hansraj said in an interview, "I'm not sure how much Sudbury wants these call centers anymore" (St. Pierre 1999a). Unfortunately, Hansraj was not responsive to my invitation for an interview.

Organizers stressed that their intention was not to chase the call center industry out of Sudbury, or to create antagonisms with OMDR and its managers. Fairness and respect were the chief goals of the drive, in addition to the establishment of a benefits package, seniority structure, and a grievance procedure. After all, the large mining companies in Sudbury had long been unionized and always profitable. But Omega used economic uncertainty and unionization to claim that a real threat to the company's financial sustainability actually existed. Many workers, of course, doubted these words from management. In addition to OMDR's decision to terminate an employee for supporting the union, and by threatening to dismiss any employee to be found working in support of the USW, the company's senior officer also remarked publicly that it would close down the facility if employees voted to be represented by the Steelworkers, committing an unfair labor practice according to Ontario's Labour Relations Act. In his letter to the employees, as per the agreement with USW organizers as an act of remediation, Hansraj was forced to concede that it violated provincial labor relations legislation. Even after certification, management reiterated these threats, despite the fact that the company was still profitable. Searson was quick to tear apart the company's case of financial hardship when we spoke.

> Originally when they were going to unionize, that was the threat, they'll shut it down. . . . Well guess what? We unionized and they didn't close the doors. Then they said, what was it, the first arbitration we had it was around layoffs and seniority, and they said if you take this to arbitration we'll close the doors. Well we took it to arbitration and they didn't close the doors. It's threats, and it's idle threats. I said, they're not going to close the doors, they are making money! (interview 2008)

Staff were also beginning to learn more about their rights in the workplace and responded to management accordingly. "The inside people that we had were really well versed in what their rights were", Dallaire explained. "Some of them, I'm telling you, I so admired them. They just would go right up to [managers] and challenge them: 'Do you realize that this is breaking article X [of the *OLRA*]?'" (interview 2008). Dallaire attributed these bold responses to the strong communications skills call center workers developed on the job, in particular their knack for managing the abuse thrown at them by prospective customers. These occasions provided reflection on how the union campaign accelerated over time, starting as a discrete, "low key" drive and moving to a point where supporters were wearing union buttons in the workplace. Establishing a sustainable organizing committee remained difficult, however. Though hundreds of people had signed cards, only a handful of employees were willing to be active in the campaign. "It wasn't an aggressive push over, we slowly took it and built on them", Dallaire said (interview 2008).

Organizers became ever-present at social events and used social networks to reach out to employees. Sudbury's Labor Day picnic was used as an occasion to sign over sixty members. Gary Patterson, then-president of USW Local 6500, invited Omega workers to the event to "give them a taste of what unionism is all about". A banner reading "Welcome Omega Employees" was the union's attempt to attract employees working for Sudbury's largest call center (see St. Pierre 1999c). Union activists had role-played the call center experience for participants at the event, helping to create an affinity between the union and OMDR employees. The strategy was innovative and effective. Role-playing helped to establish a collective identity among the workers by drawing attention to the shared stresses involved with call center work through consciousness raising. "Get a real job" was the play developed by rank-and-file organizers, and later performed by Ring Around the World players at an international conference on call centers in Toronto in 2003. The title was drawn from the abuse call center workers would receive over the phone. Each telemarketer would recite their story about how they were coping with the stressful conditions of work, presenting a realistic depiction of employment (see Pilon 2003). Adding to the influence of this performance, the reinstatement of a terminated employee and the company letter reassured people that it was safe to support the union, which assisted the campaign by giving it a "kick start", as Dallaire put it.

Rank-and-file opposition to the campaign also became more pronounced at this time. Organizers were suspicious that the anti-union activists were coached or supported by management, but the union could never confirm the claim. In a couple of instances the two parties, supporters and opponents, would rally to demonstrate their position publicly. "I remember the day we filed the application", Dallaire recalled,

> we had a rally . . . and I'm standing there and we have maybe seventy-eight [to] eighty people . . . and the anti-union group were standing next to me, but I had one of those bullhorns and they were trying to pull it away from me. . . . [They cried] how it wasn't fair, I was being heard more than they were. (interview 2008)

Antipathy and outright opposition corresponded with the history of unionism in the region. It was clear from conversations with organizers and union leaders that old tensions and union rivalries weighed on the minds and attitudes of the community. Predispositions towards unionization, both positive and negative, had real effects on the USW call center campaign. How call center workers identified themselves as knowledge workers is likely to have affected their propensity to support or reject the union as well, at least from the union organizer perspective. "You wonder why we have difficulty getting organizers. . . . [O]ur culture of being white-collar at Inco is no different, I remember visiting people that I knew seven times before they signed their card, and I knew their family members and everything. What is it?" Dallaire's comments here are telling of the challenges he and other organizers faced (interview 2008).

Local media reported the feeling of hostility experienced by some union opponents, with one employee stating in the press, "Ever since they started talking about forming a union, this has been a very stressful place to work. . . . I've been verbally abused by pro-union people" (O'Flanagan 1999). Dallaire also explained the prevalence of company managers creating myths about inside committee connections with the union:

> What do you do? You built the inside committee, some of them [are ridiculed], they call them the elite . . . I've had one place they were saying, 'do you realize that once you unionize that the inside committee will become the union bosses and will benefit from the union dues'. . . . We're demonized big time and until laws can change we're disadvantaged. (interview 2008)

In a complaint that would resonate as a standard tract against unions, some call center employees publicly suggested that the union was ignorant of what companies actually provided in wages and benefits. Reproducing anti-union arguments forwarded by employers, an OMDR employee commented in the press, "What do you think would happen if the prospective buyers or companies that bring business to all of these call centers were bombarded with demands and ultimatums? They would turn around and go with the lowest bidder and would leave the teleconferencing future of this city dead in its tracks" (Brown 2001). There appeared to be genuine fear among the workforce that unionization would scare away other employment opportunities and create an economic shock effect in the region. This sentiment was not uncommon during and after the unionization drive at OMDR, as media reports suggest (O'Flanagan 1999). Because some of the region's call centers were paying more than minimum wage without requiring postsecondary education, employees voiced support for existing benefits and feared the repercussions that would follow from unionization. It was not insignificant that the Omega employee cited above was writing *after* the successful campaign at OMDR, when the company first introduced the benefits package after a collective agreement was finally negotiated. Other statements reveal that employees were genuinely suspicious of the promises made by union organizers. One staff person argued with coworkers that "nothing is going to change" and that a union "is not always going to fix what's wrong" (St. Pierre 1999b).

Despite the anti-union efforts of OMDR, the Steelworkers successfully gained the confidence of workers, who voted 68 percent in favor of unionization during the mandatory secret ballot election. Dallaire highlighted how important this was not just for the USW, but for the labor movement as a whole. "I remember the day after winning the vote and having different unions calling me, leaving messages about finally, somebody has finally made a breakthrough of significance", he recalled (interview 2008). Indeed, the structure of outsourced and telemarketing call centers stacked the odds against the union's efforts, and Dallaire knew it. After months of campaigning, turnover threatened the sustainability of an effective organizing campaign, and other, ambivalent employees, grew disinterested in union activity. The certification process provided the employer with an advantage. Even after unions submit applications with a solid majority having signed cards, managers can commence their campaign in a short period of time and turn a lot of people around. Omega's CEO publicly stated at this time that he could not guarantee the company's presence in Sudbury if staff decided to unionize (see St. Pierre 1999d). As studies in other Canadian jurisdictions confirm, management opposition, measured by unfair labor practices, is at least twice as effective in the voting regime as compared to a card-check system (Riddell 2004).

Success was hard fought and claimed as an important victory for the Steelworkers. Even before the final certification vote, Omega employees at a Toronto facility expressed interest in organizing (St. Pierre 1999b). Obstacles seemed insurmountable at first, and organizers had to initially convince union officials that the campaign would be beneficial for the organization. But despite the certification victory, the USW and its supporters faced immediate hurdles. Not one year after electing to be represented by a union, members voted 85 percent in favor of strike action to back contract demands. OMDR had, at that point, refused to agree on a first collective agreement, prompting workers to threaten labor action. Officials with the company refused to publicly comment on the talks (*Sudbury Star* 2000). However, by the end of 2000, both the union and OMDR had settled on a collective agreement. Sustaining membership interest, despite the message conveyed by the support for a strike vote, continued to be a problem for the local. As Searson pointed out, "The most that we get out . . . is about thirty people. . . . So when you can't get the activists to come out to a meeting, how do you get the membership?" (interview 2008).

Searson's frustration with the lack of membership involvement in union activities applied to workers throughout the local, which is composed of fifty-nine units and approximately 2,900 members. It was even difficult to get unit chairpersons and shop stewards to attend. Building a union identity among the membership has been a challenge, and Omega employees, by some accounts, are still not confident enough to confront managers through the established grievance procedure. Turnover has lent to this problem, especially when it comes to the appointment of stewards, but more generally because time and experience is needed to develop a confident and empowered union membership. Wendy, then a shop steward at Omega, remarked,

> We've had a couple of people we've made shop stewards, they haven't lasted too long. They've gone to other jobs. It's not the fact that they're not committed, it's that they're young, and in a call center you don't want to be there for the rest of your life, that's for sure. It's kind of hard. Do young people really get involved? No. It's mostly, I'd say, thirty-five years of age and up. (interview 2008)

Wendy's own life history contributed to her involvement with the Steelworkers as a shop steward. From working as a coordinator of a collective kitchen to her involvement at a women's center, Wendy's commitment to social justice activism helped her develop an affinity with unionism and human rights at work.[7] When asked about the satisfaction she derives from the call center job, Wendy remarked, "I personally don't like the job, I like the people that I work with. I'll be honest, the reasons I'm still there is because I'm part of the union" (interview 2008). Other comments illustrate how influential a unionized environment can be for employee retention. "I heard some people say they would never go to another call center because the fact that none of them, there isn't another one unionized in Sudbury", she said. The lack of employment options in the region was another factor that kept some employees at the facility. While the reality of turnover could not be avoided, former employees who had moved on to other industries indicate that their interest in unionization at Omega prompted them to become union activists in their new workplace.

From the vantage point of union members, Omega's senior and front-line managers never relented on their resistance to the union. "They hate the union with a passion, always have", Searson said bluntly. Like Wendy, Searson was adamant she "would have never stayed [at OMDR] if it hadn't been for the union". In fact, the company made several attempts to remove her.

> They actually tried firing me three times. [In] 2003 I was terminated because they said I was AWOL. They said I was out trying to organize a call center in Thunder Bay. And then in 2004, August, they terminated me for low SPH [sales per hour]. (interview 2008)

Searson admits that her ability to sell was below what the company expected, and she joked that she would never leave the Chair position and return to the phones. "I know that I wouldn't have the ability to fight the way I do now", she said. But her account of the incident reveals a deeper intent behind the attempts at termination. A senior manager deliberately tried to prolong the grievance process, thinking that the longer Searson was away from work the more likely it would be that she would step down as unit chair. The attempt failed and Searson was reinstated with pay. Because of limited involvement in union activity amongst the Omega workforce, the union's influence in the company has been contingent on the experience and knowledge of longer serving activists who maintained their roles as stewards and union executive members.

One of the most contentious issues that provoked Omega employees to unionize was the use of sales per hour (SPH) statistics, which management utilized to assess and rank performance. Employees were routinely sent home because they were not making sufficient sales, but the termination of employees on these grounds ceased after the establishment of a collective agreement. Considering that Omega is an outsourced and outbound call center, attempts to change the company's performance standard was challenging for the new local. Still, the union raised the issue with OMDR, stating that if scripts are followed verbatim and call center workers are conducting their jobs according to requirements, the ability to secure sales would continue to be uncertain, at best. Searson declared that if Omega enforced a strict policy on SPH, despite the grievance procedure that permitted employees to appeal dismissals, agents are implicitly encouraged to deviate from scripts and deploy dubious methods of securing sales.

> They're what we call in the industry as "slammers". They'll lie to the customers to get the sales. I said, those are the sales that don't stay.

Those are the people who call the company and say look, this isn't what I was told and . . . I don't want this. (interview 2008)

But the frustration and stress employees felt when berated for not making sales added to the level of attrition.

The strains of making sales under intense pressure are exacerbated by the hasty training process, which took new entrants from the classroom to the sales floor in less than two weeks. At one point the process had been reduced to a single day! Management, according to the union, had no interest in introducing a more comprehensive training regime. However, representatives from an Omega client, a U.S.-based financial institution, recognized that the callers were not getting sufficient training after they monitored calls. For Wendy, Omega managers from the Toronto and Sudbury facilities eventually came to acknowledge the problem, but this issue never surfaced at the bargaining table. "When you're bargaining you're going in with what members want", Searson pointed out (interview 2008). In other words, in the surveys conducted by the union around bargaining time, training is not listed as a priority.

As the accounts provided by organizers, stewards, and chairs suggest, the union has been able to provide a voice mechanism for employees at OMDR. Workers have exercised this empowerment by countering management practices. One example is resistance to workplace surveillance. Telemarketers at Omega were aware that calls were monitored, both by clients and the company. Some employees also recognized that the purpose of surveillance had shifted from fulfilling a "coaching position" to a disciplinary mechanism. Managers, I was told, deliberately targeted union activists like Searson as a means of building a case for dismissal based on poor performance. In fact, it was widely recognized that becoming a union activist meant putting a target on your back for management. Workplace solidarity was exercised in an effort to undermine management's attempts at disciplining union activists. Searson described this as follows:

I remember this one little monitor, I'd go in the morning and she'd say, okay Judy, you're on the hit list again. And before she would monitor me she would walk by very quickly and say, okay, you're up, be really really good for me. And I would. I would be completely scripted and there would be absolutely nothing on the tape, nothing they could use against me. . . . [The] monitors liked me and they were my members! So they would come warn me . . . (interview 2008)

Monitors who colluded with managers were viewed with suspicion by colleagues since they were all part of the same bargaining unit. Actively supporting management's intent to use surveillance as a disciplinary rather than a training tool would prompt responses from other call center workers, especially those targeted for surveillance. The union structure operated as a formal and informal channel for resistance, even if the collective agreements did not contain clauses specific to the use of surveillance, audio or video, in the workplace. "We have had some monitors that went along with management and really did try to nail people and get people in trouble", Searson commented. Her response was to confront the monitor directly. After a process of complaining to management, the monitor quit that position and moved to reception. Consequently, Wendy pointed out that it is tough to find monitors because "you don't want to be hated by your colleagues" (interview 2008). Having access to this information meant that monitors possessed important knowledge as to why particular call center agents were being surveilled, be it for training purposes or disciplinary action. So while there were strategic reasons to have union activists performing that function, it still remained an unappealing task.

Despite the antagonisms faced by union organizers in the months leading up to certification, as well as the ongoing challenges in the years following their initial success, the biggest threat to the USW Local 2020 has undoubtedly been the precarity of the outsourced global call center market. It is here where unions are at their greatest disadvantage. When OMDR was acquired by the Indian firm, Silverline Technologies Ltd., in 2008, fears surfaced among the employees that the company would increase its use of offshore facilities (see *BusinessLine* 2008). Searson suggested, however, that the Sudbury workers do not understand the scope of the problem. At its peak, the Sudbury OMDR facility employed approximately 1,500 people, but by 2005 that number shrank to fewer than 300, with about 200 to 250 being part of the bargaining unit. As a staff representative for the Steelworkers indicated at the time, business has been most affected by the post-September 11 economic downturn and, by his account, the Do-Not-Call legislation in the United States (St. Pierre 2005). "I was there when they were downsizing from 750 to 200 people", Wendy said. "[B]oy were they getting rid of people left, right, and center. Sometimes I wonder if they weren't getting rid of the wrong ones" (interview 2008). Shop stewards had what was described as a case overload and the company was using simple infractions to issue verbal warnings and written reprimands, sometimes in the course of a single day. By 2008, the number of employees sank to less than 130. More problems surfaced as early as 2002 when call center staff were being sent home without pay as a result of downsizing. The union struggled with a way of dealing with this crisis because it had no control over the company's shrinking client base and revenue.

Of the few options available, the union and employees filed grievances citing Omega's denial of seniority rights. Gerry Loranger, a staff representative for the Local, indicated that stewards had received over fifty grievances from members of the unit over the issue. The director of operations at Omega responded that skills and performance history were a factor in determining layoffs, not just seniority rights, citing provisions within the collective agreement as a justification for how the process was carried out

(Wilhelm 2002a, 2002b). Rifts within the membership surfaced as a result. Younger workers were especially resentful and felt they should have the right to keep their jobs, despite the seniority provisions. Searson was very cognizant of the limits to what unions, in their present state, can do as a response to globalization and precarious aspects of call center employment. When Coronna, Ontario-based 411 call center workers employed by Nordia, a joint venture involving Bell Canada and Excel Global Services, lost their jobs due to company downsizing, the USW was presented with few options. The company cited the innovation of voice-automated technology and growing business demand for self-service offers as the reason for cutting jobs and concentrating operations in the sole, existing center in Kitchener, Ontario. Workers had voted in favor of certification at the facility just two years earlier, following an application to the Canada Industrial Relations Board (CIRB). Talks to bargain a closure agreement between the union and the company broke down as Nordia refused to provide an enhancement to severance packages mandated by employment standards legislation. Eventually it complied with existing legislation but quickly cut funding to an employee adjustment center it established to assist retrenched workers (Canadian Press 2006; Casselman 2003; *Sarnia Observer* 2006). Similarly, just four years after Telespectrum employees in St. Catharines certified with the USW, the U.S.-based company closed its doors almost overnight. The company said it regretted the loss of jobs but insisted that fluctuating client demands forced the business decision to close (see Adamczyk 2004; Fraser 2008). The rising Canadian dollar was cited as the cause for the company's poor economic performance.

Searson was adamant that as the USW became a global union it could wield greater influence over transnational employers. This would still take vast support *within* unions. "[Y]ou have to educate our members about their power", she continued, "[u]nions have the power if they wanted it" (interview with Searson 2008). Indeed, the union's success at Omega was followed by the unionization of several other call centers in Ontario, including the Telespectrum facility in St. Catharines. In 2001, USW International President Leo Gerard told members that the union "will not let Sudbury became a low-wage community. . . . We're looking aggressively to unionize these folks" (cited in Bradley 2001). Gerard was concerned that the growth of call centers in the region would mark a lowering of wages and hurt the area's economy. In 2001, Dallaire, inspired by the victory at Omega, took on the task of organizing TeleTech, part of Colorado-based TeleTech Holdings, then Sudbury's second largest call center after Omega. Ultimately the certification campaign was unsuccessful, due to what was seen as the company's more effective and professional anti-union strategy (see Whitehouse 2001; interview with Dallaire 2008). Local call center companies learned a lesson from OMDR's mistakes. But Wendy was certain that the USW's presence in the sector made a difference in Sudbury's non-unionized call centers.

Well, I'll tell you that call centers now, if it wasn't for the union at Omega, I don't think people from TeleTech and Persona and even at Rogers. . . . I think they're treated a lot better because of the union, because we are unionized and they don't want to be. (interview 2008)

In 2009, OMDR shut its doors in Sudbury for good. And without success at Teletech, the USW no longer represents call center workers in this northern Ontario mining community. Searson left OMDR to manage a small motel in Southern Ontario, finally putting to use her education and formal training as a hospital sector manager. Despite the closure, the union's successes and experiences with OMDR were deployed at other call centers in Ontario.

POLITICAL COMMUNICATIONS

Political Communications (PC) is a Canadian-owned outbound call center that conducts surveys and polling for unions, social movements, non-profits, political parties and other progressive advocacy groups.[8] With two locations in Canada, one in Toronto and the other in Vancouver, PC has been providing services for clients in Canada, the U.S., and the UK since 1991. The focus here will be on the unionized Toronto facility, which has been in operation since 1994. Not unlike the appeal of social justice that attracted a handful of Omega workers to shop steward and unit chair positions, several of the union activists with the USW local at PC followed a similar path. This matched the company's self-image, which is fashioned as a "socially progressive firm". Donna, the unit chairperson, had been with the company for ten years and had previous experience working in a government job and then subsequently fundraising for environmental groups. Donna was active in the initial union organizing campaign at PC three years prior, and considered herself a high-profile union activist at the time.

Because of its political and social orientation, USW officials conveyed to me that PC was different than most call centers, especially in comparison to OMDR. Fair wages and a progressive attitude towards work were ostensibly embedded within PC's organizational framework and management practices. But, like any workplace, dissatisfaction prompted employees to think about unionization. For Donna, the rapid growth of the company in a short period of time contributed to discontent as managerial policies were not developing along with PC's expansion. What appeared from a caller's perspective to be arbitrary wage increases left an impression with some workers that favoritism motivated management decisions. Donna helped to provide an account of developments at PC.

So the growth was just amazing. It was still being run very haphazardly. I mean this is a personal perspective on it, not just my own, but some of the reasons for it were the wages were really bad and any attempts to give wages were sort of arbitrary and sporadic. They [management] would just announce that some people were going to get a raise [laughs]. . . . We got to the point where enough was enough, we need to even things out and make it more acceptable to everybody. (interview 2008)

While dissatisfaction with certain policies was prevalent among the callers, some of the senior call center staff were not in favor of unionization. Most agreed that change in the workplace needed to happen, but no consensus emerged about whether or not union representation was necessary. By this point there had already been an attempt to organize PC, but the campaign was met with opposition from employees and the employer due to the particular union's stance on environmental issues. This was before the USW entered the scene some years later. As Donna recalled, the union in question represented forestry workers in British Columbia and had pursued legal action against Greenpeace, a PC client. The owner of Political Communications "came into the phone room and had a captive audience and talked about why he didn't like this particular union", Donna explained (interview 2008). This account suggests that the employer did not openly oppose unionization per se, but the company was not supportive of the union in question, and it quickly became evident that the initiative would fail, which it did.

Without a union the employees were left with few recourses of action in their attempts at transforming workplace policies. Management responded by working with callers to form a staff association as a way of negotiating wage and benefits, and for establishing an informal grievance mechanism. As the senior Toronto PC manager, Teresa (interview 2008), acknowledged, these agreements were effectively based on an "honor system" determined by the employer's willingness to comply. Donna labeled the agreement as "very corporate", and the absence of a binding grievance procedure furthered employee dissatisfaction with the existing association. Activists started to "shop around" for unions not long after the failed attempt at organizing, and finally approved of the Steelworkers after interviewing union officials. The USW's commitment to industrial democracy and rank-and-file participation in running the local and the broader union structure was seen as an appealing advantage over other unions. An emphasis on union training and education, a hallmark of the Steelworkers' approach to addressing grievances, among other issues, were cited as additional strengths. During the second organizing campaign, Donna noted, the employer was far more removed from the process and did not exert an anti-union sentiment. "I think when we chose the Steelworkers", Donna (interview 2008) said, "they sort of went along with it. They didn't actively oppose anything".

As bargaining began, management was less antagonistic to the union and employee demands when compared to the OMDR case. Contract negotiations and the organization of work, however, still remained fixed to workplace politics governed by a division between management and employees. It was for this reason that the staff association and its non-binding agreement failed to address workers' concerns or mitigate the perception of arbitrary decision making. The staff agreement also lacked a representative structure, so callers were still required to address problems as individuals rather than making appeals through collective action in a representative organization. When asked about the relationship between callers and management, the unit chair responded,

> It's mixed. I think most people approach a union shop steward, even with minor stuff. There are a few people who will talk to management. If they aren't able to get a satisfactory answer, they will come to the union. Management here is not hard to approach. But, what people find generally is when a [steward], or myself, approaches them with something they get a much quicker response. (interview with Donna 2008)

With regard to employee satisfaction and the professionalism of managerial staff, the difference between OMDR and PC was palpable. "There are a lot of reasons why people would stay", Donna (2008) argued. "[I]t's also a relaxed and friendly environment, and that's what keeps people here. They have flexible work schedules". From management's position, the company has a "good relationship with the USW" and the employees as a whole are described as a "very active group of people, a really intelligent group of people" (interview with Teresa 2008). Employee commitment to PC can be attributed both to the attitudes of managers and the company's socially progressive vision, as well as the protections now offered through a collective agreement. This is why PC boasts of a retention rate above the industry average for outbound centers. According to Teresa, the average length of stay for employees is two years, with turnover being highest in the first three months.

Teresa, who started as a caller with PC, provided insights into how work at the company changed since unionization. In many respects the senior manager agreed that a union presence has improved the quality of employment, overall.

> It has some positive effect on our quality . . . in that we have become more organized in how we do the training, performance improvement, review. . . . [B]efore we had one person doing all that stuff. . . . We're now in a position that I can make a good argument for having more call center staff. Not management staff, but support staff, like trainers. It has had an improvement there.

Teresa also conceded that a formal grievance process has revoked management's ability to dismiss employees without a strong justification, to the benefit of both callers and the company. "The way it's affected the quality of work positively, it has put us in a position where we had to learn about getting more professional about how to manage [the work] across the board", she explained. Despite the contentious issues that have arisen, she believed that both parties came out "with an improved relationship". But from a manager's vantage point, Teresa addressed some negative elements that have arisen since unionization. Antagonisms at the bargaining table, as well as over grievances and disciplinary cases, mean that emotional ties between managers, employees, and union representatives surface at the professional level in a relatively small workplace with less than 100 employees. There is a tendency for animosity that is directed at the in-house manager to persist during and after problems have been raised. Teresa's sentiment is a symptom of PC's progressive self-image as well as her own experience as a caller at one point. On the subject of quality of work as a consequence of unionization, the conclusion she drew was quite different.

> I don't think it has improved the quality of work being done. . . . It might have a slight negative impact, we do have people who feel—not that the union or union representatives have told them this—untouchable. 'I can under perform because I'm in a union and you can't fire me'. . . . There's more of that sort of thing now. When you put in a safety net . . . some people will go that way.

Admittedly, Teresa recognized that this is a sentiment rather than a quantitative shift in caller performance. In certain scenarios, though, employees will attempt only the bare minimum standard, according to the manager. A work-to-rule attitude—especially with regards to literal readings of a script—is a response to management's efforts at intensifying performance, even though job description titles are used to push callers into doing more than the minimum. Never was it indicated that the union or union officials condone or support this attitude. Despite these subtle attitudes that suggested dissatisfaction with the union, the senior manager was actually supportive of the outcomes and process. As a response to colleagues in other call centers, Teresa remarked that the most anti-union managers often "don't know how to manage in a unionized environment, which is just managing properly".

VISA FINANCIAL

By the time Dallaire had begun organizing Omega in Sudbury, the USW already had a history of representing call center workers in the banking sector since 1990, when employees at the Visa Financial center in Toronto certified. Eight years later, the Vancouver branch of VF followed in 1998.[9] This was no small accomplishment for the Steelworks. Visa Financial is the credit card division of one of Canada's largest financial institutions, which I will call Canada Bank, boasting over 40,000 employees and 11 million clients across the globe. Unions have been relatively unsuccessful at organizing employees in the country's banks, and this one in particular was recognized, historically, for its anti-union animus. The USW's influence has been until recently restricted to the Visa Financial call centers located in Toronto and Vancouver. In March of 2013, Visa Financial (Vancouver) announced to its employees, only days after bargaining had commenced, that it was shutting its doors within the year. According to sources in the union, all of the 120 positions are to be transferred to the Toronto branch in an effort to save costs. Like all of Canada's major financial institutions, Canada Bank reaped astounding profits in 2012, which at $3.3 billion was up 14 percent from the previous year. Its CEO is one of the highest paid executives in Canada.

What stood out to me in interviews with workers was their penchant for solving problems and dealing with people. Union stewards in particular possessed an affinity for helping customers and unionized colleagues in times of need. In fact, two customer service representatives I interviewed at the Visa Financial Toronto facility were trained as social workers and found the task of representing and assisting peers to the be most appealing aspect of working at the company. Take Sandra for instance. Sandra's initial interest in taking on the job of steward was sparked after the union resolved a grievance in her favor. When a position became available she said, "Why not? Just utilize my skills here". Because the customer service representative job also involves resolving human problems, albeit for customers, both managers and colleagues positively received her interest in being a union representative. "[Managers] always compliment in terms of how I was able to deal with the situation, they always want to have me at their meetings. [They see me] as a fair person", Sandra boasted.

Karen, another steward at Visa Financial's Toronto facility, shared this common experience. After ten years as a social worker, Karen appreciated a job where she could leave her work behind at the end of a shift. This sentiment is what initially prevented her from taking on a steward position, as well as the time commitment of being a parent. Karen became increasingly involved in union activism after assisting shop stewards, until she was approached to be part of bargaining. Then, she explained, she ended "up doing the shop steward work as well. Because people would approach me with all the issues and they kind of have this kind of trust with me. So, I said okay" (interview 2008). Susan, a shop steward in Vancouver who was inspired by the Solidarity movement in Poland and her previous work history, reflected that "corporations and people who have money own all the rights, so someone has to get together and have a voice, to have some basic rights of privileges if you're the person who's losing them". These initial experiences are contrasted with those of Catherine, unit chairperson at the Vancouver facility, who was employed in the center during unionization. Hers was an unlikely road from customer service agent to union leader.

Catherine came from a business family, and her affinity towards union-ism had to develop over time. "I actually started out not happy that the union came", she confessed. This sentiment was shared by others as well, and to some extent this resentment towards the union never completely dissipated. At the time of unionization, British Columbia's labor law did not require a secret ballot certification vote, and the workplace was certified once the union signed a requisite number of cards. The organizing drive took place over a six-month period, according to Catherine's account, and the lack of a vote generated further tensions.

> When they came in I said alright, they're here, I'm going to learn as much as I can about them so I'm not ignorant. . . . I thought people expected more than what the union could do. . . . Not realizing that there's a lot of good that unions can do.

Catherine also resented the fact that the Toronto Visa Financial call center employees received wages and benefits that Vancouver customer service representatives (CSRs) were unable to attain, but this was prior to unionization. She came to realize that these privileges were a result of negotiations and collective bargaining that had taken place for almost a decade. Other CSRs in Vancouver eventually recognized this as well. In addition to this glaring difference between the centers, Catherine explained that an HR manager transferring from the Toronto office had built a reputation of being "very disrespectful of women". His response to complaints by employees was what assisted the union efforts: "He said, if you're unhappy, get a union". Workers did just that. However, the union's success was eventually countered by a decertification attempt just as the USW was in the process of negotiating its first contract less than a year after formation. Union supporters were suspicious that management supported anti-union activists, but this allegation was never confirmed. Ultimately their efforts to undermine the union failed.

One ongoing matter that CSRs have taken issue with is the company's use of workplace surveillance. As electronic monitoring at Visa Financial expanded with the development of technology, employees at the center were increasingly under the impression that the company perceived them as potential "fraudsters". This prompted complaints, directed through the union representatives, but the issue of monitoring failed to materialize at the bargaining table. According to the workers I spoke with, it was simply a no-go area for management. That is, until a round of bargaining just prior to the company's decision to shut down the facility in Vancouver. Unlike Omega where monitors were part of the bargaining unit and worked in-house, Visa Financial has centralized its audio surveillance and monitoring system in a separate facility in Montreal. Susan, a shop steward at the Vancouver facility, explained another type of response to monitoring, suggesting that surveillance is at times both an accepted and merited practice.

We realize that it's something they have to do. Not so much checking up on us as making sure that the customer gets the best service, and that's perfectly fine. Then there's training issues. If I come along and do something and I forget to do something and I do it wrong, I need to know that I'm not doing it wrong twenty times. . . . [Customers] deserve the best you can give them. . . . Some people feel that they are under the whip, but they don't understand that that's the culture.

General security concerns and privacy protection are included in the sur-veillance practices at work. CSRs are not permitted to have iPods or cam-era devices at their docks, and managers frequently monitor whether or not call center workers keep their terminals locked if they leave the worksta-tion. Infractions for these violations of company rules will generally involve the chairperson or stewards. Indeed, monitoring has become an "accepted" dimension of the job, but CSRs have mixed views of its purpose, from ambivalence to outright support.

What appears to be of greater concern from a CSR and trade unionist perspective is training. "There's gaps in between, shortcomings", as Sandra indicated. "I think it's a rush to get the class completed". At one point, Karen explained, a high turnover rate prompted reforms to the introductory training system, after union representatives voiced their recommendations with management. As far as the Vancouver Local is concerned, training has never been considered a bargaining issue, partly due to the fact that the material is based on standardized approaches developed in Toronto. While Catherine was content with the training, some shop stewards have indi-cated that the training period is too short and that the time is condensed to meet the company's immediate "business needs" (interview with Sandra 2008). Intervention by stewards on behalf of individual CSRs has been the most common strategy in helping colleagues improve, but managers are reluctant to implement broad changes unless it meets the financial needs of the company. In other words, the statistics-based performance evaluation is the key determinant of a CSR's worth, and subsequently a justification for remedial training.

Basic evaluation criteria related to time per call and bonuses have so far been left out of negotiations, either because the bank refuses to con-sider these bargaining issues, or because the union does not feel that it has required support from members to engage with management further, or a combination of both. As Susan indicated, base salary and grievance policies have been the main achievements of the union; measurement tools and the right of management and supervisors to do their jobs according to company mandates are effectively off the table. Questions around promotions have been equally absent from negotiations, even though the opportunities for upward mobility at Visa Financial are far more plentiful than they are for PC and Omega employees. However, all promotions require employees to step outside of the bargaining unit. As an in-house operation, the bank has provisions that allow CSRs to move into management positions or outside of the call center entirely and into other departments. When asked about aspirations beyond working as a CSR, Karen expressed interest in a human resource management position, but indicated there are informal obstacles for union activists.

> And the reason why they put road blocks [up] is because as a union steward they think we don't really care about the business, because we're union. It would be harder for them to put you in that department for the fact that you were a steward (interview 2008).

Catherine emphasized the mobility restrictions in the Vancouver branch, saying that the chances for promotion in the call center were "virtually nothing". The flat hierarchical structure that is characteristic of call center workplaces exists at Visa Financial. While not unheard of, she went on, "it would create so much hostility for a representative, regardless of who it is, to become a manager suddenly".

Union interventions have, however, resulted in qualitative gains that might otherwise have been left unresolved. When the Vancouver center refused to introduce ergonomic changes to workstations for employees with medical needs, the problem was resolved in a few hours after Catherine, at a time prior to her appointment as unit chairperson, appealed the decision with a shop steward. For the most part transformation takes time and employees "don't realize that a contract will take years and years to build. Each little thing is an achievement", she stressed (interview 2008). Some of the impatience reflects the age gap within the bargaining unit, and the demands associated with various generational cohorts, as Karen explained.

> A lot of the younger reps, when they come in and look at the collective agreement say, okay, why can't you get this, this, and this, not realizing how long it took for us to make all of the new changes in the agreement. But after a while they come to understand what the union has done so far for the bank. (interview 2008)

Catherine shared this sentiment, arguing that basic bread-and-butter issues are the chief priority for a workforce dominated by CSRs in their early 20s. This creates a secondary problem for the union—recruiting shop stewards and building a sustainable community of union activists. "They don't have an idea", Karen pointed out with frustration. "They chuck [the collective agreement] in their desk and if they need to know anything they still have to come back to you" (interview 2008). Karthik Shekhar, the General Secretary of UNITES, would express similar frustrations about the call center and ITES workforce in India.

Perhaps the greatest challenge that the shop stewards identified was the lack of negotiation and conflict resolution skills among the younger workers. Karen and Sandra, for example, said that without the abilities both had acquired as social workers, newly appointed stewards might not have the proficiency to deal with problems in such an efficient and professional manner. Since the union in both centers has become an institutional dimension of work in both Visa Financial facilities, the lines of communication between the union and management have so far proven to be an effective channel of conflict resolution, mediation, and workplace participation. Still, Catherine briefed me, some workers in her unit are still too intimidated to read union newsletters and bulletins in the workplace. "They are terrified", she said (interview 2008). The Steelworker reps have been successful at including an introduction to unionism in the initial training session organized by management, albeit a short amount of time, but this nonetheless normalizes the union into the fabric of work.

Issues surrounding participation in union work are common in both Vancouver and Toronto, lending to the frustration felt by unit chairpersons and stewards. Part of this is due to the ignorance common among "office workers", Catherine insisted, who are reticent to acknowledge the strength of collective action, or to recognize how their unionized workplace has secured benefits that they take for granted. Rank-and-file participation is instrumental in securing these hard-fought gains, and management is aware of this. All of the union activists I spoke with shared similar concerns. In the time leading up to bargaining, the senior manager in the Vancouver facility makes additional appearances on the floor and sales targets are rewarded with food and other prizes. "Usually more food comes out a month before bargaining", Catherine joked. Indeed, a disengagement from identifying as workers functions in the interest of managers, who try and persuade employees of their benevolence through open door policies and generous benefits. In this respect there are similarities between the outsourced call center environment reflected in the Omega case, and the relatively well-compensated and secure employment conditions that characterize in-house call centers situated in the financial sector. But even incredible profits and effective performance are no protection from the efforts of Canada's banks to rationalize costs.

Another round of bargaining had commenced at Visa Financial in March of 2013. Catherine, as a member of the union's bargaining team, had just commenced research for negotiations. It was March 15. Four days later the union's leadership was notified that the company was closing its doors in eight months and sending the center's jobs to the Toronto facility. It turned out that Canada Bank had sold the building that housed one of its Visa Financial call centers and data processing centers, which was also being shut down. For the 120 CSRs in Vancouver, this was an absolute shock. Why should any of them have expected it? Business was good for Canada Bank and its credit card division had recently acquired a new Mastercard account in a multibillion dollar purchase. There was no doubting that the call center workers at Visa Financial were providing high caliber service. In fact, when the decision was formally announced, management insisted that the closure had nothing to do with performance but with saving costs. A union staff representative remarked, however, that having a center on both sides of the country also provided a backup option in the case of weather or technical difficulties in one or the other facility (interview with Brian 2013). In retrospect, Catherine realized the writing was on the wall at least twelve months earlier.

For the last few years Visa Financial had put a halt on new hiring, as well as their training and employee development programs. A planned renovation of their Vancouver building was also put on hold indefinitely. Most telling was the fact that during the last round of negotiations, management had pushed for a shorter, one-year collective agreement. Catherine believed that the employer sought to undo important gains made by the union during bargaining in the next round of negotiations, thus the brief tenure of the collective agreement. What the USW had achieved was significant and hard-fought, specifically the implementation of a letter of agreement that curbed management's unlimited access and review of recorded calls for performance management purposes. The appeal process in the letter was not perfect, she emphasized, but at least it was a process. Management wanted total control and fought the union's proposal. What current management practices meant for some workers is that their performance ratings could be continuously decreased every time fault was interpreted from these recordings upon review. Management could effectively listen to a call over and over again and find new problems each time, thereby damaging an employee's performance score.

There was also some disenchantment with Visa Financial's performance incentives. The company's Quarterly Incentive Program (QUIP) allowed CSRs to earn up to $2000 per fiscal quarter if they achieved particular performance targets. If an employee appealed and recorded calls were used to reassess the rating, they could be further penalized if supervisors chose to recognize additional and previously unseen flaws. Catherine also believed that CSRs were being punished for not promoting the company's aspirations in their conversations with customers. It also appeared to the union that the QUIP guidelines were interpreted in such a way that the program was designed to prevent employees from earning the entire bonus altogether. During bargaining, the USW negotiators had made this appeal process a priority over wages and benefits, which distinguished this round from previous sessions. Management, the union representatives believed, wanted to remove this hard-fought gain, giving the USW the impression that the one-year CBA was intended to reopen this check on managerial decision making. They were wrong.

Around eighty CSRs were on-shift that Monday when the news was announced that in less than a year their workplace would be gone. Some of the workers started to cry, others walked out immediately. Management was sensitive enough to not dock the pay of employees who stopped answering calls that day. Half of these workers failed to show up for their next shift. To soften the blow, Visa Financial even hired counselors to speak with workers and provide them with the "think of this as an opportunity" routine. Some CSRs, however, feared that these professionals were simply feeding information they received back to management. Such a sentiment was fueled by the perception that surveillance in the workplace was already being intensified, presumably out of fear that workers would engage in theft or sabotage. But what did these managers feel about losing their jobs in Vancouver? When I asked Catherine about how she thought the front-line call center supervisors felt about the closure, she joked about the uniform and drab attitudes that these mid-level officials possess, and suggested they are not unlike the drone "Stepford Wives" characterized in film and in Ira Levin's classic novel (interview 2013).

Catherine and the USW staff representatives were now tasked with negotiating a closure agreement. Despite the circumstances, members of the union's negotiating team were relatively pleased with the closure agreement. Brian, the chief negotiator and USW staff representative, described the agreement as "fair" and that he had "seen worse" (interview with Brian 2013). Catherine, meanwhile, was happy with what her members would receive, in the context of what was happening. While workers possessed no financial assurances in the collective agreement upon a facility closure, the final agreement provided settlements and compensation above what was required by the Canada Labor Code, which governs this federally regulated industry. When asked about what leverage, if any, the USW had at the bargaining table, Brian remarked that the bank fears bad press. Had the workers in the Vancouver facility received only the legal minimum severance, Brian said, the union would have been pushed to ramp up a public campaign against Visa Financial. At the time of writing, not a single media report documents the call center's closure. In the end, employees would be eligible to receive outplacement support through career counseling and a transition allowance, closure payments, a termination payment, retirement payment, and a $5,000 to $10,000 moving allowance if they chose to relocate to Toronto. Both the company and the union agreed to binding arbitration in the event that there was a dispute arising from the application or interpretation of the closure agreement. Compared to the overnight closures that have beset countless call center workers in Canada and India, the situation facing the Visa Financial CSRs in Vancouver was far less painful. Still, as pleased as most workers were with the agreement, Catherine reflected, "for the most part they want their jobs" (interview 2013).

As for the closure negotiations, Catherine described the weekly meetings as frustrating, and from her perspective the employer was ill-prepared and not ready to address union and employee concerns. Ultimately, it appears that with the company eager to keep the closure quiet, the union and workers at Visa Financial Vancouver came out satisfied. But there was still much to dwell on. Developments at RBC and its decision to outsource IT services and recruit temporary foreign workers seemed to weigh on the minds of those union officials I spoke with. Brian's position was clear: financial information about Canadians needs to stay in Canada. His main concern was with ensuring that the jobs were in fact going to Toronto, where 800 call center workers represented by the USW are already employed. Catherine suggested that if the Toronto center was identified as too costly in the long run, the bank's Visa Financial services could be sent to the telephone banking centers outside of Ontario that are not unionized. In an industry that defines itself by cost efficiencies, massive executive compensation, and shareholder returns, there is no reason to neglect the possibility of further restructuring.

CONCLUSION

As an example of labor convergence, the USW is at the same time responding to the challenges posed by the "new economy", just as it is to structural shifts in corporate organization and globalization. Even moving outside of its core membership in manufacturing and mining towards representing service sector workers has proven less of a challenge than competing against the nature of outsourcing and offshoring. The Steelworkers' success at Omega is significant for this reason. While this endeavor was followed by both victories and failures, the experience provided the union with insights into how unions reflect and revise their traditional approach to organizing. A commitment to transforming these strategies has proven useful in responding to sociologist and call center researcher Mercedes Steedman's (2003) question: what will the effect of offshore outsourcing be on union presence in the call center industry if unions are organizing only in the large centers where the highest union density in the industry exists? Ten years on, the query is still pressing and unresolved.

What I found remarkable in these conversations with Canadian trade unionists is the parallel frustrations and hopes members of the USW share with their counterparts in India, particularly UNITES and the YPC. Generating a trade union consciousness among young people is especially challenging, even in unionized workplaces. It was also evident that during bargaining, the strength of the union negotiators could not exceed the activism or interest amongst the membership. Tackling concerns beyond the basic bread-and-butter issues of wages and benefits was difficult, particularly where managers were reticent to even talk about anything beyond money. Brian noted that in banking especially, corporate philosophies about labor relations and benefit structures are often impassible, even where mature bargaining relationships exist. But there is more to defining union strength than what is achievable in a collective agreement. Union stewards and chairpersons were attentive to the importance of grievance and representative structures that help to mitigate the working conditions that accompany employment in call centers. Union strength, in these examples, has been conditional upon the skill, experience, and commitment expressed by activists inside the workplace. While it is certainly the case that a handful of devoted unionists in the call centers provide most of the immediate services for the bargaining unit, the institutionalization of a union's representative structure, or more plainly the normalization of a union's presence, demands sustainable participation. The precarious nature of call center employment that characterizes outsourced and outbound facilities jeopardizes this possibility.

What the union activists I spoke with acknowledged was an uncertainty that their colleagues, and they themselves, felt toward the future of unionization in Canada's call centers. Even individuals trained to be managers, like Searson, developed an affinity toward holding a union position once they recognized the arbitrary and unfair practices exercised by superiors. Others saw the need for empowerment and wanted to ensure that labor had a voice in the decisions at work. As Catherine at Visa Financial emphasized at the end of our interview, "[W]e need any help we can get in the call center to make it a better work environment. I'm really thankful to the Steelworkers for that, because they've really educated me a lot. I didn't realize the rights I had" (interview 2013). In this regard unionization is not a conscious act of resistance, but a means through which workers regulate the terms of employment and make meaningful interventions in the governance of labor practices. For the final chapter I address how unions attempt to address the uncertainties of call center and ITES employment on a global scale, and what modes of resistance and regulation are deployed in the process.

7 Global Division of Knowledge Labor, Global Unionism

UNITES, and the ITPF before it, were both new union ventures in India and both received support from European trade unions to facilitate their formation and growth. The Young Professionals Collective, on the other hand, was an indigenous project that was established by activists and lawyers who sought to build a network of call center workers. In Canada, the United Steelworkers has since the late 1990s branched out, with mixed success, into call centers and the service sector generally. These examples suggest that unions, both new and old, are undergoing a transformation because of the development of a global division of knowledge labor. Outsourcing, off-shoring, and subcontracting are all part of the process of global economic and technological change. Chapter 7 explores the cases of Union Network International (UNI) and Workers Uniting, two relative new international trade union initiatives that are exploring new approaches to building global unionism. But how new is this concern over the impacts a globalized economy can have on the relationship between capital and labor?

Drawing from Jay Youngdahl's (2008) prognosis on the future of cross-border unionism, the two leading trends in the union movement identified here are, one, the formation of global union federations (GUFs) and, two, international mergers between national unions. To this list I add a third trend—the development of Global Agreements (GA), which has created a nexus between GUFs, transnational unions, and national labor organizations. While all three trends constitute attempts at union renewal through which national unions can bargain with MNCs, global unionism is defined by administrative, not bottom-up rank-and-file, action. Indeed, as labor scholar Kim Voss (2010) cautions, union revitalization is premised on reversing the decline of union density and enhancing the collective bargaining power of trade unions, not membership mobilization and union democracy. Even former heads of GUFs, like Dan Gallin (2009), have recognized this as a serious shortfall (see also Cox 1977). As global federations become more involved in the building of organizing campaigns, what does this mean for national projects? As labor scholars like Herod (2001), Breitenfellner (1997), and Lambert and Webster (2001) discuss, global unionism is successful to the extent that it recognizes the significance of local organizing, the building of alliances with social forces, and acknowledging the pragmatic importance of national strategies.

Debates on the growth and effectiveness of transnational unions have a long and contentious history. What I illustrate here are the challenges confronting unions and global union federations—successors of international trade secretariats (ITS)—and their attempts at building transnational alliances and organizing strategies focused on post-industrial workplaces. These strategies have been informed by the characteristics of a global division of knowledge labor. Union Network International (UNI), the Swiss-based GUF, has been instrumental in establishing IT labor organizing in India, first with the founding of the IT Professionals Forum in 2000, and later in assisting with the emergence of UNITES in 2005. UNI is the world's leading service sector federation and a worthy subject of study in the case of call center employment because of its attentiveness to organizing the IT and ITES sectors.

In Canada, the USW has made some inroads in the call center industry, but remains a distinct case from UNITES for several reasons. Unlike UNITES, the USW employed its own organizers and relied on national approaches and finances when organizing call center workplaces in Canada. Yet there is an important global dimension to the union. As part of an international organization headquartered in Pittsburgh, Pennsylvania, with members in Canada, the United States, and the Caribbean, the USW is truly a transnational union. In 2007, the international stature of the union grew even further. By merging with Unite the Union (Unite) from the UK, the new global entity, Workers Uniting, became the first trans-Atlantic labor union. Only Ver.di, the German Unified Service Sector Union formed in 2001, exceeds Workers Uniting in size and still ranks as the world's largest trade union with over two million members. While the union merger that formed Workers Uniting may have little immediate impact on the ground in Canada, the international union now has allies which help fund and support initiatives like UNITES in India through direct union activity and through the support of UNI.

Both UNI and Workers Uniting illustrate important examples of union convergence. Such mergers are promoted as new initiatives and part of reinventing labor organizations, but by itself convergence cannot provide a solution to declining union density rates. Nor can the formation of bigger organizations resolve long standing political disputes within trade unions or the international trade union movement. As political economists and labor scholars Mosco and McKercher (2008, 108) write, labor union convergence "is difficult to achieve, full of contradictions, and offers no guarantees of success at the bargaining table". However, this is not to say that the merger of labor organizations at the national and international levels is without purpose. Convergence provides workers and their representative organizations with some institutional capacity to confront corporations and increasingly pro-business governments by taking advantage of the synergies brought about through the combination of once-independent trade unions and global federations. In some instances, there are equal disadvantages associated with *not* adopting union convergence if changes in the economic and technological world outstrip a union's ability to negotiate with radically transformed, and likely converged, corporations.

Communication and knowledge workers are well positioned to draw from the importance of convergence, considering that workers in these sectors are at the forefront of "producing for a converging arena of electronic information services or knowledge" (Mosco and McKercher 2008, 41). This was the thrust behind the formation of Ver.di (*Vereinte Dienstleistungsgewerkschaft* or Unified Service Sector Union) in March of 2001, which marked the emergence of a converged post-industrial union that aimed to develop an integrated trade union policy for the entire service sector in Germany. As corporate and technological convergence accelerates in a globalized economy, there is strategic sense for international and national trade unions to do the same. The five unions that founded Ver.di conceived of the new union as a reaction to the shift from an industrial to a service-oriented "knowledge-based" society, seeing convergence as a necessary step towards renewal and survival (see Keller 2005). But at the same time, there are limitations. Affinities between workers across borders are not by any means natural, and labor unions themselves are imperfect institutions that are not consistently well equipped at responding to structural economic changes. Nor does convergence immediately invigorate rank-and-file mobilization, increase the rate of membership growth, or improve the chances of organizing campaigns. Programs that aim to address these difficulties must do so through active interventions and solidarity-building initiatives, as the trade union officials interviewed in this study propose. Union convergence is fraught with pitfalls, but it also opens up new prospects for building stronger trade union movements by bringing together a coalition of unions and trade union cultures. What I maintain is that the marshaling of union resources around organizing and the implementation and enforcement of Global Agreements (GAs) have the potential to draw from the strongest dimensions associated with convergence by facilitating multi-sector and internationally coordinated organizing drives and solidarity campaigns. Chapter 7 works to establish this conclusion by looking at the development of such initiatives.

INTERNATIONALISM

Sociologist and labor process scholar Michael Burawoy (2010) sparked a controversial debate in the pages of *Global Labour Journal* for remarks he made about research and literature on global labor movements. Specifically, Burawoy cast doubt on the efficacy of "counter-movements" that oppose the processes of commodification, marketization, the deterioration of labor standards, as well as ecological devastation. Responses from leading figures in the field of labor studies, like Dan Clawson, were swift. The conclusion to Clawson's (2010, 400) retort was succinct and important: "We should celebrate, not mock, those analysts who identify struggles that have not won yet, but which may provide the building blocks for future successes". Peter Waterman (2010), another important figure in global labor studies research, also waded into the debate by voicing as a matter of regret the dissolution of conversation on global labor studies—a field founded on strategies, histories, and examples of movements of resistance to global capitalism—to one of attack / defense. What resonates in the written back-and-forth is acknowledgement that as a field of study, research on global unionism and related areas is fraught with disagreement and debate. The same can be said for the organizations being discussed.

Throughout the 20th century, trade union movements in the industrialized countries embodied a range of political commitments that evolved from socialist, anarchist, and liberal traditions. The establishment of the Soviet Union in 1917 and Cold War politics emerging after World War Two further splintered these tendencies within union movements, nationally and internationally. As international union organizations, referred to historically as international trade secretariats (ITS), matured in the post-War period, they also came to be increasingly defined as institutions dominated by union federations of the wealthiest economies. International trade secretariats developed as a result of national trade unions representing specific industries, crafts, and professions. Major crafts had all established their own secretariats and by around 1914 there were over thirty such institutions in operation tasked with exchanging information, organizing solidarity action, research, and liaising with organizations at the national and international level, government and private. In some respects, there was very little about ITSs that resembled conventional trade unionism, that is, organizing and collective bargaining (Busch 1983; Windmuller 2000). Most of these organizations also reproduced colonial-era power imbalances between workers in what came to be acknowledged as a new international division of labor. Whether or not these same colonial legacies persist in the global division of labor, or the global division of *knowledge* labor specifically, is still a matter of contestation.

Union internationalism is characterized today by global union federations (GUF), which represent the transnational dimension of trade union movements. Like their national counterparts, GUFs are similarly undergoing a process of identity and strategic renewal. Most recently, the International Metalworkers' Federation (IMF), International Federation of Chemical, Energy, Mine and General Workers' Unions (ICEM), and International Textiles Garment and Leather Workers' Federation (ITGLWF) merged to form IndustriALL Global Union in 2012, which now represents over 50 million workers in 140 countries. Despite their massive membership, global unions do not wield a power commensurate with their size.

Because industrial relations frameworks exist almost exclusively at the national level, GUFs are similarly required to secure gains for members by winning rights and standards within the parameters of what is negotiable within the nation state. What Peter Waterman (2001a, 2001b, 1992) and his collaborators (Waterman and Wills 2001; see Wallerstein 2000) argue is that the renewal of union internationalism will be premised on finding alternatives to neo-liberal globalization by strengthening ties with social movement struggles, like Occupy, inside and outside the workplace. Ultimately, commitments to union renewal and revitalization are made possible only by moving beyond the confines of collective bargaining and existing industrial relations regimes. This is why Waterman's (2001a, 319) typology of international*isms* is of practical significance. Whereas *labor internationalism* "refers to a wide range of past and present labor-related ideas, strategies and practices, including those of cooperatives, labor and socialists parties, socialist intellectuals, culture, the media and even sport", *union internationalism* is restricted to a specific and arguably the most central form of worker "self-articulation" and representation today. It is through these models that I assess UNI and the USW's convergence model of renewal.

Interviews with labor leaders suggest that there is acknowledgment that a global division of labor demands a global union network. For scholars and trade unionists themselves, the question is *how* to make this transnational cooperation function and the extent to which revitalization and a new upsurge can be projected at the global level. If the original ITSs were mandated with being information clearinghouses that coordinated national union activity and informed members about the regulation of craftwork, today's global union federations are moving toward developing into solidarity centers that are capable of collaborating with unions, labor associations, non-governmental organizations (NGOs), social movements, as well as governments. This is where solidarity building draws from sociological questions of mobilization. For global union federations, the challenge is one of invoking the collective activity of regional locals, and of sustaining solidarity across national and North-South divides (see Frundt 2005).[1] This is especially important in cases where GUFs have helped facilitate national organizing efforts and then face the subsequent challenge of addressing problems that lie ahead for the nascent labor organizations.

UNI AND THE GLOBAL DIVISION OF KNOWLEDGE LABOR

Offshoring and outsourcing have for at least a decade created obstacles for global union federations. Unable to regulate the mobility of capital, GUFs are at a disadvantage when attempting to represent the interests of members who face deteriorating conditions of employment and redundancies. The leading question now confronting international labor organizations is:

How are bargaining efforts possible with companies that operate complex international commodity and service chains beyond the reach of national unions? Despite the importance of national industrial relations and employment standards regimes, these institutions provide limited frameworks for unions to negotiate with global corporations beyond the national context, with the exception of the European Union. As the largest service and knowledge sector GUF, UNI has worked to establish agreements directly with major multinational enterprises to overcome these limitations. After undergoing a review of its operations, UNI's leadership recognized the strategic importance of operating as a global *union* rather than a *federation*. This is part of focusing the union's energy on expansion since its founding convention in Chicago in 2000, when over 1,000 leaders of service and technology unions and representatives from FIET (International Federation of Employees, Technicians, and Managers), MEI (Media and Entertainment International), IGF (International Graphical Federation), and CI (Communications International) merged to form UNI. UNI currently represents over 15 million workers from over 900 unions worldwide.

In the picturesque Swiss town of Nyon, home to UNI's global headquarters, the GUF deputy general secretary, Philip Bowyer, who boasted of once living in the attic of eminent Marxist historian E.P. Thomson as a struggling graduate student, provided insights to the federation's developing strategies.

> We are a very financially sound organization. So that was a lot of work. More recently, this year [2009] we are trying to make a major change in the organization to be much more focused. . . . [T]his really revolves around the idea of Global Agreements [GAs], the agreements with global companies acting like a global union instead of some loose federation of people. (interview with Bowyer 2009)

Global Agreements (GA) serve as "soft law" agreements that help secure a voluntary commitment to core labor standards as well as an act of rule setting between two non-state actors. Global Agreements also operate as non-binding conflict resolution mechanisms with the intent of resolving problems before they become damaging to either party involved, much in line with OECD Guidelines on Multinational Enterprises (see TUAC and OECD 2004; OECD 2000). Despite their lack of judicial recognition, GA's establish best practices and mutually recognized standards, often based on ILO Conventions and principles (see Fichter and Sydow 2008; ILO 2008). On paper, these agreements also help to develop the legitimacy of GUFs by securing support and recognition of UNI within the companies. So far GAs have yet to be part of any substantive global industrial relations regime building, but they do operate as a strategic ambition for global federations such as UNI in their efforts at securing a dialogue with leading MNCs. UNI has so far signed global agreements with over thirty multinationals and has made the expansion of GAs a priority. Unfortunately no GAs have been signed with dedicated IT or ITES multinationals, like HP, Microsoft, or Wipro, and UNI has yet to be recognized in the social dialogue process by industry leaders in Europe. Success, however, has been achieved with major telecommunications and service companies like Quebecor and Telefónica, both of which possess significant information technology components.

As Bowyer reflected on the GUF's signing of its first Agreement in 2001,

> Our idea at the time was, if there's a global company and we have an agreement with it that they will recognize unions all over the world— that was about as far as we went. That was where the idea originated. So we started by trying to talk to different companies and it was pretty hit and miss and haphazard. . . . [The] GA is not just what it says in the agreement, it's the fact that the companies at the global level recognize us and talk to us. *It's our foot in the door. . . . The issue is an object, it gives people something to work towards, but it's not the end.* (interview with Bowyer 2009, emphasis added)

Referred to as the UNI-Telefónica Code of Conduct, the agreement was reached in March of 2001 and later revised in December of 2007. As a global telecommunications provider with a presence in Latin America and Europe, UNI regarded the signing of this agreement as a major success. From the union federation's standpoint, the Code of Conduct helped to entrench the company's favorable industrial relations practices by ensuring non-discrimination in employment, freedom of association and trade union rights, employment stability, minimum wages, and workers' representation at the workplace, regardless of where the company operated. For Telefónica, the motivation to engage in negotiations was based on a pragmatic interest in promoting the firm's corporate social responsibility (CSR) strategy and enhancing employee satisfaction (European Foundation for the Improvement of Living and Working Conditions 2008). But, the deputy general secretary reflected, the efficacy of such agreements are limited.

> Companies just wanted to make an agreement with us, we made it, but frankly they have not done very much. . . . So we've tried to get away from that. Now what we do is create these trade union alliances which start by bringing unions together. . . . *The idea is to keep the unions involved and keep them mobilized around the issues in the company. That's the key.* (interview with Bowyer 2009)

In the case of Telefónica, two Spanish trade union organizations, the Trade Union Confederation of Workers' Commissions (Confederación Sindical de Comisiones Obreras, or CC.OO) and the General Workers' Confederation (Unión General de Trabajadores, or UGT), were instrumental in developing and enforcing the Code. UNI's engagement with employers can help secure industry standards across a company's global operations but ultimately the ambition is to expand the number of trade unionists at the national level, where these companies operate. Indeed, as UNI officials insisted, the effectiveness of GAs is dependent on the power of national unions responsible for their implementation. The federation's newly established organizing fund helps to resource local union campaigns that use global agreements as a preliminary encounter with specific companies. Marcus Courtney, head of UNI Telecomm and veteran organizer with the Washington Alliance of Technology Workers (WashTech) in the United States, explained how GAs facilitate a growth in union membership.

Our Telefónica [agreement] has been very successful in certain parts of the country, in terms of what's going on in Brazil, in terms of San Paolo, it's been successful. They have been able to organize thousands of workers there. Other parts of South America they've talked about how it's been able to resolve a lot of national issues between the companies and the unions, in terms of positive outcomes. . . . Then again, we do have problems. In Ireland there's problems, there's problems in Mexico we're trying to resolve—it's not the silver bullet. (interview with Courtney 2009)

Courtney recognized parallels between his experience as president and organizer with WashTech and how leverage over powerful companies is only possible with a sustainable membership base and contractual agreements. "Global Agreements", he continued, "are a piece around the international component. . . . I think you really need to have every country pushing for improved comprehensive national standards around bargaining and organizing rights". UNI Europa officials shared the concern, insisting that what UNI does is sign and then monitor these agreements. As Birte Dedden (2009), UNI Europa's policy officer, suggested, "the more agreements are based on national law and are part of collective agreements that are covered by [national legal jurisdictions] where you have a legal empowerment . . . [t]hat is a better instrument". UNI's European office and its union affiliates have the advantage of engaging with multinationals through works councils and a comprehensive social dialogue mechanism that assists in the *enforcement* of a GA framework.

Global Agreements function as a tool to address the comparatively large gaps in labor protections offered by other developed countries, notably the United States. Despite the rhetoric of stateless and decentered globalization, unions and their international federations are empowered (or disenfranchised) by national legislation or regional employment standards. Rather than accepting a blanket statement on the effectiveness of GA's, UNI policy-makers are conscious of the fact that the implementation of agreements is conditioned by the nature of political regimes and industry standards.

Indeed, the existence of a GA does not guarantee that a multinational company, or its subsidiaries and affiliates, will necessarily abide by it. Despite the generally positive outcomes that have followed from UNI's agreement with Telefónica, the company's subsidiary call center in Puerto Rico, Atento Puerto Rico, fired union organizers who were active in a campaign led by the Communication Workers of America (CWA). Atento management violated both the terms of the GA and U.S. National Labor Relations Board (NLRB) regulations in the process. On the other hand, UNI affiliates in Brazil cited the GA as instrumental in their successful efforts at securing a collective agreement with Atento in 2006, indicating that Global Agreements can offer leverage to unions, even though they are not guarantees of success (see Mosco and Lavin 2008).

A third component of global agreements is the potential to build cross-border solidarity. In its "Tell-Tell-Telefónica" campaign, which focuses on entrenching the freedom to organize across the company's global operations, UNI mobilized international union and labor support to ensure that workers in Mexico and Ireland are able to experience the pledge to which the MNC committed. Framework agreements are used as leverage for local organizing activities and operate as rallying points for international solidarity. They also open spaces for NGOs and consumer and civil society groups to hold companies accountable for their voluntary obligations, as well as build connections with trade unions through voluntary networks (Riisgaard 2005). UNI is attentive to reproducing these strategies in several African countries, where the federation is helping local telecommunications unions draft an agreement with MTN, a leading telecommunications provider on the continent. This has also broached the tripartite strategy of engaging with industry groups and governments in an effort to set out the groundwork for a rudimentary regulatory framework that could potentially establish sector-wide standards and collective agreements.

For UNI's leadership, reversing union decline is a principal objective for the federation. Broader debates of global governance and international labor relations practices are not abandoned, but the immediate goal is one of increasing union strength and density rates. "Organizing", Bowyer stressed, "becomes the key to everything" (interview 2009). Agreements also facilitate UNI's entry into national economies, especially when MNC's expand their operations into the developing world. GAs with leading financial institutions, security firms, insurance, telecommunications, and other service sector companies are pivotal for entry into India, where UNI has been making strides with Group4 Security and other multinationals. Similar projects have been established for IBM, a global IT company that has long been successful at resisting unions. Coordinated projects and the establishment of an Organizing Department within the GUF assist such ambitions. Operating as a global union has meant mobilizing support among constituents to build new union projects where existing labor organizations had failed. This was the thrust behind getting the ITPF, and subsequently UNITES, off the ground. The strategy is also aimed at allowing for UNI to operate independently from member unions as a global organization, rather than a confederacy. By marshaling financial support through dues and establishing a centrally-administered organizing fund, UNI's aim has been to work at strengthening existing GAs and to fund local organizing campaigns. Seed money is deployed for the purpose of establishing sustainable national unions that can exist independently from the global federation—a principle goal that the ITPF and UNITES were unable to achieve.

UNI also functions as a liaison between labor organizations and union projects in developing countries like India, where it is most active. SASK, the Finnish trade union center that has provided financial support for UNITES, is one of the most committed allies to unions in the Global South. Twenty-six years ago SASK was formed as an alliance of two independent, national union federations, SAK (*Suomen Ammattiliittojen Keskusliitto*) and STTK (*Suomen Teollisuus Työntekijöiden Keskuliitto*), which represented blue and white-collar workers respectively. Both served to represent member unions in national tripartite collective bargaining. As an official representing SASK explained, the federation's "main purpose is to ensure an interactive link between the Finnish trade union movement and Southern partner unions, so that solidarity support can be established, mutual learning can take place, and also that the work to defend workers' rights and to advocate pro-worker policies can happen effectively, mainly in South but also in the North" (personal correspondance 2012). This has meant supporting projects like UNITES in India, mediated by UNIDOC offices, to mining and steel industry organizing in partnership with the International Metalworkers Federation (IMF). About 85 percent of SASK's funding comes from the Government of Finland. UNI's UNIDOC and regional offices in South Asia operate as bases for solidarity initiatives, and the GUF's Indian connections help to provide the human and organizational infrastructure for specific projects. This is one example of GUFs operating as real unions, rather than administrative centers alone.

Union Network International has made GAs a priority in its model of organizing for these reasons. Another objective is the concentration of financial resources on key projects, namely securing agreements and establishing union organizing campaigns at flagship companies in an effort to establish sector-wide gains. UNI's organizers have also recognized the importance of entering sectors where union interventions are minimal or nonexistent. The case of UNITES in India is one such example. Broadly, developments in information technology usage within corporations have raised obstacles to traditional union efforts, forcing UNI to reflect on its internal organizational strategy through a committed organizing department. One response has been the merger of the IT and telecommunications departments at the UNI Europa level. A research associate with UNI commented that the union federation is changing the way it is working by concentrating on organizing and not just servicing existing gains and unions. As for IT, "that is really important for us because the IT part of the new sector doesn't have any global agreement at the moment, whereas the [telecommunications] part has some. That will be a great help if we can work with some union that is already there that has experience campaigning for global agreements . . . " (interview with research associate 2009).

What he and others indicate is that a union renewal process is unfolding within UNI, structurally and culturally. UNI's organizing strategy and interest in building alliances with unions and worker associations is part of a broader project. For IT and ITES initiatives, the strategy involves transforming the kinds of messages unions convey to prospective members. Andrew Bibby, a journalist who has provided extensive coverage of UNI and its projects, maintains that unions have failed to "stimulate broader public debate on globalization or to make wider alliances", hindering the appeal of organizations that are ineffectual at representing the interests of workers in particular sectors (Bibby 2004). Union Network International has been working on addressing such concerns, with UNITES and the ITPF being one such example of building alliances and new unions. WashTech in the United States, the Communication Workers Union (CWU), and UNIFI, a banking union in the UK, provide additional examples of innovative forms of knowledge-sector unionism. The debate about union renewal has also provoked interest in how global federations are relevant at the national and international levels.

UNI's strategy has been to develop a more complex position on offshoring, outsourcing, and the global division of information labor beyond acceptance or opposition. UNIFI's Globalization Charter with banking giant HSBC has sought to *manage* the process of change arising from the globalization of the financial institution's operations, and for the firm to adopt ethical employment standards in all its sites. UNI's Call Center Charter similarly emerged as an attempt to apply employment standards and best practices to company operations no matter where they are located. UNITES has included the Charter in its collective agreements with Indian companies in an effort to establish basic standards that are universally accepted and premised on the standardized nature of call center work. Similarly, UNI's position on electronic monitoring and surveillance in the workplace helped draw attention to the threat to employment standards in workplaces where information and communication technologies are prevalent or central to the work process, particularly call centers (UNI 2006a, 2006b). These initiatives have been derived from extensive dialogue with labor organizations from around the world that are part of the UNI fold and made possible by a converged GUF framework. UNI-sponsored conferences in Europe have also helped raise awareness to wider privacy concerns relevant to ITES and IT employment. Birte Dedden, a policy officer for IT and knowledge workers with UNI Europa, the federation's European operation, spoke to the need of reaching out to young workers at UNI-organized conferences.

Our thing, in terms of the target groups you're trying to hit in terms of organizing, my experience in that conference for instance, is that they loved the fact and were surprised to find trade unions addressing the issue of Web 2.0 and on-line rights at the workplace. We were giving them input on their rights when they are Facebooking on your laptop at work. Or, are you entitled to this union? Stuff like that. Or, what happens is, and to what extent, can the employer prohibit things and to what extent can we integrate that into collective bargaining or negotiations, etc. (interview 2009)

Union relevance, and indeed the sustainability of trade unions general, is premised on recruiting young members in previously unrepresented workplaces, as Dedden suggests. As the cases of the USW and UNITES suggest, mobilizing young workers has been especially challenging, but critical for union success. Conferences and other face-to-face interactions facilitate engagement between union leaders and workers from various settings as well as invoke a dialogue across countries on the subject of unionization. UNI, in this example, is not simply an intermediary, but an active participant in union organizing.

The question of how to organize young, professionalized IT workers has been of growing importance for all unions, not just UNI. For the young research associate at UNI who spoke to me, "[T]here's still the image problem for the unions, especially towards the young people. Even more towards young IT professional who are, as far as I can see, not really interested in joining unions" (interview with research associate 2009). As he went on to say, "So I think that's really a problem that has to be solved. Here I'm not sure UNI can play a role apart from telling affiliates that there's a problem, but then it's up to affiliates on a national level to act". Cultural transformations within unions are not just a matter of reflecting the economic realities of 21st century economies, it is also a matter of survival. UNI's leadership has recognized that unions need to change their strategies, and from their vantage point, it is vital that the global union does the same. Speaking to the issue of high-tech workers in Europe, the researcher continued that UNI needs to "go away from the traditional union message" which is primarily focused on salary rates and holiday privileges. UNITES activists realized this in their efforts to speak with IT and ITES workers in India as well. As a young knowledge worker himself, the researcher was speaking from experience when he addressed the challenges unions face with IT employees in particular.

I think the majority of IT workers . . . already have very good working conditions, so they are not interested in hearing from someone in a union that we are going to give you what you already have. . . . I think unions should, towards IT people at least, base their message on training, on the idea that young people will move from one workplace and job more frequently than their parents were doing. *The idea would be to have a union for life, but knowing that they will change workplaces a lot of times in their career, and they will have the support of the union.* These are things that can be more appealing to these target groups. (interview 2009, emphasis added)

"New Generation Networks" (NGN) are being developed to represent these concerns by challenging conventional union organizing strategies and engaging with participatory decision-making. Similar issues have been addressed through UNI's Professional and Managerial Staff groups, which take issue with service sector labor concerns such as workplace surveillance and maintaining a basic standard of benefits across particular sectors. At the European level, UNI is similarly engaged in a re-branding exercise. "Our task", UNI Europa's Dedden pointed out, "is actually to respond to current changes in the sector" (interview 2009). One approach has been to merge the UNI-Europa Telecommunications and IT offices in a broader ICTS (Information, Communication, and Telecommunication Services) department, reflecting the converged nature of corporations and labor groups operating in increasingly indistinguishable sectors. UNI's role as a global union is to operate as an "international coordinator" of established practices and to offer a bird's eye perspective, rather than offering career guidance and services directly. For Gerhard Rohde, a thirty-year veteran of the German and European trade union movement and head of UNI's IBITS division, local unions are the providers of such services and ultimately take on these newly established best practices. As he remarked in conversation, UNI is tasked "to pick up on positive examples and to organize a kind of knowledge transfer so the member organizations can learn from each other, and [do not] have to reinvent things everywhere" (interview with Rohde 2009).

The attempt at constructing a renewed union image was especially important following the 2008 financial crisis. Marcus Courtney, who was particularly equipped to discuss the conditions of information technology employment, realized that while IT workers were hit by the economic downturn, the consequences were of a different severity compared to other sectors of the economy. Part of the crisis, he maintained, could actually *enforce* the professional identity, as workers could cite their superior skills and education qualifications as a buffer against longterm unemployment and economic decline. While scholars have long maintained that white-collar and high-tech workers are increasingly subject to the same precarity and eroded standards of labor experienced by labor in other industries, the message Courtney conveyed was that despite the possible onset of this reality, the crisis did not automatically hit the "reset button", as he put it (interview 2009). Fractures may appear in the privileged and self-identified professionalized vocation of high-tech IT employment, but not to the degree that knowledge workers would necessarily turn in large numbers to collective labor associations.

One of the most substantial challenges for UNI and other unions has been to use the crisis as a platform on which to launch new union campaigns. Organizers, by Courtney's account, are required to ask questions and raise concerns that skilled and semi-skilled IT workers would be receptive to: In a post-recession scenario, would high-tech workers regain their wage advantage? Could their health benefits be maintained? Would pensions and employer contributions to retirement schemes continue? "I think you have to really dive down into those issues and figure out," he argued, "the only way you can get out of that is bargaining collectively. *That's the only way to reset, but it's not an automatic reset here*", he continued (interview 2009, emphasis added). Of course, the character of collective bargaining need not reflect the existing notions and legally recognized practices, as UNI Europa's Policy Officer argues, but instead to develop "services [unions] can provide within this sector", such as training, and bargain for support from employers (interview with Dedden 2009). The acceleration of offshoring and outsourcing has become a rallying point for workers in these sectors, one that labor associations and unions have used to assist in their organizing campaigns.

What makes offshoring a challenging subject for a global union, especially one representing workers in the Global North and South, is how the organization maintains a commitment to a diverse membership that has been advantaged and disadvantaged by the changing pattern of a global division of knowledge work. In 2005, UNI released its Charter on Offshore Outsourcing, a document that was attentive to the internationalized distribution of high-value services associated with finance, insurance, media, graphics, IT, health care, and telecommunications. The document was particularly salient in the highly mobile and globalized call center industry. The Charter envisions labor market policies and public investments in education and training to mitigate the social consequences of offshoring, not unlike the liberal resolutions promoted by labor economists and international organizations like the OECD (see TUAC and OECD 2004). Global Agreements function as a pivot point for the Charter. Like the GAs, UNI's Charter called on unions and corporations to negotiate a settlement on the terms of offshoring and outsourcing, to ensure that there was both a labor- and business-side agreement to the decision (see UNI 2005). What a number of UNI officials stressed is that the federation does not oppose outsourcing, but instead seeks an arrangement where companies could not escape labor or environmental standards by relocating. "Ideologically we are not against outsourcing", UNI's research associate stressed; "We think people should be unionized in the destination countries as well" (interview 2009). UNITES represents an extension of this policy, and the union's official position has supported the internationalist perspective on establishing and enforcing global standards, rather than resisting globalized service and production chains.

Building on these offshoring policies, members of UNI Europa and UNI IBITS, as well as a handful of other unions, helped to launch the Making

Offshore Outsourcing Sustainable (MOOS) project as an initiative to formulate coherent union responses to the movement of work across Europe and internationally. Indeed, UNI's European offices and members contend with the "nearshoring" phenomenon that takes place with Eastern economies (UNI 2008a). When MOOS first convened in 2005, the focus was placed on the offshoring of ICT-intensive employment among European member unions. By 2006, the Vancouver-based workshop included trade unionists and academics from North America working to establish practices that could enable national unions to engage with multinationals over the question of offshoring and outsourcing (MOOS 2006a, 2006b, 2007). UNI-Europa's handbook on offshore outsourcing, which emerged from these discussions, urged unions to be proactive in their response to globalization by confronting companies before they took the steps to relocate work. Collective bargaining and inter-union solidarity action were recognized as tactics to hold companies responsible for their operations (see De Bruyn and Ramiou 2006). The global union's first ever call center conference, held in Athens in 2005, was part of this effort to expand unionization in the ITES sector as a platform to confront a global industry and to regulate what was understood as part of the "global mobility revolution" (UNI 2006c).

WORKERS UNITING

At a convention hall in Las Vegas in July 2008, the United Steel, Paper and Forestry, Rubber, Manufacturing, Energy, Allied Industrial and Service Workers International Union, or United Steelworkers (USW), already a confederation of numerous mergers, joined with the British Unite the Union, itself a by-product of an Amicus-Transportation & General Workers Union arrangement formed in 2007. This resulting merger formed Workers Uniting, the first trans-Atlantic union. In its founding constitution the new amalgamated union declared that its members will "build global union activism, recognizing that uniting as workers across international boundaries is the only way to challenge the injustices of globalization" (Workers Uniting n.d.c.). With over three million members, the international organization represents an effort at convergence across sectors and borders. Leading organizers and union activists were also aware of the need to confront multinational capital at the local and international levels. In this regard union convergence is understood as a necessary strategy to confront the local, national, and international expanse of economic inequality within sectors commonly perceived to be outside the reach of unions.

The process of convergence is fraught with challenges, particularly as it relates to balancing the necessity of constructing a functional international union, coordination of bargaining, solidarity work, and the realities of local organizing. The question is complicated when the merger is transnational, and becomes increasingly problematic when factoring in developing economies with developed ones. This has prompted some scholars to ask, "can regular workers organized in unions, mainly based in the North, and the hundreds of millions of non-regular or informal workers, mainly in the South, understand each other and begin to define common goals" (Bieler, Lindberg, Pillay 2008, 265)? These are problems UNI continues to face. With the accelerated convergence of corporate organizations, unions are under further pressure to take similar steps as a strategic response to the growth and decentralizations of operations. Technological and industry convergence has furthered the affinity unions have with tactics that equip their organizations with the ability and resources to mount effective campaigns that seek to regulate a near free-for-all scenario and force companies into a position of making concessions with their workers. If UNI's perspective on Global Agreements is any indication, local bargaining initiatives and mobilizing will condition the political and economic success of the global union as well. Having a well-resourced and influential union with connections across borders may indeed be part of the solution.

There has been both fanfare and pessimism over the USW's merger with Unite. As one report in *Time* magazine glibly noted, "Workers of the world, unite, indeed. But don't expect a revolution" (Grose 2008). Labor scholars have yet to come to a consensus on the issue, and the emergence of Workers Uniting has reignited debates about the effectiveness of global union federations and the future they may or may not hold in the era of globalization. Either way, as Andrew Murray, a spokesperson for Unite, suggested in a media interview, "We're dealing with global companies that can move capital—and employment—around the world, at will in many cases. . . . While big business is global, and labor is national, we're going to be at a disadvantage" (Associated Press 2008). And indeed, several developments have been marked as successes for the new union and its international allies. In 2008, ArcelorMittal, the International Metalworkers Federation (IMF), the European Metal Federation, and the USW signed an important agreement that guarantees minimum safety standards for the company's 320,000 workers (Holecek 2008). As the world's largest steel manufacturer with operations in over sixty countries, establishing a meaningful (and enforceable) agreement with the sector's leading company could have significant implications.

The agreement with ArcelorMittal signaled an ongoing move to negotiate and build alliances transnationally. Workers Uniting, and its British and North American constituents, have sought to expand their reach into Eastern Europe, Latin America, and Asia. Derek Simpson, Unite's joint general secretary, has already held talks with his counterparts in Australia and Eastern Europe about future collaboration (Kleinman 2008; Aslam 2008). Outside the formal bounds of trade unions, the USW has been working since the 1990s on strengthening its network of strategic alliances with foreign unions, with connections being established with mining and manufacturing unions in Brazil, South Africa, Australia, Mexico,

Germany, and Britain (USW 2007). The union has also sought to collaborate with worker-owned cooperative initiatives, such as Mondragon in Spain, by building its own framework agreement with the longterm goal of seeing co-operatives established in North America (USW 2009). Unlike GUFs, such as UNI, established unions are capable of invoking rank-and-file support for these activities, reinforcing the importance of acting through and with international federations. Working in the interests of solidarity, the Steelworkers' multimillion-dollar Humanity Fund has been an effective tool for union renewal by helping to sustain global alliances of workers and a commitment to social justice (Marshall and Garcia-Orgales 2006). These sources of funding have helped build global union councils and strengthen the USW's influence amongst miners' unions throughout Latin America.[2] Now, with a broader union structure in place, the partnership could potentially lead to the "synchronization of collective bargaining in companies with operations on both sides of the Atlantic", using existing solidarity networks as the hinge for these efforts (USW n.d.; Workers Uniting n.d.a).

One of the pressing challenges facing Workers Uniting is that it represents workers in countries with vastly different economies of scale and divergent interests. This will test both the commitment of rank-and-file members and union officers to this new organization. While the international union's structure is still in the development process, the two component parts will maintain separate identities for the time being. Beyond the international scope of Workers Uniting, the union will nonetheless become a registered labor organization in the UK, U.S., Ireland, and Canada, representing all of its founding unions (*Metal Producing & Processing* 2008). The blueprint for this design is intended as an example to other trade unions throughout the world seeking to take part in the creation of a global union without completely altering their own internal representative structures.

Unite and its allies in Workers Uniting have had to reconcile with the challenges affiliated with how unions build programs to manage the global scope of multinationals. And, as UNI's reorganizing strategy suggests, there is nothing organic about constructing larger organizations. After the creation of Workers Uniting, Peter Skyte (interview 2009), National Officer for Unite, glibly called the moment a time of "post-merger introspection", much like what both Unite and the USW had gone through in previous amalgamations. In some ways, he added, the combination of unions is not altogether different than company level mergers, where the organizational structure and human resources need to be coordinated around a central objective. It took UNI eight years to reach a point of developing a coherent organizing strategy. When Unite was first formed, the union's new executive prioritized three pillars of activity: organizing, politics, and the international, as the organization's international officer, Simon Dubbins (interview 2009), suggested in an interview. Indeed, organizing has been part of the convergence project at Unite.

What has separated the cases of Workers Uniting, USW, and Unite from earlier ITSs has been the initiative to move outside their role as "information clearinghouses". For Workers Uniting, this also created tensions with existing GUFs and the relevance of their role as international representatives of national unions. As a source in Unite said to me, there "was also this fear from the global union federations as to what [the creation of Workers Uniting] meant for them, and how they would relate to it" (interview 2009). Reactions were mixed. UNI, by this person's account, had a positive reception, whereas the IMF (International Metalworkers Federation) was initially more concerned for reasons of jurisdictional overlap. From another vantage point, unions from the South feared that this was an attempt by unions in the North to close ranks as a form of mutual protection against labor movements in poorer parts of the world. Dubbins insisted that there has been no intention to withdraw from existing global federations, but instead to build something more effective than what had otherwise been seen as a loose federation of unions. Through an engagement within the IMF framework in 2003–2004, British and North American union officials discussed the idea of constructing an international union that could function like a conventional labor organization. However, "there was a feeling that the IMF", Dubbins added, "was not really capable of giving it that extra lift it [the trade union movement] needed". Unite's and the USW's familiarity with the merger process provided an impetus to take the dialogue to the next step.

Both UNI and Workers Uniting have also worked to implement the guiding rationale behind their mergers, which focused on addressing global capitalism and organizing. Gerhard Rohde took this notion of renewal further by pointing to the cultural elements of trade unions. As a survival mechanism the strategy is not likely to be successful, he argued, but there are different examples as to how mergers can be structured. A labor organization, he explained,

> needs to give some identity to individual members. The organization has to be a kind of a community, it's not only a powerful organization to get things right and to stand up to employers, its membership also has to come with a certain pride. (interview 2009)

When unions in particular sectors are associated with negative connotations, individual workers are reluctant to join because of the professional and personal stigma accompanying the affiliations. Developing a strong affinity between the organization and its membership can, Rohde suggests, greatly increase the association's influence and capacity to engage with multinationals. Peter Waterman's (2008) observation that rank-and-file members are largely ignorant of their union's international affiliations is pertinent here. GUFs and international unions are tasked with building a global identity as part of the renewed union culture. Contextualizing union mergers in a historical framework also helps to address how these challenges were resolved in the past. Workers Uniting may indeed be a new and innovative venture in union internationalism, but there still remain plenty of cross-border examples to reflect upon. Kari Tapiola, at the time the ILO's standards director with decades of experience in the Finnish and international trade union movement, cautioned during a conversation that the jury is still out on the effectiveness of union mergers, notably regarding the example of Workers Uniting. But, he proceeded to raise further critical questions related to the USW's experiences in North America, and how this might impinge upon its capacity to build cross-border agreements.

> [Y]ou have traditionally had US-Canada unions which probably is a reflection of the US-Canadian economic situation in production. That seems to have worked well. It does raise a question: why haven't these unions done mergers with Mexican unions? We have had some similar discussions in Europe, for instance on possible mergers between Finnish and Estonian trade unions where the economic activities are closely linked. But even in areas like the Nordic [region], where culture is similar, the way collective bargaining is conducted differs from one country to another and even between sectors. *I have difficulties in seeing that an international union could internationalize collective bargaining . . .* (interview 2009, emphasis added)

Tapiola insisted that trade unionists "have to make sure that the immediate link between the worker and his/her union representative does not seem to disappear" (interview 2009).

Two concerns are left unresolved in the convergence and merger process. First, union convergence requires an internal mitigation of administrative and cultural tensions. Because unions suffer from competing interests in their pursuit of acquiring new members, it is necessary to establish bonds of solidarity even when conditions are not inherently conducive to collaboration. Mergers between once-competing unions in the national arena are made possible by concessions and negotiations—at the international level this challenge remains as well. From this social perspective, unions must establish not only an economic or legal presence in the workplace, but more importantly, the rank-and-file must support its new representative structure in order for such endeavors to be feasible and prove successful. Even after signing the Ottawa Accord in 2007, the blueprint for Workers Uniting was met with administrative hurdles. "Even if you want to go in that direction [of merging]", Dubbins argued, "there's a whole load of obstacles that present themselves, not least of which is the legal requirements and legal registrations" (interview 2009). Convergence is met not only with contradictions and internal power dynamics, but also the immediate regulatory processes that make the creation of an effective and organized union an incredible challenge.

Second, a workable global industrial relations regime has yet to develop and unions remain dependent on national institutions and systems (see Bognanno, Budd, and Kleiner 2007). Like UNI, Unite and their colleagues in allied unions have recognized the need for multiple strategies as a means of negotiating with multinational enterprises. Global Agreements have been recognized as one approach. For Peter Skyte, national officer for Unite the Union and former liaison with UNITES in India, the question is not an either/or distinction between GA's and national collective agreements—both are required tools to engage global companies, and both are dependent on an active and mobilized membership for success (interview 2009). Unite, as a member of UNI, has experienced negotiating global agreements and seeing them through into the implementation phase. The eventual signing of a GA with Quebecor World, a Canadian-based printing company that employs 35,000 workers in more than 160 printing and media facilities worldwide, was cited as a success precisely because membership action and international solidarity put unions and GUFs in a position to negotiate with the corporation.[3] Dubbins' own account of this development is worth repeating.

At first the company refused to meet us, refused to answer any of our letters. They were, particularly in the United States, using union busters and actively doing everything they could to stop a global agreement, and to stop recognition and organization at their sites there. We, via the European well-organized sites, along with sites that were organized in the States and other parts of the world, *we researched the company, built a network, had an academic involved in categorizing and cataloguing the abuses, we targeted the suppliers, their customers, and in the end we ended up with the company agreeing to sign an agreement.* (interview 2009, emphasis added)

Quebecor was a hard-fought victory for UNI and its national affiliates who worked on establishing the agreement over a seven-year period. An agreement between UNI and Quebecor, the world's second largest printing company, was eventually signed in April of 2007 (see Mosco and Lavin 2008). Working from a strong network of union activists was pivotal. In comparison, Dubbins noted the case of signing a GA with a Swedish-based printing company, which involved comparatively little struggle, but with minimal member participation the agreement is not recognized as being effective or "owned" by the rank-and-file. Unite's approach to building GA's is consistent with the union's renewal strategy which hinges on making organizing a chief priority. "We've moved away from the servicing model", said Dubbins (interview 2009), "and much more towards issues-based organizing". Global Agreements have been approached with the same vision, as a solidarity-building effort dependent on new strategies and a focus on expansion, not just servicing. This is what differentiates between an effective GA, and one that only includes the company and union signatures.

In the information technology sector, unions have been far less successful in making strides with multinationals. Unite shares UNI's acknowledgement that unions, and GUFs, have been unsuccessful at building any sector-wide recognition with major IT firms. If we look at the USW in Canada, its entry into ITES is relatively minimal compared to its European counterpart, Unite. Reiterating the union's commitment to expansion, Dubbins also pointed to the process of renewal through organizing new sectors. As he reflected, "Rebuilding the membership and breaking into new sectors has been the big issue and I think we've gotten much better from the last few years about what works and what doesn't". Successful attempts at organizing call centers have relied on this tendency, especially those facilities not already affiliated with companies that have a history of union representation. One of the major hindrances has actually been due to the dominance of IT and ITES by American multinationals like IBM and CSC, which have avoided a union presence in their U.S.-based operations for years (see Morgan and Sayer 1988). Without a strong labor presence in the home country, Unite and UNI are finding it difficult to organize in particular European countries as a result. Global Agreements with companies such as Deutsche Telecom and Telefónica—which have a significant IT presence but are primarily invested in telecommunications—are a start, but the objective is to establish GA's with major players like IBM, Sysco, and others. Works Councils have been established with other U.S. companies in Europe, such as EDS and HP, but nothing as substantial as a collective agreement or sector-wide negotiating potential.

Skyte suggests that changes in the IT sector may in fact boost union organizing. While the most privileged IT professionals are well paid, how employers are behaving, he argues, has changed. IBM workers in the United States led an online campaign, sponsored by Alliance@IBM CWA Local 1701, against the company to protest a 15 percent pay cut imposed by management. In 2007, international union support led to the first-ever virtual strike on Second Life, which disrupted the company's activities in the 3-D environment. UNI, Unite, UNITES, Alliance@IBM, and a handful of other unions participated in the action, working in solidarity with the demands being made by Rappresentanza Sindacale Unitaria IBM Vimercate (RSU) in Italy (UNI 2007; CWA 2008, 2007).[4] Similar decisions by management sparked opposition to IBM in the UK as well. This led to Unite being able to recruit hundreds of workers at HP and IBM over the issue of pay freezes, pension schemes, redundancies, and internal restructuring. The next step is to enhance the ability to represent the interests of these workers and mobilize rank-and-file efforts, then to gain recognition. Federations and informal networks are seen as valuable resources in this regard.

Like the support drawn on the international scene by the USW and Unite for mining and manufacturing workers, GUFs and union networks help construct models of labor organizing for IT and ITES. Unite's interaction with UNITES in India has been taken up through UNI as well as through independent correspondence with Karthik Shekhar and UNITES Professional activists. This has aided European trade union efforts at charting the offshore activities of British firms, like HSBC, and their operations abroad. UNITES' emergence as a new union project through UNIDOC offices in India has also charted the prospects for founding greenfield initiatives throughout IT industries in Europe, such as ITT.eu in Ukraine. There is truth in the claim that Western unions are servicing their own interests by sustaining a dialogue with counterparts in emerging economies like India, as an Indian labor scholar voiced with suspicion during an interview, but for good cause. It means that overtures towards international solidarity are just as much about protecting national interests and the well-being of existing members as it is about strengthening the union movement abroad. However, the trade unionists I spoke with were quick to respond that it is not a question of ending the corporate practice of offshoring, but to ensure fair and decent standards of employment. What these conversations enforced was that national unions must reconcile how to best represent the interests of their membership and at the same time develop a pragmatic internationalist response the globalization of work. Dubbins made this point clear: "We have obviously had the challenge of trying to take a positive view of jobs relocating and the role it has in development, *whilst at the same time the number one priority has to be to look after the interests of the membership*". Labor internationalism, in Waterman's vernacular, might aid in developing a coherent global solidarity network, but as union activists consulted in the research stress, the needs of the membership must be addressed first.

CONCLUSION

If any consensus has been established among trade union activists nationally and internationally, it is that collective bargaining relationships with multinational corporations need to be confronted through a global framework. International trade secretariats, as mechanisms of communication and information exchange, have evolved into more focused organizations that attend to the ambition of organizing. This does not mean their contemporary equivalents, GUFs, have resolved debates about political affiliation and strategy—quite the contrary. The establishment of larger, converged union federations has been a consequence of the dual purpose of survival and innovation. Traditional craft barriers within labor organizations at the international level have slowly eroded, just as their smaller national counterparts have been forced to reconcile with economic transformations that have seriously eroded political influence and the capacity to bargain for sector-wide interests. An adherence to traditional approaches to engagement with corporations, however, is no longer compatible with whatever can be deciphered as a global labor relations regime, and this appears to be recognized by some members of the union leadership. As sectors evolve and converge, unions too have gone back to the drawing board to reconfigure their strategies and conventional approaches.

UNI's emergence as the leading service sector federation comes from the reality that fragmented and often-competitive relations between international union alliances and representative institutions were no longer sustainable. Political and industrial considerations are indeed intertwined, and GUFs have responded accordingly. But this is also why GUF projects are works in progress, considering the inconclusive resolution about the effectiveness of tactics that are currently in the test phase. Global Agreements are manifestations of these factors, as well as prototypes of union renewal at the global level. Organizing efforts and rank-and-file mobilization are as important, if not more so, than the regulatory potential of these agreements. It is likely that organic manifestations of union alliances, such as solidarity networks forged from events and crises, are as effective as formal arrangements and agreements with companies. This, and the interaction UNI has capably formed with unions in the South, are examples of hybrid union-labor internationalism.

Union renewal has taken many forms as labor organizations struggle to service existing members. Social movement unionism and solidarity campaigns have the potential to bridge unions with consumer groups, NGOs, and others, but renewing the labor movement need not be conceived as a forfeiture of traditional institutions. Renewal is simultaneously an empowerment of labor organizations. Global union federations and international unions have sought to use these networks as a means of establishing support where formal union efforts had previously failed. As a way of capturing the attention of workers in IT and ITES, unions have necessarily taken this approach by constructing associations from the ground up. These organizations are unlikely to reflect the revolutionary ambitions held by the most radical elements of previous international labor movements, but the aim to increase membership through rank-and-file activism—even if these terms are no longer appealing—and forging new institutions and compacts with employers is a legacy of these early movements. Globally coordinated mobilization is widely recognized as important for trade unions and their allies in GUFs. Conceptual visions of globalization aside, unions are required to think internationally but act locally; this is not merely a platitude. The question now is to chart the ability of unions to confront companies at home and abroad.

8   Conclusion

When Daniel Bell wrote *Post-Industrial Society* in the 1970s, he anticipated new ways of working, of living, of engaging in politics, and new
forms of consciousness that were being pieced together in a transforming
social order. Even though Bell and other futurists at the time were reticent
to acknowledge the appropriateness of a single moniker to define this era,
be it the Information Age, the Global Village, or Post-Industrialism, scholars and forecasters agreed that the emergent order defied existing categories
of economic and social organization. Nowhere has this been more evident
than in the world of work. For the processes of labor, technology has
indeed created seismic shifts in the patterns of a global division of knowledge labor. Yet the contributions of critical scholars such Harry Braverman
and Michael Burawoy spoke of a consistency in the maintenance of capitalist modes of production in what has been described in the book as post-
industrial capitalism. Call centers especially, as part of the wider terrain
of information technology and IT enabled services, represent the anxieties
and challenges facing workers and unions in advanced capitalist society. It
is through mutual constitution that the terrain of work, globalization, and
labor organizing are connected.

Labor organizations that make interventions into post-industrial workplaces have faced many of the social hurdles that futurist scholars have long
anticipated. Indeed, the political economy of offshoring and outsourcing
has fashioned a serious structural obstacle for unions not only because of
the technical characteristics of this aspect of globalization, but also due to
the pro-business response by governments to the global division of knowledge labor. The challenges are as much questions of the social dimensions
of work as they are related to the economic and political positionality of
workers in the call center industry, for example, public sector, telecommunications, telemarketing, offshored, and so on.

In Canada, the union stewards, organizers, staff representatives, presi-
dents, and rank-and-file members I spoke with expressed both optimism and
uncertainty about the future for labor unions in global capitalism. Union
activists recognized that unions are at an impasse when dealing with the
offshoring and outsourcing of work, particularly the types of employment

that are routinized and conditioned by ever-evolving information and communication technologies. The creation of Workers Uniting, although still in its infancy in 2007–2009, was looked upon with optimism because it presented a hope that as corporations go global, so too could trade unions. There was also a feeling of uncertainty on the part of some union activists that younger workers were reluctant to mobilize around collective issues, preferring instead to focus on their individual lives in flexible and ostensibly temporary workplaces. When problems arise these workers turn to their unions, but interest subsides when an issue is resolved. This is not unlike the problems UNITES officials have confronted. In fact, the Indian IT union's inability to gain traction among a serious number of the country's two million IT workers, particularly those in the flagship information technology companies, is not unlike the struggles facing established Canadian unions. Nor does global or national labor convergence offer convenient remedies to these deep-seated problems, despite the urgency for union renewal and international solidarity and organizing.

What these hurdles yield is recognition that call centers, as an industry and place of employment, cannot be reduced to simple metaphors like "electronic sweatshops" or "assembly lines in the head". These general claims certainly have some purchase in particular facilities and segments of the industry, like telemarketing, but as general descriptions they fail to embrace the divergent nature of call center employment. Certainly, the call center labor process has some uniform characteristics that have developed around a particular technological interface between workers and clients. Work in this industry is also shaped by unique organizational routines, management practices, spatial locality, and generally, a political economy of global telecommunications. Workers are also able to make meaningful changes to the work process, and even find satisfaction in the human interaction itself. At other times, of course, the interaction might also be a source of frustration and dissent. For these reasons Appadurai's (1996) articulation of a consumer and production fetishism resonates in the study of call centers. Social relations of production, crystallized in material form as commodities, also include the totality of production *and* consumption, the social construction of space, and a global division of knowledge labor, which are all fixtures in Appadurai's framework.

Fetishism and the process of commodification has not developed unassisted. Businesses have employed a multitude of organizational forms as a way of structuring increasingly complex global call center production chains that purposefully obfuscate the relations in and of production. Call centers are deliberately placeless. International service provision has been made possible by such IT-enabled processes, which allow companies to manage a network of subsidiaries and subcontractors. Standardized formats for customer interaction, emotional commodification, and other elements of delivering services as both core and non-core activities are made possible by these innovations. Internationally accepted notions of professionalism have made the integration of global labor forces into Western markets conceivable in the last decade and a half, which is especially true for call centers and other components of ITES. This constitutes a second barrier for unionization. Managerial as well as productive functions are subsumed under the watchful gaze of scientifically-established mechanisms of understanding the processes of control at work. This is a quintessential dimension of post-industrial capitalism, which is organized around knowledge for, as Bell (1999/1973, 20) maintained, the "purpose of social control and the directing of innovation and change".

All of these conditions have been made possible by a political economic infrastructure that began to emerge in the 1970s with the development of neo-liberalism as policy. A global, liberalized telecommunications regime has provided the arteries for an international call center industry, as much as changes to industrial and labor relations laws have worked to undermine the influence of trade unions in the workplace. And, despite the moniker of free market reforms, neo-liberalism is premised on intensive government intervention in economic affairs, albeit defined by pro-business policies. Together these changing patterns of regulation have expanded opportunities for commercialization and operate as a force for capitalist development in emerging economies like India.

Even though business and industry literature speaks of a general benefit to the population as a result of liberalized markets, the effects have been unequal and uneven. This does not mean that earlier, Fordist and Keynesian modes of regulation were egalitarian. Chakrabarti and Cullenberg (2003), in their study of economic transition in India, cautioned against the nostalgic return to the highly regulated economy that marked the years before the New Economic Policies of the early 1990s. The scholars go so far as to label an appeal to these previous economic strategies as "indefensible", considering they were predicated on a system of production that sustained high rates of poverty, illiteracy and ill-health, and furnished a licensing system that maintained structural corruption which benefited the rich and elite of society. But the current system has not resolved these entrenched inequalities, despite some of the opportunities offered by the post-industrial economy, of which IT-ITES is a part. Liberalization has, of course, made conditions more precarious for unions and their members, as well as for a growing segment of the white-collar population.

In light of India's entry to the offshore call center economy there is also the question of what precipitated the rise of a global division of knowledge labor, and information production more broadly. The new international division of labor (NIDL) established by Fröbel et al.'s (1980) was replaced by the GDL hypothesis as a more capable means of understanding the contemporary structure of global capitalism. This is a consequence of the former's insufficient attentiveness to the mechanisms that generate and sustain labor forces besides technological innovations, international telecommunications, and the availability of inexpensive labor. At the same time,

Machlup's (1962, 1980) schema of knowledge production, with its built-in division of labor predicated on the complexity and value of work, as well as the relative inputs of information and skill, is critical in developing an adequate theory of how call centers fit a global division of information labor. Importantly, Machlup's definition of knowledge work opened up the question of how the technical separation of tasks allowed for an internationalization of knowledge production to previously uncharted regions that were, historically, on the periphery of these high-value industries. From here we come to the question of labor.

Trade unionism is situated at the intersection of a global division of knowledge labor and the processes of production that define call center employment. Unions and labor associations, in the case of the ITPF, were for a time successful in recruiting members based on a purposefully constructed identity as a professional organization. UNITES was marginally more successful in this endeavor, but a mix of employer opposition, the relative privilege associated with IT-ITES employment, and a lack of access to workplaces prohibited a sustained growth of membership. Still, in some cases, structural problems within the industry led IT and ITES workers to turn to unions as a means of resolving problems or gaining collective representation, or both. Mobilization was made possible because, as in the case of UNITES, problems experienced by professional employees such as harassment, breach of basic labor rights, and arbitrary management decisions were structural and not isolated instances. As Kelly (1998) suggests, it is not effective to make hardened distinctions between people as individualists or collectivists. The capacity of professional organizations like UNITES and the ITPF to mobilize has depended on embracing the individualistic demands of IT-ITES workers and empowering them *through* collective action. This is certainly true for workers in the ITES-BPO and call centers especially. Following the global financial crisis, even the mainstream press and business publications identified the possibility of widespread layoffs that were unimaginable only a year earlier. However, the trend was short lived and the momentum generated by this uncertainty among some of the more privileged information technology professionals lost steam.

Talk of a new upsurge or union revitalization among scholars and labor activists calls into question the ambition of trade unions in post-industrial capitalism—specifically, the ways in which organized labor mobilizes support among workers across knowledge industries. At the international level, UNI is at the forefront of this debate for service sector unions. UNITES, and earlier the ITPF, are some examples of union revitalization and an ostensibly new upsurge. For academics, there is much work to be done in the field. Since UNI has made organizing a priority and intends on financing local union initiatives through a centrally administered fund, it will be important in the years ahead to investigate the nature of these coordinated initiatives. In India, one such project involves considering global union federation efforts at organizing workers in the country's private sector banks and financial institutions as part of UNI's "New Generation Network" (NGN) project.

UNI has focused its attention on sectors where traditional union organizing efforts have been met with limited success. The Union for Commerce Employees in India (UNICOME), the Union for Logistics Employees (UNILOGE), the Union for Finance Employees (UNIFINE), and the Union for Mobile Employees (UNIMODE) are all part of UNI's NGN initiative, and all of these start-up organizations have targeted private sector service industries that have grown since liberalization. For UNITES, it will be important to focus on the union's ability, or lack thereof, to become financially self-sufficient and organize workers in the coveted multinational firms that dot India's IT and ITES landscape. At this point it appears that the experiment might be winding down, although it is far from deceased. Because union officials have taken aim at spreading the UNITES model throughout South East Asia, there is value in charting the export of this success to other information technology hubs that service export markets, the Philippines especially. UNITES and other IT-ITES unions will ultimately be on the front lines of the changing global division of labor as business and IT-ITES processes spread across Asia. A project such as this would find value in drawing from political economy to dissect the power relations within international union structures as proposals are formulated and enacted. The engagement between local union organizers and global federation headquarters requires a critical investigation of potential inequalities and power imbalances between the social actors on the ground, and how, if at all, GUFs have worked to resolve the reproduction of relations that characterize the political dynamics that exist between Global North and Global South in the process.

In the Canadian context, there is value in pursuing the question of how unions like the USW, traditionally embedded in the primary commodity and manufacturing sectors, have organized workplaces that employ information technology workers and at the same time are using international affiliations to confront multinational employers. As unions turn increasingly to new sectors, such a project must confront debates within organized labor and the challenges, logistical and political, facing labor organizations in their venture into post-industrial workplaces. With the recent merger of two of Canada's most important unions, the Canadian Auto Workers (CAW) and the Communications, Energy and Paperworkers Unions (CEP), which created Unifor in 2013, it is important to come back to the question of what value convergence brings to the labor movement. Questioning the USW example, is the merger with Unite and the formation of Workers Uniting an inspiration or a survival mechanism at a time of growing assaults on trade unionism in the United States and the UK? This also begs the question about the possibility of a global post-industrial relations regime and international bargaining. Will GUFs and transnational unions be able to negotiate these challenges in the years ahead?

Finally, there is the question of what the future holds for call centers as the staple of customer-organization interaction. Developments in social media and smart phone technology could radically alter the interface between consumers of service and call center production that depends on telephone-based voice communication as the principle interface. As global IT-BPM spending is set to reach $2 trillion before the end of 2013, what consequence will SMAC (Social, Mobility, Analytics, Cloud), the new moniker used by Nasscom (2013) to define a terrain of interactive technologies, have for knowledge producers, particularly in tele-mediated workplaces? As Kathik Shekhar reflected in conversation, these developments will further complicate the prospects for the formation of high-tech unions (interview 2012).

For unions, revitalization means not only an increase in membership but also the capacity to bargain and establish new rights and benefits for members. Indeed, free and fair collective bargaining is a significant gain in itself, and one that is being eroded by neo-liberalism and anti-union policies. Without these hard-fought accomplishments, how does the trade union movement hope to achieve economic and political victories for workers? This book has admittedly covered several topics that are "in progress", meaning that they are transitory initiatives and without a definitive resolution to immediate problems. Other challenges, like addressing the offshoring and subcontracting of work, are currently unresolved by unions such as the USW. But there is cause for optimism. Trade union activists and their allies spoke of the dignity and empowerment that accompanies collective mobilization and union representation. This is a research topic and a cause worth pursuing.

Notes

NOTES TO CHAPTER 1

1. The film based on Bhagat's novel was released under the title *Hello*.
2. In 2010, India's GDP in U.S. currency stood at $1.43 trillion compared to Canada at $1.563 trillion, according to International Monetary Fund (2010) figures. However, 2015 estimates conclude that the Indian economy will reach a GDP of $2.412 trillion, outpacing Canada's GDP of $1.880 trillion.

NOTES TO CHAPTER 2

1. Similar to the organizational strategy adopted by IBM, Convergys, a globally recognized firm in the outsourcing market, opened up an Indian subsidiary in 2004. This strategy was meant to develop a lower cost structure and offer greater control over operational resources for clients seeking to enter the off-shore outsourcing market (Convergys n.d.). The company was also responsible for spearheading "accent-modification" and "cultural-appreciation classes" for its Indian employees through the CAN 8 Virtual Lab Language Laboratory.
2. In the third quarter of 2010, *The New York Times* reported, American businesses earned profits at an annual rate of US$1.659 trillion, the highest recorded figure since the Commerce Department began keeping track (Rampell 2010). Canada's figures in the fourth quarter of 2010 were more modest, at CAN$65.5 billion, up 7.9 percent from the previous quarter.
3. *Toronto Star* columnist David Olive (2007) waxed nostalgic about the influential pressure that then-Deputy Finance Minister David Dodge brought to bear on the Chrétien Liberals in the early 1990s. Olive's commentary emerged when the world's wealthiest economies were on the brink of recession. Under the leadership of Finance Minister Paul Martin, the Canadian government embarked on a plan, under the tutelage of Dodge, to cut the country's ballooning deficit. This involved, among other austerity measures, the gradual erosion of social program funding, cuts to federal transfer payments to provinces, and reneging on the party's promise to scrap the Goods and Services Tax (GST). The "tough-love" prognosis was perceived as a necessary move in order to salvage the sinking Canadian economy and rescue the currency from an eroded rate of exchange.

NOTES TO CHAPTER 3

1. Based on the IMF's Balance of Payments Statistics Yearbook in 2002, Germany, the United Kingdom, Japan, the Netherlands, and Spain were recorded

as the top five importers of business services. The United States trailed as a close sixth. China was ranked not far behind, in tenth. In terms of "computer services" trade surpluses, the UK led with approximately US$20 billion followed by the U.S. at $17 billion. Hong Kong was not far behind at $15 billion, and India came in fourth at $6.8 billion. The figures for "computer and information services" surpluses ranked Ireland as number one ($9.8 billion), followed by the U.S. ($3.8 billion), the UK ($3 billion), and Canada fourth ($1 billion) (Amiti and Wei 2004a, 24).

2. The United States ranked 117th, the UK 85th, and China 99th, ahead of the U.S.

3. This is based on OECD calculations tabulated from the IMF's Balance of Payments Database published in February 2005. Ireland, by contrast, experienced the worst and most dramatic trade deficits in these categories throughout the same period, despite its status as a major exporter of business and IT services. In fact, the "Celtic Tiger" is heavily dependent on these service exports, which grew at a rate of over 40 percent between 1995 and 2003.

4. IT infrastructure management has recently been identified as an emerging offshore market since that labor is seen as the most addressable cost. Standardization of repetitive tasks, the capacity to fragment more complex work processes, rising costs, and the technical ability to manage tasks from remote locations have opened up this market to offshoring. According to one study, Fortune 50 companies could save as much as $500 million on their IT infrastructure budgets by offshoring and outsourcing at least a portion of this operation to vendors (Pandit and Srinivasaraghavan 2008).

5. Take, for instance, the case of General Motors and the sixty-five microprocessors specially built for a typical GM vehicle. With the exception of the microprocessor for the power train, the company writes very little of the software in-house. Instead, GM contracts with major suppliers like IBM, Siemens, and Motorola, which in turn source labor from their production networks throughout the United States, Europe, and Asia (Carmel and Tjia 2005).

6. Offshoring, some studies suggest, must be measured by combining macroeconomic aggregates such as FDI, trade balance data, industry production and employment numbers, with microeconomic causes and effects of foreign investments (Le Goff 2005).

7. Evalueserve's (2003) report presents an alternative scenario as well. Predicted labor shortages can be compensated for by increasing the use of immigrant and non-immigrant (temporary) labor. In the U.S. this has been especially contentious, as the H1-B temporary visa debate has summoned opposition from the labor movement as well as xenophobic sentiments within the population.

NOTES TO CHAPTER 4

1. Ellen Roseman, author of the 2008 *Toronto Star* article, hosted a comments board on her personal blog (Roseman n.d.). One person remarked, "A few weeks ago, while trying to get some information from my bank on an unrelated issue, I discovered that "MY" bank, TD, now has a customer service call center in INDIA !!! . . . Many readers may not think this is a problem because we are so in love with globalization. But I'm personally so upset with this situation I am seriously considering withdrawing ALL of my money and retirement funds from this bank". While the vendor in India was only part of a pilot project being tested by TD Bank, with most of the 700 customer service representatives still located in Canada, customer responses and

commentators were quick to chastise the financial institution for its decision to offshore work. Some appealed to the inability of Indian agents to speak with clear English accents, while others criticized the bank, which registered record level profits, for not hiring Canadian workers.

2. This 2002 report relied on the North American Industry Classification System (NAICS) as a definition for call center employment: "These establishments are engaged in activities such as soliciting or providing information; promoting products or services; taking orders; and raising funds for clients. This industry also includes establishments primarily engaged in answering telephone calls and relaying messages to clients; and establishments primarily engaged in providing voice mailbox services". The NAICS category *excludes* establishments primarily engaged in taking orders in offices of mail-order houses, providing paging services, gathering, recording, tabulating, and presenting marketing and public opinion data, and organizing and conducting fund-raising campaigns for others (see Statistics Canada n.d.a); included are answering services, floral wire service, telephone answering and message service, telemarketing bureaus, telemarketing service on a contract or fee basis, telephone call centers, telephone solicitation service, voice mail box service, and wake-up call service (see Statistics Canada n.d.b).

3. Compensation rates in Fredericton, New Brunswick, are the lowest at 17 percent below the national average, while Kingston sits at 7 percent below; Toronto and the Greater Vancouver Area are 2 and 7 percent above average, respectively (Contact Center Canada 2006b).

4. Of course, these losses were at the same time accompanied by the establishment of new centers, such as the expansion of Virtual-Agent Services—an American-owned company serving hospitality, catalogue sales, insurance and roadside assistance clients—in the province (Canadian Press 2008).

5. Whereas the same Contact Center Canada (2006a) report estimated that offshoring would affect between 7,000 and 9,000 call center positions in Canada annually, 1 and 1.5 percent of the base, subsequent studies have not been able to substantiate these claims.

6. A benchmarking study conducted by the Australian-based Callcenters.net (2007a) produced the opposite conclusion: 33 percent of call centers were involved in international services, and the majority, 67 percent, in local servicing. One account of the varying result may be a consequence of a less representative sample in the Callcenter.net report than in the Global Call Center project. There also appears to be some inconsistencies in Callcenters. net's data. In the "Countries Service by Contact Centers" profile, the report reveals that 74 percent of the centers service India, 22 percent the United States, and 18 percent the UK.

7. Rodrik and Subramanian (2001, 38) list a series of internal liberalization measures that were implemented between 1985 and 1986, which supported the pro-business agenda in India. These include: eliminating the licensing of twenty-five categories of industries subject to certain fairly onerous conditions; extending de-licensing to large companies in industries that were previously restricted by the Monopolies and Trade Restrictive Practices Act (MRTP) and Foreign Exchange Regulation Act (FERA); allowing companies in over twenty industries to expand the scope of their operations into related activities; and allowing companies to surpass existing and highly regulated capacity utilization rates. Such regulatory reforms promoted competition by clearing the way for new domestic firms to enter the market. A case has also been made for the harmonization of India's value added tax (VAT) system throughout the country's twenty-eight states and territories to cover all manufacturing goods and services, with proceeds shared

between the central and state governments. Liberalization was similarly called for to be an increasingly ambitious project, deepening attempts to deregulate retailing, banking, news media, electricity, and even defense (see Pandit 2005).

8. Nasscom (2004) provides a rubric for the various phases in the ITES-BPO sector's development. Phase I is marked by the entry of large corporate pioneers who test the political waters by offshoring crucial operations. In Phase II the risk profile improves and companies start to set up new and more strategic initiatives offshore. Phase III, roughly between 2003 and 2008, has shown offshoring in India to be a proven model, sustainable in the medium and long terms. Quality remains high, labor costs remain under control, regulatory interference is minimized, and the public relations of sending work offshore is manageable. This later period is the phase in which skilled labor markets outside of the Western economies can be successfully integrated into the global production and service chains.

9. Convergys signed a contract with the state-owned telecommunication firm, Bharat Sanchar Nigam Ltd. (BSNL), to take care of the company's billing processing. This follows a strategy used by the same outsourcer in Canada. Other Indian companies have started to outsource some of their back office operations, including customer service, all of which has reportedly been kept within India. Financial corporations such as Standard Chartered Bank, which runs India's largest foreign bank, have also sought to increase the number of call center employees (Reuters 2009).

10. This is part of the Integrated Train Enquiry System, which has the appropriate acronym, ITES. Indian Railways receives about 140,000 to 150,000 phone calls every day (S. Singh 2007).

11. Ranger (2006) reports on the over 10,000 outsourced call center agents working from Eastern Europe and 7,800 in North Africa, largely driven by Egypt. The Kenyan government's attention to improving the country's IT infrastructure is an additional benefit that could lure foreign clients. At present the cost of a fiber optic connection to Kenya far exceeds that of India, but the World Bank has recently provided funds to help subsidize the construction of a new submarine cable, part of the 5,000 km East African Marine System (*Sydney Morning Herald* 2007).

NOTES TO CHAPTER 5

1. This has been especially true of the Indian National Trade Union Congress (INTUC), affiliated with the Congress Party, which by some historical accounts is largely the labor arm of the party. Contrasted with the All India Trade Union Congress (AITUC), born of the Communist tradition and having arisen from the rank-and-file, INTUC would wield local unions as a convenient political tool (see Bhattecherjee 1999).

2. Shetty provided his account of what led to the incident:

   One of the main reasons that we've found that these attacks have taken place [against] women . . . by the drivers . . . [is] because the drivers are not employed full-time by the companies. Companies are trying to save money by outsourcing the supply of drivers. . . . So this kind of movement and turnover of drivers has caused a lot of problems, there is no verification of backgrounds . . . The companies' response is to hush up any such cases. . . . (interview with Shetty 2008)

3. "To start with we will ask IBM to make the same commitments for the company in India as they have agreed to do in Australia . . . then we will take the

agitation to other companies", Shekhar stated in a major Indian publication (Shankar 2006).
4. Other research indicates that 50 percent of workers quit for a higher paying position in a similar job, followed by 30 percent who leave to seek higher education (Rajeev and Vani 2007).

NOTES TO CHAPTER 6

1. Union density among the 650,000 employees at AT&T reached a peak of 56 percent in 1983, but fell to 24 percent in 2001. Among the conglomeration of Bell companies, union rates for union-eligible network technicians declined to about 57 percent in 2001 from 82 percent in 1983; among customer service and sales workers, 26 percent and 66 percent for the same years (Katz, Batt, and Keefe 2003, 576).
2. Between 2005 and 2007 the unionization rate for IT workers in Canada experienced little variation, growing from 16.3 to 16.4 percent (Software Human Resource Council 2005, 2007). Professional, scientific, and technical services constituted the single largest segment, at 44.9 percent (Software Human Resource Council 2005, 2007).
3. For instance, as the number of people employed by firms with less than 100 workers increases, where unionization is traditionally less prevalent, this creates a downward pressure on union rates. Changing demographics related to age and gender, the authors argue, are also key variables. As industries with longer histories of proportionally higher unionization rates diminish and workers are forced to look for work in non-unionized workplaces and sectors, rates subsequently decrease. Morisette, Schellenberg, and Johnson (2005) also suggest that a "reduction in employee need for union representation" is one possibility for declining rates, as is increased management opposition to unionization, but they stop short of substantiating their tentative conclusions.
4. This is still below the average hourly earnings for unionized employees according to 2006 figures, which stood at $23.34 for full-time employment (Statistics Canada 2007).
5. Western call centers exceeded the national average, as 70 percent of agents are women, compared to Ontario at 65 percent and Atlantic Canada at 67 percent (Carroll and Wagar 2007, 15).
6. Organizational issues related to women's empowerment began at the Steelworkers' first International Women's Conference in February of 2000, which gave rise to *Women of Steel*. This initiative, Fonow (2003) reflects, involved a range of discursive practices and formal structures that sought to institutionalize equity concerns and feminism in the USW. Marshall and Garcia-Orgales (2006) have drawn attention to the Steelworkers' efforts at building a sustainable international solidarity movement that emphasizes the importance of strengthening the ties between workers in the Global North and Global South. The creation of the USW's Humanity Fund, established in 1985 as a response to the famine in Ethiopia, is examined as a central example of union resources deployed to help support trade unions in South America, where Canadian mining companies occupy a dominant role in the sector.
7. Just prior to working at Omega in 2002, Wendy was employed with a local taxi company and had been involved with a union campaign at the workplace, which ultimately ended in defeat. She was terminated from the company shortly afterwards and was encouraged by friends to apply at OMDR.

8. "Political Communications" is a pseudonym. All interview participants have similarly been provided an alias to protect their identity.
9. "Visa Financial" is a pseudonym.

NOTES TO CHAPTER 7

1. Informal versus formal sector employment dominates the challenge of union organizing in the Global South, where national and international union efforts have been met with difficulty. But the issue is one that cannot be left unresolved in the broader debate of international unionism (see Bieler, Lindberg, and Pillay 2008; Davies and Ryner 2006; Stevens 2010).
2. International solidarity demonstrations were held by unions representing mining sector workers in 2009, of which Workers Uniting members were a part, as a protest against the Mexican government's support for the anti-union actions taken by the nation's largest mining interest, Grupo Mexico (Canadian Press 2009).
3. In 2010, Quebecor World was acquired by Wisconsin-based Quad/Graphics to become Worldcolor.
4. IBM has been at the center of international union efforts to negotiate with the company, either through legislated means or solidarity campaigns. In 2008, the company refused to negotiate a collective agreement with employees represented by the Australian Services Union, forcing workers to engage in rolling work stoppages (UNI 2008b). Success was achieved by employees at IBM Argentina when workers, affiliated with CEPETEL (Centro de Profesionales de Empresas de Telecommunicaciones) were finally given the opportunity to elect their union representatives, a first in the company's 85 year history (UNI 2010b).

References

Acharya, Keya. 2009. "Labor-India: Getting 'Bangalored' back," *Global Issues*, January 2, http://www.globalissues.org/news/2009/01/02/189 (accessed January 12, 2009).

Ackers, Peter. 2006. "Leaving labor? Some British impressions of Indian academic employment relations," *Economic and Political Weekly*, September 30, 4187–4194.

Adamczyk, Bryan. 2004. "Steelworkers celebrate agreement with Telespectrum Worldwide Inc.," *Canadian Press*, June 30.

Aggarwal, Aradhna. 2006. "Special economic zones: Revisiting the policy debate," *Economic and Political Weekly*, November 4, 4533–4536.

Akyeampong, Ernest B. 2005. "Business support services," *Perspectives on Labor and Income*, May 5. Ottawa: Statistics Canada.

Amin, Ash. 1995. "Post-Fordism: Models, fantasies and phantoms of transition." In *Post-Fordism: A Reader*, edited by Ash Amin, 1–40. Cambridge: Blackwell.

Amin, Samir. 2003. *Obsolescent Capitalism: Contemporary Politics and Global Disorder*. New York: Zed Books.

Amiti, Mary, and Shang-Jin Wei. 2006. "Service offshoring and productivity: Evidence from the United States." Working Paper 11926. Cambridge, MA: National Bureau of Economic Research. http://www.nber.org/papers/w11926 (accessed May 18, 2010).

———. 2004a. *Fear of Service Outsourcing: Is it Justified?* Cambridge, MA: National Bureau of Economic Research.

———. 2004b. "Demystifying outsourcing: The numbers do not support the hype over job losses," *Finance and Development*, December, 36–39.

Anthony, Regina. 2007. "IT companies queue up for SEZ license to extend tax holiday," *livemint.com*, October 15, http://www.livemint.com/2007/10/14235449/IT-companies-queue-up-for-SEZ.html (accessed October 15, 2007).

Appadurai, Arjun. 1996. *Modernity at Large: Cultural Dimensions of Globalization*. Minneapolis: University of Minnesota Press.

Arrighi, Giovanni. 2007. *Adam Smith in Beijing*. New York: Verso Press.

AsiaOne Business. 2008. "Outsourcing may still mean big business," November 3, http://business.asiaone.com/Business/News/SME%2BCentral/Story/A1Story20081103-98034.html (accessed November 4, 2008).

Aslam, Abid. 2008. "Union alliance seeks global power," *Asia Times*, May 29, http://www.atimes.com/atimes/Global_Economy/JE29Dj03.html (accessed May 29, 2008).

ASSOCHAM. 2009. *Globalisation: Growth and people*. New Delhi: Associated Chambers of Commerce and Industry of India.

Associated Press. 2011. "Where are the jobs? For many companies, overseas," December 28, http://www.google.com/hostednews/ap/article/ALeqM5iFY0R

9agrMVljqtaB6ccsILSKd3Q?docId=771fbe245e624cbd95ab5a49122dd701 (accessed January 10, 2011).

———. 2008. "British union sets merger with Steelworkers," *New York Times*, May 26, http://www.nytimes.com/2008/05/26/business/worldbusiness/26labor. html?partner=rssnyt&emc=rss (accessed May 26, 2008).

———. 2007. "E.D.S. offers exit incentives to 12,000 workers," *New York Times*, September 13.

A.T. Kearney. 2004. *Making Offshore Decisions: Offshore Location Attractiveness Index*. Chicago: A.T. Kearney, Inc.

Austen, Ian. 2004. "Canada, the closer country for outsourcing work," *New York Times*, November 30.

Babe, Robert E. 2008. "Innis and the emergence of Canadian communication/ media studies," *Global Media Journal*, 1:1, 9–23.

———. 2000. "Foundation of Canadian communication thought," *Canadian Journal of Communication*, 25:1. http://www.cjc-online.ca/viewarticle.php? id=560&layout=html (accessed December 29, 2007).

———. 1994. "The place of information in economics." In *Information and Communication in Economics*, edited by Robert E. Babe, 41–68. Boston: Kluwer.

———. 1990. *Telecommunications in Canada*. Toronto: University of Toronto Press.

———. 1975. *Cable Television and Telecommunications in Canada*. East Lansing: Michigan State University.

Bain, Peter, and Phil Taylor. 2002. "Ringing the changes? Union recognition and organisation in call centers in the UK finance sector," *Industrial Relations Journal*, 33:3, 246–261.

———. 2000. "Entrapped by the 'electronic Panopticon?' Worker resistance in the call center," *New Technology, Work and Employment*, 15:1, 2–18.

Bajaj, Vikas. 2011. "Philippines overtakes India as hub of call centers," *New York Times*, November 25, http://www.nytimes.com/2011/11/26/business/ philippines-overtakes-india-as-hub-of-call-centers.html?pagewanted=all&_r=0 (accessed May 25, 2013).

Baldry, Chris. 1999. "Space—The final frontier," *Sociology*, 33:3, 535–553.

Baldry, Chris, Peter Bain, and Phil Taylor. 1998. "Bright Satanic offices: Intensification, control, and team Taylorism." In *Workplaces of the Future*, edited by Paul Thompson and Chris Warhurst, 163–183. New York: Palgrave Macmillan.

Baldwin, John R., and Wulong Gu. 2008. *Outsourcing and Offshoring in Canada*. Ottawa: Statistics Canada.

Ball, Kirstie. 2003. "Organization, surveillance and the body: Towards a politics of resistance," *Organization*, 12:1, 89–108.

Baran, Paul, and Paul Sweezy. 1966. *Monopoly Capital*. New York: Monthly Review Press.

Barnes, Taylor. 2010. "US healthcare reform is boon for India outsourcing companies," *Christian Science Monitor*, March 25, http://www.csmonitor.com/ World/Asia-South-Central/2010/0325/US-healthcare-reform-is-boon-for-India-outsourcing-companies (accessed January 14, 2011).

Basi, J.K. Tina. 2009. *Women, Identity and India's Call Centre Industry*. London and New York: Routledge.

Basu, Indrajit. 2009. "IT workers join unions to fight job cuts," *UPI Asia.com*, May 6, http://www.upiasia.com/Economics/2009/05/06/it_workers_join_ unions_to_fight_job_cuts/9707/ (accessed May 8, 2009).

Basu, Sreeradha. 2013. "BPO companies report decline in women workforce after Delhi gang-rape: Assocham," *The Times of India*, January 3, http://timesofindia. indiatimes.com/tech/careers/job-trends/BPO-companies-report-decline-in-women-workforce-after-Delhi-gang-rape-Assocham/articleshow/17872778. cms (accessed January 23, 2013).

Batt, Rosemary. 2002. "Managing customer services: Human resource practices, quit rates, and sales growth," *Academy of Management Journal*, 45:3, 587–597.

Batt, Rosemary, and Lisa Moynihan. 2002. "The viability of alternative call center production models," *Human Resource Management Journal*, 12:4, 14–34.

Batt, Rosemary, Virginia Doellgast, Hyunji Kwon, Mudit Nopany, Priti Nopany, and Anil da Costa. 2005. *The Indian Call Center Industry: National Benchmarking Report*. Ithaca, NY: Cornell University, School of Industrial and Labor Relations.

Bayliss, Kate, and Christopher Cramer. 2001. "Privatisation and the post-Washington consensus: Between the lab and the real world?" In *Development Policy in the 21st Century*, edited by Ben Fine, Costas Lapavitsas, and Jonathan Pincus, 52–79. London: Routledge.

BCLRB see British Columbia Labor Relations Board.

Beirne, Martin, Kathleen Riach, and Fiona Wilson. 2004. "Controlling business? Agency and constraint in call center working," *New Technology, Work and Employment*, 19:2, 96–109.

Bell, Daniel. 1999/1973. *The Coming of Post-Industrial Society*. New York: Basic Books.

———. 1976. *The Cultural Contradictions of Capitalism*. New York: Basic Books.

Belt, Vicki. 2002. "A female ghetto: Women's careers in call centers," *Human Resource Management Journal*, 12:4, 51–66.

Belt, Vicki, and Ronald Richardson. 2000. "Women's Work in the Information Economy: The case of telephone call centers," *Information, Communication & Society*, 3:3, 366–385.

Bentham, Karen. 2002. "Employer resistance to union certification: A study of eight Canadian jurisdictions," *Relations industrielles/Industrial Relations*, 57:1, 159–185.

Bernard, Elaine. 1982. *The Long Distance Feeling: A History of the Telecommunications Workers Union*. Vancouver: New Star Books.

Bhaghat, Chetan. 2005. *One Night @ the Call Center*. New York: Ballantine Book.

Bhagwati, Jagdish. 1968. "Distortions and immiserizing growth: A generalization," *Review of Economic Studies*, 35:4, 481–485.

Bhattacherjee, Debashish. 1999. "Organized labor and economic liberalization in India: Past, present and future," discussion paper, Labor and Society Programme, International Institute for Labor Studies, Geneva.

Bibby, Andrew. 2004. "The global mobility revolution," *UNI In Depth*, March 17, http://www.union-network.org/uniindep.nsf/51520e5cabae0089c12569b 4004fe4c2/79fcc3c0a19684c9c1256e5a004517b6?OpenDocument (accessed September 12, 2007).

———. 2002a. "IT professionals' forums in India," *World of Work*, 42, http:// www.ilo.org/public/english/bureau/inf/magazine/42/itindia.htm (accessed October 20, 2007).

———. 2002b. "Labor organisation in India's IT industry," *Financial Times*, http:// www.andrewbibby.com/telework/india.html (accessed November 19, 2007).

———. 2002c. "A new union mould," *Financial Times*, February 27, http://global. factiva.com/ha/default.aspx (accessed May 14, 2006).

———. 2000. "Organising in financial call centers: A report for UNI." Discussion paper. http://www.andrewbibby.com/docs/ofcc1.html (accessed November 19, 2007).

Bieler, Andreas, Ingemar Lindberg, and Devan Pillay, eds. 2008. *Labor and the Challenges of Globalization: What Prospects for Transnational Solidarity?* Scottsville, SA: University of KwaZulu-Natal Press.

Birla, Ritu. 2010. *Stages of Capital: Law, Culture, and Market Governance in Late Colonial India.* Durham and London: Duke University Press.

Bognanno, Mario F., John W. Budd, and Morris M. Kleiner. 2007. "Symposium introduction: Governing the global workplace," *Industrial Relations,* 46:2, 215–221.

Bounds, Andrew. 2013. "Survey says reshoring "symbolic" and will not lead to jobs boom," May 10, http://www.theglobeandmail.com/report-on-business/economy/jobs/survey-says-reshoring-symbolic-and-will-not-lead-to-jobs-boom/article11855864/#dashboard/follows/ (June28, 2013).

BPO India. 2012. "NASSCOM calls for rebranding BPO to BPM," September 11, http://www.bpoindia.org/columns/nasscom-calls-for-rebranding-bpo-to-bpm/ (accessed September 11, 2012).

Bradley, Lara. 2001. "Steelworkers set sights on call center industry," *Sudbury Star,* February 22, A1.

Braverman, Harry. 1974. *Labor and Monopoly Capital.* New York: Monthly Review Press.

Breitenfellner, Andreas. 1997. "Global unionism: A potential player," *International Labor Review,* 136:4, 531–555.

Brenner, Robert. 2011. "The political economy of the rank-and-file rebellion." In *Rebel Rank and File,* edited by Aaron Brenner, Robert Brenner, and Cal Winslow, 37–76. Brooklyn, NY: VersoBrignall, Miles. 2006. "Powergen brings call centers back to UK," *Guardian Unlimited,* June 15, http://business.guardian.co.uk/story/0,,1798579,00.html (accessed September 3, 2007).

Briskin, Linda. 2008. "Cross-constituency organizing in Canadian unions," *British Journal of Industrial Relations,* 46:2, 221–247.

British Columbia Labor Relations Board. 2003. "Convergys Customer Management Canada, Inc. and B.C. Government and Service Employees' Union." BCLRB No. B62/2003.

Brophy, Enda. 2009. "Resisting call center work: The Aliant strike and convergent unionism in Canada," *Work, Organisation, Labor and Globalisation,* 3:1, 80–99.

———. 2006. "System error: Labor precarity and collective organizing," *Canadian Journal of Communication,* 31:3, 619–638.

Brown, Leslie, and Susan Strega. 2005. "Transgressive possibilities." In *Research as Resistance: Critical, Indigenous, and Anti-oppressive Approaches,* edited by Leslie Brown and Susan Strega, 1–17. Toronto: Canadian Scholar's Press.

Brown, Terrance. 2001. "Steelworkers aren't needed at call center," *Sudbury Star,* March 5, A7.

Bryant, Jennings, and Dorina Miron. 2004. "Theory and research in mass communication," *The Journal of Communication,* 54:4, 662–704.

Buchanan, Ruth. 2000. "1–800 New Brunswick: Economic development strategies, firm restructuring and the local production of 'global.'" In *Globalizing Institutions: Case Studies in Regulation and Innovation,* edited by Jane Jenson and Boaventura de Sousa Santos, 53–79. Burlington, VT: Ashgate.

Buchanan, Ruth, and Sarah Koch-Schulte. 2000. *Gender on the Line: Technology, Restructuring and the Reorganization of Work in the Call Center Industry.* Ottawa: Status of Women.

Burawoy, Michael. 2010. "From Polanyi to Pollyanna: The false optimism of global labor studies," *Global Labour Journal,* 1:2, 301—313.

———. 1985. *The Politics of Production.* London: Verso.

———. 1979. *Manufacturing Consent: Changes in the Labor Process Under Monopoly Capitalism.* Chicago: University of Chicago Press.

Busch, Gary K. 1983. *The Political Role of International Trade Unions.* London: MacMillan Press Ltd.

Business Standard. 2008. "India call center revenue to touch Rs 8,500 cr.," February 14, http://www.business-standard.com/common/news_article.php?leftnm =8&subLeft=2&chklogin=N&autono=313573&tab=r (accessed February 13, 2008).

BusinessLine. 2008. "Silverline Tech acquires N American contact center in shares swap deal," January 7, http://www.thehindubusinessline.com/blnus/15071604. htm (accessed January 8, 2008).

Callaghan, George, and Paul Thompson. 2002. "We recruit attitude: The selection and shaping of routine call center labor," *Journal of Management Studies*, 39:2, 233–254.

Callcenters.net. 2009a. "Infosys expects to grow on tough times," March 19, email list-serve.

———. 2009b. "Fielding proposes anti-offshoring bill," March 31, email list-serve.

———. 2009c. "Obama announces offshoring blow," May 6, email list-serve.

———. 2009d. "Fair Work Bill has 'significant implications' for contact centers," April 16, email list-serve.

———. 2007a. *Contact Center Industry Benchmarking Report: India*. Sydney: Callcenters.net.

———. 2007b. "Indian BPOs to investigate employees," December 12, e-mail list-serve.

Campbell, David. 2012. "Why call centers no longer ring up big job gains," *Globe and Mail*, March 8, 2012, http://www.theglobeandmail.com/report-on-business/economy/economy-lab/why-call-centres-no-longer-ring-up-big-job-gains/article535838/ (accessed June 26, 2013).

Canadian Customer Contact Center Industry. 2002. *The Canadian Customer Contact Center Landscape: An Industry in Transition*. Canadian Customer Contact Center Industry and Human Resources Development Canada. http://www.contactcentercanada.ca/en/about-the-industry/sector-study.aspx (accessed June 8, 2010).

Canadian Press. 2009. "Union to demonstrate globally against Mexican shipments," March 3, http://proquest.umi.com/pqdweb?index=2&did=1667553421 &SrchMode=2&sid=2&Fmt=3&VInst=PROD&VType=PQD&RQT=309&V Name=PQD&TS=1238614568&clientId=14119 (accessed April 1, 2009).

———. 2008. "American company to create more call center jobs in New Brunswick," *Truro Daily News*, April 14, http://www.trurodaily.com/index. cfm?sid=125909&sc=518 (accessed April 16, 2008).

———. 2006. "Nordia to shut down October 4: 411 call center workers denied equitable severance," August 29.

———. 1999. "Call centre union drive gets nasty," *Cape Breton Post*, October 20.

Caporaso, James A. 1987. "The international division of labor: A theoretical overview." In *A Changing International Division of Labor*, edited by James A. Caporaso, 1–42. Boulder: Lynne Rienner Publishers.

Carmel, Erran, and Paul Tjia. 2005. *Offshoring Information Technology: Sourcing and Outsourcing to a Global Workforce*. Cambridge: Cambridge University Press.

Carroll, Wendy R., and Terry H. Wagar. 2007. *Contact Centers in Canada: Understanding Human Resource Management and Organizational Culture in Contact Centers in Canada*. http://wrcarroll.blogspot.com/ (accessed June 7, 2010).

Cassedy, Ellen, and Karen Nussbaum. 1983. *9 to 5: The Working Woman's Guide to Office Survival*. New York: Penguin Books.

Casselman, George. 2003. "Nordia call-center employees win union representation," *Canadian Press*, January 27.

CBC News. 2008. "Call center industry needs to change, say economists," March 3, http://www.cbc.ca/canada/new-brunswick/story/2008/03/03/nb-callcenter. html (accessed March 4, 2008).

―――. 2007a. "Workers met by locked doors at 2 N.B. call centers," August 29, http://www.cbc.ca/canada/new-brunswick/story/2007/08/29/nb-connectclose. html (accessed August 30, 2012).

―――. 2007b. "Company president blames N.B. for call center closures," September 10, http://www.cbc.ca/canada/new-brunswick/story/2007/09/10/nb-connectblame.html (accessed September 11, 2007).

―――. 2007c. "Moncton call center to shed almost half its workers," October 17, http://www.cbc.ca/canada/new-brunswick/story/2007/10/17/call-center.html (accessed October 19, 2007).

Chakrabarti, Anjan, and Stephen Cullenberg. 2003. *Transition and Development in India.* New York: Routledge.

Chakravartty, Paula. 2008. "Labor in or as civil society? Workers and subaltern publics in India's information society." In *Global Communications: Toward a Transcultural Political Economy,* edited by Paula Chakravartty and Yuezhi Zhao, 1–20. Lanham, MD: Rowman & Littlefield.

―――. 2005. "Weak winners of globalization: Indian H-1B workers in the American information economy," *Asian American Policy Index (AAPI) Nexus,* 3:2, 59–84.

Chakravartty, Paula, and Yuezhi Zhao. 2008. "Introduction: Toward a transcultural political economy of global communications." In *Global Communications: Toward a Transcultural Political Economy,* edited by Paula Chakravartty and Yuezhi Zhao, 285–308. Lanham, MD: Rowman & Littlefield.

Chandler, Alfred D. 1977. *The Visible Hand: The Managerial Revolution in American Business.* Cambridge, MA: Harvard University Press.

Chaturvedi, Anumeha, and Rahul Sachitanand. 2013. "A million engineers in India struggling to get placed in an extremely challenging market," *Economic Times,* June 18, http://articles.economictimes.indiatimes.com/2013–06–18/news/40049243_1_engineers-iit-bombay-batch-size (accessed June 26, 2013).

CIOL Network. 2009. "Trade union says it alerted Govt on Satyam," January 8, http://www.ciol.com/News/News-Reports/Trade-union-says-it-alerted-Govt-on-Satyam/8109114568/0/ (accessed January 12, 2009).

Clawson, Dan. 2010. "'False' optimism: The key historic breakthroughs? A response to Michael Burawoy's 'From Polanyi to Pollyanna: The false optimism of global labour studies'," *Global Labour Journal,* 1:3, 398—400.

―――. 2003. *The Next Upsurge and the New Social Movements.* Ithaca and London: ILR/Cornell University Press.

Clement, Wallace. 1997. "Introduction: Whiter the new Canadian political economy?" In *Understanding Canada: Building on the New Canadian Political Economy,* edited by Wallace Clement, 3–18. Kingston: McGill-Queen's University Press.

Cohen, Laurie, and Amal El-Sawad. 2007. "Lived experiences of offshoring: An examination of UK and Indian financial service employees' accounts of themselves and one another," *Human Relations,* 60:8, 1235–1262.

Conference Board. 2008. *Performance 2008: Productivity, Employment, and Growth in the World's Economies.* New York: Conference Board.

Conference Board of Canada. 2005. *Business Process Offshoring Outsourcing: Will Canadian Businesses Sink or Swim?* Ottawa: Conference Board of Canada.

Contact Center Canada. 2006a. *Customer Contact Centers in Canada: The Impact of Offshoring, Technology and Regulation on Human Resources.* Contact Center Canada and Prism Economics and Analysis.

―――. 2006b. *Contact Centers in Canada—The Competitive Landscape for Pay.* Contact Center Canada and Mercer Human Resource Consulting Limited.

Convergys. n.d. *Convergys Offshore Services: India.* http://www.convergys.com/pdf/factsheets/offshore_india_fact.pdf (accessed June 12, 2007).

Cox, Robert. 1977. "Labor and hegemony," *International Organization*, 31:3, 385–424.

Coyle, Angela. 2010. "Are you in this country? How 'local' social relations can limit the 'globalisation' of customer services supply chains," *Antipode*, 42:2, 289–309.

Crilly, Rob. 2007. "Why Kenya could be world's latest call center capital," *The Times*, December 22, http://business.timesonline.co.uk/tol/business/markets/africa/article3084915.ece (accessed December 22, 2007).

Crozier, Michel, Samuel P. Huntington, and Joji Watanuki. 1975. *The Crisis of Democracy: A Report on the Governability of Democracies to the Trilateral Commission.* New York: New York University Press.

CWA. 2008. "IBM tech workers use technology to fight back," CWA newsletter, February 21.

———. 2007. "Virtual strikers take on IBM in Second Life," CWA newsletter, September 20.

CWA, CEC, JwJ, NTUI, and YPC. 2006. *Bi-national Perspective on Offshore Outsourcing: A Collaboration between Indian and US Labor.*

D'Cruz, P., and E. Noronha. 2006. "Being professional: organizational control in Indian call centers," *Social Science Computer Review*, 24:2, 342–361.

Das, Gucharan. 2006. "The India model," *Foreign Affairs*, 85:4, 2–16.

Dash, Dipak Kumar. 2007. "60% of small call centers to be shut," *The Times of India*, July 4, http://timesofindia.indiatimes.com/India_Business/60_of_small_call_centers_to_be_shut/articleshow/2172679.cms (accessed September 6, 2007).

Datamonitor. 2006. "Selling Canada as a nearshore option," Market series, March.

Davenport, Thomas H. 2005. *Thinking for a Living: How to Get Better Performance and Results from Knowledge Workers.* Boston: Harvard Business School Press.

———. 1993. *Process Innovation: Reengineering Work through Information Technology.* Boston: Harvard Business School Press.

Davenport, Thomas H., and Laurence Prusak. 1998. *Working Knowledge: How Organizations Manage What They Know.* Boston: Harvard Business School Press.

Davies, Matt, and Magnus Ryner, eds. 2006. *Poverty and the Production of World Politics: Unprotected Workers in the Global Political Economy.* New York: Palgrave.

De Bruyn, Tom, and Monique Ramiou. 2006. *Offshore Outsourcing: A Handbook for Employee Representatives and Trade Unionists.* Brussels: Union Network International-Europa. http://www.union-network.org/unisite/sectors/ibits/moos/moos_handbook.htm (accessed July 22, 2008).

Deccan Herald. 2005. "Allow IT women pros to choose work hours," December 19.

Desai, Ashok V. 2007. *India's Telecommunications Industry: History, Analysis, Diagnosis.* New Delhi: Sage Publications.

Deshpande, Satish. 1997. "Unionization in the United States and India: An empirical investigation," *The Journal of Psychology*, 131, 512–518.

Downey, Greg. 2003. "Commentary: The place of labor in the history of information technology revolutions". In *Uncovering Labour in Information Revolutions, 1750—2000*, edited by Aad Blok and Greg Downey, 225—261. New York: Cambridge University Press.

———. 2001. "Virtual webs, physical technologies, and hidden workers: The spaces of labor in information internetworks," *Technology and Culture*, 42, 209–235.

Drucker, Peter. 1959. *Landmarks of Tomorrow.* New York: Harper.

Early, Steve. 2011. *The Civil Wars in U.S. Labor: Birth of a New Workers' Movement or Death Throes of the Old?* Chicago: Haymarket Books.

The Economic Times. 2010. "Nasscom rules out threat from US bill on Indian BPOs," June 4, http://economictimes.indiatimes.com/infotech/ites/Nasscom-rules-out-threat-from-US-bill-on-Indian-BPOs/articleshow/6009328.cms (accessed June 4, 2010).

———. 2009. "Indian BPOs lost 'voice' to Philippines," December 28, http://asterisk.tmcnet.com/news/2009/12/28/4551008.htm (accessed December 29, 2009).

———. 2008a. "BPOs to see major dent in their revenues: TCS likely to suffer the most," September 6.

———. 2008b. "IT-BPO union flays Nasscom stand on layoffs," December 7, http://economictimes.indiatimes.com/Features/The_Sunday_ET/Companies/IT-BPO_union_flays_Nasscom_stand_on_layoffs/articleshow/3803038.cms (accessed December 11, 2008).

———. 2008c. "No meltdown job cuts, assure Tata Consultancy, Infosys," October 30, http://economictimes.indiatimes.com/No_meltdown_job_cuts_assure_TCS_Infosys/articleshow/3655595.cms (accessed October 31, 2008).

The Economist. 2013. "Reshoring manufacturing: Coming home," January 19, http://www.economist.com/news/special-report/21569570-growing-number-american-companies-are-moving-their-manufacturing-back-united (accessed June 28, 2013).

———. 2009. "India's Enron," January 8, http://www.economist.com/business/displaystory.cfm?story_id=12903424&fsrc=rss (accessed January 29, 2009).

———. 2007a. "Rich man, poor man," January 20, 15–16.

———. 2007b. "Hungry tiger, dancing elephant: How India is changing IBM's world," http://www.financialexpress.com/fe_full_story.php?content_id=160489 (accessed April 10, 2007).

———. 2006. "The new titans," September 16, 3–30.

———. 2004. "The thin red line," May 8–14, 40.

EDC (Export Development Canada). 2005. "Ringing in the Profits," *Export Wise,* Winter, 11–16.

Edwards, Richard. 1979. *Contested Terrain: The Transformation of the Workplace in the Twentieth Century.* New York: Basic Books, Inc.

European Foundation for the Improvement of Living and Working Conditions. 2008. *Codes of Conduct and International Framework Agreements: New Forms of Governance at the Company Level.* Dublin.

Evalueserve. 2003. *The Economic Impact of Global Sourcing on the US.* Chappaqua, NY & Gurgaon, India: Nasscom.

Ewen, Stuart. 1976. *Captains of Consciousness: Advertising and the Social Roots of the Consumer Culture.* Toronto: McGraw-Hill Book Company.

Expatica. 2007. "Support for Indian ICT workers," November 12, http://www.expatica.com/actual/article.asp?subchannel_id=24&story_id=45867 (accessed November 14, 2007).

Farrell, Diana, Noshir Kaka, and Sascha Sturze. 2005. "Ensuring India's offshoring future," *The McKinsey Quarterly,* 74–83.

Fernie, Sue, and David Metcalf. 1998. "(Not) hanging on the telephone: Payments systems in the new sweatshops." *Center for Economic Performance,* discussion paper No. 390. London: Center for Economic Performance, London School of Economics.

Fichter, Michael, and Jorg Sydow. 2008. "Organization and regulation of employment relations in transnational production and supply networks: Ensuring core labor standards through international framework agreements?" Revised project proposal submitted to the Hans-Boeckler-Foundation, January 28.

Fine, Ben. 2001. "Neither the Washington nor the post-Washington consensus: An introduction." In *Development Policy in the 21st Century*, edited by Ben Fine, Costas Lapavitsas, and Jonathan Pincus, 1–27. London: Routledge.

Fine, Ben, Costas Lapavitsas, and Jonathan Pincus. 2001. "Preface." In *Development Policy in the 21st Century*, edited by Ben Fine, Costas Lapavitsas, and Jonathan Pincus, x–xvi. London: Routledge.

Fiorito, Jack. 2004. "Union renewal and the organizing model in the United Kingdom," *Labor Studies Journal*, 29:2, 21–53.

Fishman, Charles. 2012. "The insourcing boom," *The Atlantic*, December, http://www.theatlantic.com/magazine/archive/2012/12/the-insourcing-boom/309166/3/?single_page=true (accessed January 27, 2013).

Florida, Richard. 2002. *The Rise of the Creative Class*. New York: Basic Books.

Fonow, Mary Margaret. 2003. *Union Women: Forging Feminism in the United Steelworkers of America*. Minneapolis: University of Minnesota Press.

Fournier, Valerie. 1999. "The appeal to 'professionalism' as a disciplinary mechanism," *The Sociological Review*, 47, 280–307.

Fraser, Don. 2009. "Call center business booming," *The Standard*, January 30, http://www.stcatharinesstandard.ca/ArticleDisplay.aspx?e=1412397 (accessed February 1, 2009).

———. 2008. "Day after closure announcement call center workers still stunned; TRG Customer Solutions closing on July 23," *The Standard*, May 3, http://www.stcatharinesstandard.ca/ArticleDisplay.aspx?e=1012820 (accessed May 4, 2008).

Freeman, Richard B. 2007. "The challenge of the growing globalization of labor markets to economic and social policy." In *Global Capitalism Unbound: Winners and Losers from Offshore Outsourcing*, edited by Eva Paud, 23–40. New York: Palgrave Macmillan.

Frenkel, Stephen J., Marek Korczynski, Karen A. Shire, and May Tam. 1999. *On the Front Line: Organization of Work in the Information Economy*. Ithaca: Cornell University Press.

Friedman, Thomas L. 2005. *The World is Flat: A Brief History of the Twenty-first Century*. New York: Farrar, Straus and Giroux.

Fröbel, Folker, Jurgen Heinrichs, and Otto Kreye. 1980. *The New International Division of Labor*. New York: Cambridge University Press.

Frundt, Henry J. 2005. "Movement theory and international labor solidarity," *Labor Studies Journal*, 30:2, 19–40.

Fukuyama, Francis. 1992. *The End of History and the Last Man*. New York: The Free Press.

Gallin, Dan. 2009. "Interview: Bureaucratism: Labor's enemy within," *Newunionism.net*, October, http://www.newunionism.net/library/organizing/Interview%20-%20Dan%20Gallin%20-%202009.htm (accessed October 18, 2009).

Garson, Barbara. 1988. *The Electronic Sweatshop: How Computers are Transforming the Office of the Future into the Factory of the Past*. New York: Penguin Books.

Goldfarb, Danielle, and Louis Theriault. 2008. *Canada's "Missing" Trade with Asia*. Ottawa: Conference Board of Canada.

Government of Canada. 2008. *Compete to Win: Final Report*, Competition Policy Review Panel, June. Ottawa: Industry Canada.

Government of India. 2008. "Agriculture, rural development, industry, services and physical infrastructure." *11th Five Year Plan 2007–2012*. vol. 3. New Delhi: Planning Commission, http://planningcommission.nic.in/plans/planrel/fiveyr/welcome.html (accessed May 21, 2010).

———. 2002. "Sectoral Policies and Programmes." *10th Five Year Plan 2002–2007*. vol. 2. New Delhi: Planning Commission, http://planningcommission.nic.in/plans/planrel/fiveyr/welcome.html (accessed May 21, 2010).

———. 2001. *Report of the working group on information technology for the formulation of the Tenth Five Year Plan*. New Delhi: Government of India.

Government of Maharashtra. 2003. "IT and ITES policy, 2003." Industries, Energy & Labor Department, Government resolution. No. ITP-2003/CR3311/IND-7, December 7.

Gramsci, Antonio. 1971. *Selections From the Prison Notebooks*. New York: International Publishers.

Grose, Thomas K. 2008. "Big labor goes global," *Time*, July 1, http://www.time.com/time/business/article/0,8599,1819380,00.html (accessed July 3, 2008).

Guard, Julie. 2006. *Training Unemployed Manitobans for Call Centers: A Good Public Investment?* Ottawa: Canadian Center for Policy Alternatives.

———. 2003. *Manitoba's Call Center Explosion: A Preliminary Overview*. Toronto: United Steelworkers.

Guard, Julie, Jorge Garcia-Orgales, and Mercedes Steedman. 2006. "Turning points: Call center workers organize," *Our Times*, August–September, 30–35.

Guard, Julie, Jorge Garcia-Orgales, Mercedes Steedman, and D'Arcy Martin. 2006. "Organizing call centers: The Steelworkers' experience." In *Paths to Union Renewal: Canadian Experiences*, edited by Pradeep Kumar and Christopher Schenk, 277–292. Peterborough, ON: Broadview Press.

Guard, Julie, Mercedes Steedman, and Jorge Garcia-Orgales. 2007. "Organizing the electronic sweatshop: Rank-and-file participation in Canada's steel union," *Labor: Studies in Working-Class History of the Americas*, 4:3, 9–31.

Ha, Tu Thanh. 2013. "New Delhi rape victim worked at phone center fielding calls from Canada," *The Globe and Mail*, January 8, http://www.theglobeandmail.com/news/world/new-delhi-rape-victim-worked-at-phone-centre-fielding-calls-from-canada/article7032468/ (accessed May 24, 2013).

Hammer, Michael, and James Champy. 2003. *Reengineering the Corporation: A Manifesto for Business Revolution*. New York: Harper Business.

Harvey, David. 2006a. *Spaces of Global Capitalism: Towards a Theory of Uneven Geographical Development*. New York: Verso.

———. 2006b. *Limits to Capital*. New York: Verso.

———. 2005a. *A Brief History of Neoliberalism*. Oxford: Oxford University Press.

———. 2005b. *The New Imperialism*. New York: Oxford University Press.

———. 1990. *The Condition of Postmodernity*. Cambridge: Blackwell.

Head, Simon. 2003. *The New Ruthless Economy: Work and Power in the Digital Age*. New York: Oxford University Press.

Heckscher, Eli F., and Bertil Ohlin. 1991. *Heckscher-Ohlin Trade Theory*. Cambridge, MA: MIT Press.

Hensman, Rohini. 2011. *Workers, Unions, and Global Capitalism*. New York: Columbia University Press.

Herod, Andrew. 2001. "Labor internationalism and the contradictions of globalization: Or, why the local is sometimes still important in a global economy," *Antipode*, 33:3, 407–426.

Hill, Elizabeth. 2009. "The Indian industrial relations system: Struggling to address the dynamics of a globalizing economy," *Journal of Industrial Relations*, 51:3, 395–410.

The Hindu. 2006. "BPO call centers to come up in rural areas soon," January 31, http://www.hindu.com/2006/01/31/stories/2006013117620300.htm (accessed August 30, 2007).

———. 2005. "BPO employees' union to be affiliated to INTUC," December 24.

Hirschefeld, Karin. 2005. *IT Professionals Forum in India: Organization at a Crossroads: Report on a Visit to IT Professionals Forums in February 2005*. Nyon: Union Network International.

Hirschman, Albert O. 1945. *National Power and the Structure of Foreign Trade.* Berkeley: University of California Press.

Hochschild, Arlie. 1983. *The Managed Heart: The Commercialization of Human Feeling.* Berkeley: University of California Press.

Holecek, Andrea. 2008. "Steelworkers step toward 'global union,'" *Nwi.com,* June 27, http://www.thetimesonline.com/articles/2008/06/27/updates/breaking_news/doc4865351842301181203885.txt (accessed June 28, 2008).

Holman, David. 2005. "Call centers." In *The Essentials of the New Workplace: A Guide to the Human Impact of Modern Working Practices,* edited by David Holman, Toby D. Wall, Chris W. Clegg, and Ann Howard, 111–131. West Sussex, UK: John Wiley & Sons, Ltd.

Holman, David, Rosemary Batt, and Ursula Holtgrewe. 2007. *The Global Call Center Report: International Perspective on Management and Employment.* Global Call Center Project.

Horowitz, Robert Britt. 1989. *The Irony of Regulatory Reform: The Deregulation of American Telecommunications.* New York: Oxford University Press.

Houseman, Susan. 2007. "Outsourcing, offshoring and productivity measurement in United States manufacturing," *International Labor Review,* 146:1/2, 61–80.

HRSDC see Human Resource and Skills Development Canada.

Huffington Post. 2012. "Temporary foreign workers: 18 of 50 largest Canadian employers using them," April 12, http://www.huffingtonpost.ca/2013/04/12/temporary-foreign-workers_n_3064389.html (accessed May 27, 2013).

Human Resource and Skills Development Canada. 2009. "Work-unionization rates," http://www4.hrsdc.gc.ca/.3ndic.1t.4r@-eng.jsp?iid=17 (accessed October 19, 2010).

Hunt, David, James Manyika, and Jaana Remes. 2011. "Why US productivity can grow without killing jobs," *McKinsey Quarterly,* February.

Huws, Ursula. 2009. "Working at the interface: Call-center labor in a global economy," *Work Organisation, Labor & Globalisation,* 3:1, 1–8.

———. 2003. *The Making of a Cybertariat: Virtual Work in a Real World.* New York: Monthly Review Press.

IANS. 2013. "IT imports will be worth $400 billion in 2020," *Yahoo.com,* February 20, http://in.news.yahoo.com/imports-worth-400-billion-2020-103806947—finance.html (accessed May 28, 2013).

IAOP (International Association of Outsourcing Professionals). 2012. "The 2012 global outsourcing 100," http://www.iaop.org/content/19/165/3437 (accessed May 27, 2013).

———. 2010. "The 2010 global outsourcing 100," http://www.iaop.org/content/23/152/2040/ (accessed March 17, 2011).

———. 2009. "The 2009 global outsourcing 100," http://www.iaop.org/content/23/152/1197/ (accessed March 17, 2011).

IBNLive. 2011. "Outsourcing health data to Indian call center," January 4, http://ibnlive.in.com/news/outsourcing-health-data-to-indian-call-center/139429-3.html (accessed January 5, 2011).

———. 2006. "Sting op may spell doom for BPOs," October 4, http://www.ibnlive.com/news/thursday-could-spell-doom-for-call-centers-in-india/23165-7.html (accessed September 3, 2007).

ILO see International Labour Organization.

International Labour Organization (2008) *World of Work: The Magazine of the ILO,* No. 62. Geneva: International Labour Office.

The Indian Express. 2005a. "Bangalore rape prompts police chief to meet BPO heads," December 23.

———. 2005b. "Industry meet in January to formalize code of conduct," December 23.

Industry Canada. 2013. "Canadian ICT sector profile," March 13, http://www.
ic.gc.ca/eic/site/ict-tic.nsf/eng/h_it07229.html (accessed June 26, 2013).
International Monetary Fund. 2010. *World Economic Outlook Database*, October. http://www.imf.org/external/pubs/ft/weo/2010/02/weodata/index.aspx
(accessed January 14, 2011).
ITPF (I.T. Professionals Forum). n.d. ITPF website. http://www.itpfindia.org/india/
index.php?option=com_content&task=view&id=16&Itemid=32 (accessed
November 30, 2009).
Iype, George. 2005. "Does the IT industry need a trade union?" *Rediff*, October 6,
http://www.rediff.com/money/2005/oct/06bspec.htm (accessed September 17,
2007).
Jackson, Andrew. 2004. "Forum: Reorganizing unions—Solidarity forever? Trends
in Canadian union density." *Studies in Political Economy*, 74, 125–146.
Jessop, Bob. 1993. "Towards a Schumpeterian Welfare State? Preliminary
remarks on a post-Fordist political economy," *Studies in Political Economy*,
40, 6–39.
Jin, Dal Yong. 2008. "Neoliberal restructuring of the global communication system: Mergers and acquisitions," *Media, Culture & Society*, 30:3, 357–373.
———. 2007. "Transformation of the world television system under neoliberal globalization, 1983–2003," *Television & New Media*, 8:3, 179–196.
Jomo, K.S., and Rudiger von Arnim. 2008. "Trade liberalisation for development? Who gains? Who loses?" *Economic and Political Weekly*, November 29,
11–12.
Kanellos, Michael. 2005. "India's tech renaissance," *CNET News.com*, June
28–30, http://news.cnet.com/Indias-renaissance-Move-over,-China/2009-
1041_3-5751994.html (accessed August 27, 2013).
Kapur, Devesh, and Ravi Ramamurity. 2001. "India's emerging competitive advantage in services," *Academy of Management Executive*, 15:2, 20–33.
Katz, Harry C. 1997. "Introduction and comparative overview." In *Telecommunications: Restructuring Work and Employment Relations Worldwide*, edited by
Harry C. Katz, 1–28. Ithaca and London: ILR Press.
Katz, Harry C., Rosemary Batt, and Jeffrey H. Keefe. 2003. "The revitalization of
the CWA: Integrating collective bargaining, political action, and organizing,"
Industrial and Labor Relations Review, 56:4, 573–589.
Kazmin, Amy. 2009. "Vulnerable IT workers find comfort in union," *Financial
Times*, February 12, http://www.ft.com/cms/s/0/1a6cdb42-f92d-11dd-ab7f-
000077b07658.html?nclick_check=1 (accessed February 15, 2009).
Keller, Berndt. 2005. "Union formation through merger: The case of Ver.di in Ger-
many," *British Journal of Industrial Relations*, 43:2, 209–232.
Kelly, John. 1998. *Rethinking Industrial Relations: Mobilization, Collectivism
and Long Waves*. Routledge: London.
Kiely, Ray. 2007. *The New Political Economy of Development: Globalization,
Imperialism, Hegemony*. New York: Palgrave Macmillan.
Kirkegaard, Jacob F. 2004. "Outsourcing: stains on the white collar?" CESifo
Forum. Washington, D.C.: Institute for International Economics.
Kleinman, Mark. 2008. "Unite set for historic US merger with United Steel-
workers," *The Telegraph*, May 26, http://www.telegraph.co.uk/money/main.
jhtml?xml=/money/2008/05/25/cnunite125.xml (accessed May 26, 2008).
Koshy, George. 2008. "Did govt force Jet to take back staff?" http://content.ibn-
live.in.com/article/17-Oct-2008business/did-govt-force-jet-to-take-back-staff—
goyal-sorry-76049–7.html (accessed June 28, 2013).
Kozolanka, Kristen. 2006. "Taming labor in neo-liberal Ontario: Oppositional
political communication in a time of 'crisis,'" *Canadian Journal of Communication*, 31:3, 561–580.

Krishna, Sankaran. 2005. "India: Globalisation and IT development," *South Asian Journal*, April–June, http://www.southasianmedia.net/magazine/journal/8_it_development.htm (accessed August 5, 2009).

Krishnan, Sruthi. 2009. "Bonds restrict job options," *The Hindu*, August 31, http://www.thehindu.com/2009/08/31/stories/2009083154780500.htm (accessed September 13, 2009).

Kulkarni, Vishwanath. 2008. "Convergys plans to enter Indian call center market," *Livemint.com*, May 5, http://www.livemint.com/2008/05/05222939/Convergys-plans-to-enter-India.html (accessed May 7, 2008).

Kumar, Anil. 2009. "IT companies free of labor laws for 2 years," http://www.bpovoice.com/profiles/blogs/labor-law-holiday-for-it (accessed June 6, 2013).

Kumar, Pradeep, and Christopher Schenk, eds. 2006a. *Paths to Union Renewal: Canadian Experience*. Calgary: Broadview Press.

———. 2006b. "Introduction." In *Paths to Union Renewal: Canadian Experiences*, edited by Pradeep Kumar and Christopher Schenk, 15–26. Peterborough: Broadview Press.

Kumra, Gautam, and Jayant Sinha. 2003. "The next hurdle for Indian IT," *2003 Special Edition: Global Directions, The McKinsey Quarterly*, 43–53.

Kuruvilla, Sarosh and Aruna Ranganathan. 2010. "Globalisation and outsourcing: Confronting new human resource challenges in India's business process outsourcing industry", *Industrial Relations Journal*, 41:2, 136–153.

Lakha, Salim. 1994. "The new international division of labour and the Indian computer software industry," *Modern Asian Studies*, 28:2, 381–408.

Lambert, Rob, and Eddie Webster. 2001. "Southern unionism and the new labor internationalism," *Antipode*, 33:3, 337–362.

Larner, Wendy. 2002a. "Calling capital: Call center strategies in New Brunswick and New Zealand," *Global Networks*, 2:2, 133–152.

———. 2002b. "Globalization, governmentality and expertise: Creating a call center labor force," *Review of International Political Economy*, 9:4, 650–674.

Lash, Scott, and John Urry. 1987. *The End of Organized Capitalism*. Cambridge: Polity Press.

Leadbeater, David ed. 2008. *Mining Town Crisis: Globalization, Labour and Resistance in Sudbury*. Halifax and Winnipeg: Fernwood Publishing.

Le Goff, Philippe. 2005. *Canada and Offshoring*. Ottawa: Library of Parliament.

Lefebvre, Henri. 1979. "Space: Social product and use value." In *Critical Sociology: European Perspectives*, edited by J.W. Frieberg, 285–296. New York: Irvington Publishers, Inc.

Leidner, Robin. 1993. *Fast Food, Fast Talk*. Berkeley: University of California Press.

Lerner, Daniel. 1967. *Communication and Change in the Developing Countries*. Honolulu: University of Hawaii.

Liker, Jeffery. 2004. *The Toyota Way*. New York: McGraw-Hill.

Lipietz, Alain. 1987. *Mirages and Miracles: The Crisis of Global Fordism*. London: Verso.

Lipset, Seymour Martin, Martin Trow, and James Coleman. 1956. *Union Democracy*. New York: Anchor Books.

Logan, John. 2002. "How 'anti-union' laws saved Canadian labor: Certification and striker replacements in post-War industrial relations', *Relations industrielle/Industrial Relations*, 57:1, 129–156.

Lyon, David. 2001. *Surveillance Society: Monitoring Everyday Life*. Buckingham, UK: Open University Press.

Lyon, David, and Elia Zureik, eds. 1996. *Computers, Surveillance, and Privacy*. Minneapolis: University of Minnesota Press.

Macaraig, Mynardo. 2010. "Philippines overtakes India as call centre capital," December 6, http://www.google.com/hostednews/afp/article/ALeqM5hyVa3Jh OVmfCSvjOS9oM5AX8nw9Q?docId=CNG.3c86e1065eee2cfd740284f4a84f3 555.01 (accessed December 8, 2010).

Machlup, Fritz. 1980. *Knowledge: Its Creation, Distribution, and Economic Significance. Vol. 1: Knowledge and Knowledge Production.* Princeton: Princeton University Press.

———. 1962. *The Production and Distribution of Knowledge in the United States.* Princeton: Princeton University Press.

Mah, Bill. 2008. "140 city jobs lost at TD call center," *Edmonton Journal,* February 28, http://www.canada.com/edmontonjournal/news/story.html?id=9d7f0840-d471-4d23-a762-f64728b2accf (accessed February 29, 2008).

Mahalingam, T.V. 2009. "Where dreams end . . . and nightmares begin," *Outlook Business,* June 27, 47–57.

Majluf, Luis Abugattas. 2007. "Offshore outsourcing of services: Trends and challenges for developing countries." In *Global Capitalism Unbound: Winners and Losers from Offshore Outsourcing,* edited by Eva Paud, 147–162. New York: Palgrave Macmillan.

Martin Prosperity Institute. 2009. *Ontario in the Creative Age.* Toronto: Martin Prosperity Institute, University of Toronto.

Martin, Stana. 2002. "The political economy of women's employment in the information sector." In *Sex & Money: Feminism and Political Economy in the Media,* edited by Eileen R. Meehan and Ellen Riordan, 75–87. Minneapolis: University of Minnesota Press.

Marshall, Judith, and Jorge Garcia-Orgales. 2006. "Building capacity for global action: Steelworkers' Humanity Fund." In *Paths to Union Renewal: Canadian Experiences,* edited by Pradeep Kumar and Christopher Schenk, 221–234. Peterborough: Broadview Press.

Marx, Karl. 1967. *Capital.* Vol. 1. New York: International Publishers.

Mattelart, Armand. 2003. *The Information Society: An Introduction.* Thousand Oaks: Sage Publications.

Mayer-Ahuja, Nicole, and Patrick Feuerstein. 2007. *IT-labor Goes Offshore: Regulating and Managing Attrition in Bangalore.* Gottingen, Germany: SOFI Working Paper.

Mazurkewich, Karen. 2008. "India's tech giants climb the corporate food chain," *Financial Post,* April 24, http://www.financialpost.com/story.html?id=469384 (accessed April 28, 2008).

McCarthy, John. 2002. "3.3 million U.S. service jobs go offshore". *Trends,* November 11. Cambridge, Mass: Forrester Research.

McChesney, Robert W. 2007. *Communication Revolution: Critical Junctures and the Future of Media.* New York: New Press.

———. 1999. *Rich Media, Poor Democracy: Communication Politics in Dubious Times.* Urbana: University of Illinois Press.

McFarland, Joan. 2002. "Call centers in New Brunswick: Maquiladoras of the North?" *Canadian Woman Studies,* 21/22:4/1.

McKercher, Catherine. 2002. *Newsworkers Unite: Labor, Convergence, and North American Newspapers.* Lanham: Rowman & Littlefield.

McKinsey Global Institute. 2003. *New Horizons: Multinational Company Investment in Developing Economies.* McKinsey Global Institute.

McMillin, Divya C. 2006. "Outsourcing identities: Call centers and cultural transformation in India," *Economic and Political Weekly,* January 21, 235–241.

McNally, David. 2009. "From financial crisis to world-slump: Accumulation, financialisation, and the global slowdown," *Historical Materialism,* 17, 35–83.

Metal Producing & Processing. 2008. "USW goes global in merger of unions," July 6, http://www.metalproducing.com/frontpage/news/81190/usw_goes_global_in_merger_of_unions (accessed July 8, 2008).

Mirchandani, Kiran. 2012. *Phone Clones: Authenticity Work in the Transnational Service Economy*. Ithaca: Cornell University Press.

———. 2005. "Gender eclipsed? Racial hierarchies in transnational call center work," *Social Justice*, 32:4, 105–119.

———. 2004a. "Practices of global capital: Gaps, cracks and ironies in transnational call centers India," *Global Networks*, 4:4, 355–374.

———. 2004b. "Webs of resistance in transnational call center: Strategic agents, service providers and customers." In *Identity Politics at Work: Resisting Gender, Gendering Resistance*, edited by Robyn Thomas, Albert J. Mills, and Jean Helms Mills, 179–195. London and New York: Routledge.

Mishra, Bibhu Ranjan. 2008. "IT-BPO union to file PIL against 'extended' working hours," *Rediff.com*, November 26, http://www.rediff.com/money/2008/nov/26bpo-it-bpo-union-to-file-pil-against-working-hours.htm (accessed November 30, 2008).

Mishra, Dipak. 2008. "1st rural BPO of north India in Saurath," *The Times of India*, August 22, http://timesofindia.indiatimes.com/Cities/Patna/1st_rural_BPO_of_north_India_in_Saurath/articleshow/3391233.cms (accessed August 22, 2008).

Mishra, Pankaj. 2009. "The nightmare has just begun," *The Economic Times*, January 27.

Mittelman, James H. 1995. "Rethinking the international division of labour in the context of globalization," *Third World Quarterly*, 16:2, 273–295.

Mohandas, Poornima. 2008. "Sporadic legal battles point to labor issues in IT, BPO sectors," *Livemint.com*, September 11, http://www.livemint.com/2008/09/11001323/Sporadic-legal-battles-point-t.html?d=1 (accessed October 21, 2008).

Moll, Marita, and Leslie Regan Shade, eds. 2008. *For Sale to the Highest Bidder: Telecom Policy in Canada*. Ottawa: Canadian Center for Policy Alternatives.

Moneycontrol.com. 2006. "Biggies line up for Railways call centers," August 26, http://www.moneycontrol.com/india/news/business/ittelecomindustry/biggies-lineforrailwayscallcenters/market/stocks/article/236637 (accessed September 3, 2007).

Monga, Deepshikha, and Harsimran Singh. 2007. "2008 will be a crucial year for the BPO industry," *The Economic Times*, December 31, http://economictimes.indiatimes.com/Corporate_Trends/Tough_call_for_BPOs/articleshow/2663068.cms (accessed January 3, 2008).

MOOS. 2007. "Third MOOS workshop," January 12, http://www.union-network.org/unisite/sectors/ibits/moos/newsletter.htm (accessed July 22, 2008).

———. 2006a. "Second MOOS workshop," April 24, http://www.union-network.org/unisite/sectors/ibits/moos/newsletter.htm (accessed July 22, 2008).

———. 2006b. "Third MOOS workshop," April 31, http://www.union-network.org/unisite/sectors/ibits/moos/newsletter.htm (accessed July 22, 2008).

Morgan, Kevin, and Andrew Sayer. 1988. *Microcircuits of Capital: 'Sunrise' Industry and Uneven Development*. Cambridge: Polity Press.

Morisette, Rene, and Anick Johnson. 2007. *Offshoring and Employment in Canada: Some Basic Facts*. Ottawa: Statistics Canada.

Morisette, Rene, Grant Schellenberg, and Anick Johnson. 2005. "Diverging trends in unionization," *Perspectives on Labor and Income*, April, 5–12. Ottawa: Statistics Canada.

Morris, Chris. 2007. "Experts say loss of N.B. call centers highlights transient nature of industry," *Canada East Online*, August 30, http://www.canadaeast.com/news/article/62294 (accessed August 31, 2007).

Mosco, Vincent. 2009. *Political Economy of Communication.* 2nd ed. Thousand Oaks: Sage Publications.

———. 2004. *The Digital Sublime: Myth, Power, and Cyberspace.* Cambridge: MIT Press.

———. 1988. "Introduction: Information in the pay-per society". In *The Political Economy of Information,* edited by Vincent Mosco and Janet Wasko, 3–26. Madison: The University of Wisconsin Press.

———. 1982. *Pushbutton Fantasies: Critical Perspectives on Videotex and Information Technology.* Norwood, NJ: Ablex Publishing Corporation.

Mosco, Vincent, and Andrew Stevens. 2007. "Outsourcing knowledge jobs: Workers respond to the new international division of labor." In *Knowledge Workers in the Information Society,* edited by Catherine McKercher and Vincent Mosco, 147–162. Lanham: Lexington Books.

Mosco, Vincent, and Catherine McKercher. 2008. *The Laboring of Communication: Will Knowledge Workers of the World Unite?* Lanham, MD: Lexington Books.

———, eds. 2006. *Canadian Journal of Communication,* 31:3.

Mosco, Vincent, Catherine McKercher, and Andrew Stevens. 2008. "Convergences: Elements of a feminist political economy of labor and communication". In *Feminist Interventions in International Communication,* edited by Katharine Sarikakis and Leslie Regan Shade, 207–223. Lanham: Rowman & Littlefield.

Mosco, Vincent, and Dan Schiller, eds. 2001. *Continental Order? Integrating North America for Cybercapitalism.* New York: Rowman and Littlefield.

Mosco, Vincent, and David O. Lavin. 2008. "The laboring of international communication." In *Internationalizing Media Studies,* edited by Daya Thussu, 148–162. London: Routledge.

Mulholland, Kate. 2004. "Workplace resistance in an Irish call center," *Work, Employment & Society,* 18:4, 709–724.

Mytelka, Lynn Krieger. 1987. "Knowledge-intensive production and the changing internationalization strategies of multinational firms." In *A Changing International Division of Labor,* edited by James A. Caporaso, 1–42. Boulder: Lynne Rienner Publishers.

Nanda, Meera. 2011. *The God Market: How Globalization is Making India more Hindu.* New York: Monthly Review Press.

Nandy, Debopriya. 2008. "Major IT firms expected to announce job losses," *ITExaminer.com,* September, 17, http://www.itexaminer.com/major-it-firms-expected-to-announce-job-losses.aspx (accessed November 30, 2008).

Narasimhan, Laxman. 2011. "Can India lead the mobile-Internet revolution?" *McKinsey Quarterly,* February.

Narasimhan, T.E. 2008. "BPOs make a mark in former Naxal land," *Business Standard,* June 16, http://www.business-standard.com/common/news_article. php?leftnm=lmnu9&subLeft=&autono=326149&tab=r (accessed June 16, 2008).

Nasscom. 2013. *Annual Report 2012–2013.* Delhi: Nasscom.

———. 2009. "Executive summary," *Nasscom Strategic Review 2009,* 5–10. Delhi: Nasscom.

———. 2008a. *Indian IT/ITES Industry: Impacting Economy and Society 2007–08.* New Delhi: National Association of Software and Services Companies.

———. 2008b. *Executive Summary: 2008.* New Delhi: Nasscom.

———. 2008c. "NASSCOM Announces Roadmap for FY 2009," http://www. nasscom.in/Nasscom/templates/NormalPage.aspx?id=53718 (accessed October 24, 2008).

———. 2006. "Global Contact Center Evolution," *Market Intelligence Service*, 65, 1–24.

———. 2004. *Nasscom Handbook of the Indian ITES-BPO Industry: Background and Reference Resource-2004*. New Delhi: Nasscom.

Nathan, Dev. 2007. "Globalisation of labor," *Economic and Political Weekly*, September 29, 3995–4001.

National Foundation for American Policy. 2007. "Anti-outsourcing efforts down but not out," NFAP Policy Brief, April. National Foundation for American Policy.

Nilekani, Nandan M. 2008. "Sourcing without borders: Sourcing in a flattening world." In *Building a Future with BRICs: The Next Decade for Offshoring*, edited by Mark Kobayashi-Hillary, 117–131. London: Springer.

Nixon, Gordon. 2013. "RBC CEO Gord Nixon's open letter," *CBC News*, April 11, http://www.cbc.ca/news/canada/story/2013/04/11/rbc-gord-nixon-apology-letter.html (accessed May 24, 2013).

Norling, Per. 2001. "Call center companies and new patterns of organization," *Economic and Industrial Democracy*, 22, 155–168.

Noronha, Ernesto, and Premilla D'Cruz. 2009. "Engaging the professional: Organising call center agents in India," *Industrial Relations Journal*, 40:3, 215–234.

———. 2006. "Organizing Call Center Agents: Emerging Issues," *Economic and Political Weekly*, May 27, 2115–2121.

Nuttall, Jeremy. 2013. "Unions threaten to pull billions out of RBC," *Canoe.ca*, April 18, http://www.canoe.ca/Canoe/Money/News/2013/04/18/20751756.html (accessed May 24, 2013).

O'Flanagan, Rob. 1999. "Union seeks quick deal with Omega," *Sudbury Star*, A2.

OECD. 2009. *Guide to Measuring the Information Society, 2009*. Paris: Organization for Economic Cooperation and Development.

———. 2007. *Offshoring and Employment: Trends and Impacts*. Paris: Organization for Economic Cooperation and Development.

———. 2006a. "The share of employment potentially affected by offshoring: An empirical investigation," Working Party on the Information Society, Directorate for Science, Technology and Industry, February 23. Paris: Organization for Economic Cooperation and Development.

———. 2006b. "Potential impacts of international sourcing on different occupations," Working Party on the Information Society, Directorate for Science, Technology and Industry, October 19. Paris: Organization for Economic Cooperation and Development.

———. 2000. *The OECD Guidelines for Multinational Enterprises*. Paris: Organization for Economic Cooperation and Development.

Olive, David. 2007. "The nerve of David Dodge," *Toronto Star*, April 27, http://www.thestar.com/business/article/207808 (accessed May 14, 2010).

Pandit, Ranjit V. 2005. "Why believe in India: 2005 special edition: Fulfilling India's Promise, *The McKinsey Quarterly*, 133–139.

Pandit, Vivek, and Rajesh Srinivasaraghavan. 2008. "A fresh wind for offshoring infrastructure management," October, *The McKinsey Quarterly*.

Paranjoy, Guha Thakurta, and Akshat Kaushal. 2010. "Underbelly of the Great Indian telecom revolution," *Economic and Political Weekly*, December 4, 49–55.

Parthasarathi, Vibodh, ed. 2007. *Beneath IT: Formations of Industry, Work & Labour in the Information Technology Sector*: New Delhi: Center for Culture, Media & Governance and Center for Jawaharlal Nehru Studies, Jamia Millia Islamia.

Paul, Shamik. 2009. "Dish it out differently," *Business Line*, June 15, http://www. thehindubusinessline.com/todays-paper/tp-eworld/dish-it-out-differently/article1084343.ece?ref=archive (accessed August 23, 2013).

Paus, Eva. 2007. "Winners and losers from offshore outsourcing: What is to be done?" In *Global Capitalism Unbound: Winners and Losers from Offshore Outsourcing*, edited by Eva Paud, 3–20. New York: Palgrave Macmillan.

Paus, Eva, and Helen Shapiro. 2007. "Capturing the benefits from offshore outsourcing in developing countries: The case for active policies." In *Global Capitalism Unbound: Winners and Losers from Offshore Outsourcing*, edited by Eva Paud, 215–228. New York: Palgrave Macmillan.

Pawar, Rajendra S. 2008. "Indian offshoring: Building sustainable excellence." In *Building a Future with BRICs: The Next Decade for Offshoring*, edited by Mark Kobayashi-Hillary, 147–159. London: Springer.

Pearce, Frank, and Steve Tombs. 1998. *Toxic Capitalism: Corporate Crime and the Chemical Industry*. Brookfield: Ashgate.

Peet, Richard. 1989. "Part III: Introduction." In *New Models in Geography*, Vol. 1, edited by Richard Peet and Nigel Thrift, 105–114. London: Unwin Hyman.

Pilon, Claire. 2003. "Call center workers hit Toronto stage," *Sudbury Star*, October 1, B7.

Piore, Michael, and Charles Sabel. 1984. *The Second Industrial Divide*. New York: Basic Books.

Polanyi, Karl. 1944. *The Great Transformation*. Boston: Beacon Press.

Porat, Marc Uri. 1977. *The Information Economy: Definition and Measurement*. Washington, DC. US Department of Commerce, Office of Telecommunications, May.

Poster, Winifred R. 2007. "Who's on the line? Indian call center agents pose as Americans for US-outsourced firms," *Industrial Relations*, 46:2, 271–304.

Power, Bill. 2009. "Town: closing hurts," *ChronicleHerald.ca*, October 17, http://thechronicleherald.ca/Business/1148049.html (accessed October 19, 2009).

Prasad, Anshuman. 2003. "The gaze of the other: Postcolonial theory and organisational analysis." In *Postcolonial Theory and Organisational Analysis*, edited by Anshuman Prasad, 3–43. London: Palgrave.

Prasad, Kiran. 2009a. *Communication for Development: Reinventing Theory and Action. Vol. 1: Understanding Development Communication*. Delhi: B.R. Publishing Corporation.

———. 2009b. *Communication for Development: Reinventing Theory and Action. Vol. 2: Advanced Development Communication*. Delhi: B.R. Publishing Corporation.

Pratap, Surendra. 2010. "Challenges for organizing the BPO workers in India," *Asian Labor Update*, 76, 36–40.

Rajan, Raghuram G. and Shang-jin Wei. 2004. "The non-threat that is outsourcing," *The Business Times*, June 8, http://users.nber.org/~wei/data/rajan&wei2004/rajan&wei2004.pdf (accessed August 23, 2013).

Rajeev, Meenakshi, and B.P. Vani. 2007. "Chapter 10: BPO industry from the employee's perspective." In *India's Export of Selected BPO Services: Understanding Strengths and Weaknesses*, Research report No. ECO/76. Bangalore: Institute for Social and Economic Change.

Rajghatta, Chidanand. 2011. "Indian book of jobs in US: 60,000 and adding," *The Times of India*, March 31, http://articles.timesofindia.indiatimes.com/2011-03-31/india-business/29365829_1_indian-businesses-indian-companies-jobs (accessed April 8, 2011).

Ramamurti, Ravi. 2001. "Finance Minister Yashwant Sinha on India's changing role in the world economy," *Academy of Management Executive*, 15:2, 8–12.

Ramaswamy, E.A. 1985. "Managerial trade unions," *Economic and Political Weekly*, 20: 21, M75–M88.
———. 1977. *The Worker and His Union: A Study in South India*. Bombay: Allied Publishers.
Rampell, Catherine. 2010. "Corporate profits were the highest on record last quarter," *New York Times*, November 23, http://www.nytimes.com/2010/11/24/business/economy/24econ.html?_r=1 (accessed March 3, 2011).
Ranger, Steve. 2006. "Offshore outsourcing upstarts bite at India's heels," *silicon. com*, June 7, http://services.silicon.com/offshoring/0,3800004877,39159364,0 0.htm (accessed September 3, 2007).
Remesh, Babu P. 2004a. *Labor in Business Process Outsourcing: A Case Study of Call Center Agents*. New Delhi: V.V. Giri National Labor Institute.
———. 2004b. "'Cyber coolies' in BPO: Insecurities and vulnerabilities of non-standard work," *Economic and Political Weekly*, January 31, 492–497.
Remesh, Babu P., and N. Neetha. 2008. "Gender implications of outsourced work in the new economy: A case study of domestic call centers," *The Indian Journal of Labor Economics*, 51:4, 717–730.
Reuters. 2009. "Stan Chartered may double India call-center staff," April 27, http://in.reuters.com/article/domesticNews/idINBOM44272120090427 (accessed April 28, 2009).
Ribeiro, John. 2008. "Job cuts in India's call centers and BPO likely," *Network World*, October 29, http://www.networkworld.com/news/2008/102908-job-cuts-in-indias-call.html (accessed November 30, 2008).
Ricardo, David. 1911. *The Principles of Political Economy and Taxation*. London & New York: Everyman's Library.
Riddell, Chris. 2004. "Union certification success under voting versus card-check procedures: Evidence from British Columbia, 1978–1998," *Industrial and Labor Relations Review*, 57:4, 493–517.
Rideout, Vanda. 2002. *Continentalizing Canadian Telecommunications: The Politics of Regulatory Reform*. Montreal: McGill-Queen's University Press.
Rifkin, Jeremy. 1996. *The End of Work: The Decline of the Global Labor Force and the Dawn of the Post-market Era*. New York: G.P. Putnam's.
Riisgaard, Lone. 2005. "International framework agreements: A new model for securing workers rights?" *Industrial Relations*, 44:4, 707–737.
Rodrik, Dani, and Arvind Subramanian. 2001. "From 'Hindu Growth' to productivity surge: The mystery of the Indian growth transition." IMF Working Paper, 04/77. Washington, D.C.: International Monetary Fund.
Roseman, Ellen. n.d. "Straight talk on personal finance and consumer issues," personal blog, http://www.ellenroseman.com/?p=95#comments (accessed August 1, 2010).
———. 2008. "TD clients rerouted to India call center," *The Star.com*, January 16, http://www.thestar.com/columnists/article/294386 (accessed January 17, 2008).
Roychowdhury, Supriya. 2003. "Public sector restructuring and democracy: The state, labor and trade unions in India," *The Journal of Development Studies*, 39:3, 29–50.
Rule, James B. 1996. "High-tech workplace surveillance: What's really new?" In *Computers, Surveillance, and Privacy*, edited by David Lyon and Elia Zureik, 66–76. Minneapolis: University of Minnesota Press.
Russell, Bob. 2009. *Smiling Down the Line: Info-service Work in the Global Economy*. Toronto: University of Toronto Press.
Sahay, Sundeep, Brian Nicholson, and S. Krishna. 2003. *Global IT Outsourcing: Software Development Across Borders*. Cambridge: Cambridge University Press.

Sampat, Preeti. 2008. "Special Economic Zones in India," *Economic & Political Weekly*, July 12, 25–29.

Samuelson, Paul A. 2004. "Where Ricardo and Mill rebut and confirm arguments of mainstream economists supporting globalization," *Journal of Economic Perspectives*, 18:3, 135–146.

———. 1947. *Foundations of Economic Analysis*. Cambridge: Harvard University Press.

Sandhu, Amandeep. 2006. "Why unions fail in organising India's BPO-ITES Industry," *Economic and Political Weekly*, October 14, 4319–4322.

Sarikakis, Katharine, and Leslie Regan Shade. 2008. "Revisiting international communication: Approach of the curious feminist." In *Feminist Interventions in International Communication: Minding the Gap*, edited by Katharine Sarikakis and Leslie Regan Shade, 3–16. Lanham: Rowman & Littlefield Publishers.

Sarnia Observer. 2006. "Corunna call center to close: Company moving jobs to Kitchener," August 10.

Sayeed, Vikhar Ahmed, and A. Saye Sekhar. 2009. "Thousands of IT professionals have lost their jobs in the major cyber cities," *Frontline*, February 28, http://www.hinduonnet.com/fline/stories/20090313260501400.htm (accessed March 3, 2009).

Schacht, John N. 1985. *The Making of Telephone Unionism 1920–1947*. New Brunswick, NJ: Rutgers University Press.

Scharf, Adria. 2003. "Scripted talk: From 'welcome to McDonalds' to 'paper or plastic?' employers control the speech of service workers," *Dollars and Sense*, 249: September/October, 35–37, 53.

Schiller, Dan. 1999. *Digital Capitalism: Networking the Global Market System*. Cambridge: MIT Press.

Schiller, Herbert I. 1996. *Information Inequality: The Deepening Social Crisis in America*. New York: Routledge.

———. 1973. *The Mind Managers*. Boston: Beacon Press.

Schumpeter, Joseph A. 1972. *Capitalism, Socialism, and Democracy*. New York: Harper Torchbooks.

Schussler, Stefan. 2007. "Call centers facing labor shortage," *Leader-Post*, September 27, http://www.canada.com/reginaleaderpost/news/business_agriculture/story.html?id=9af0012a-f9e2–4478–9ebf-26399f79ea3f (accessed September 28, 2007).

Scott, Robert, Thomas Garner, and David Ticoll. 2004. *A fine balance: The Impact of Offshore IT Services on Canada's IT landscape*. PriceWaterhouseCoopers.

Sengupta, Somini. 2009. "Attack on women at an Indian bar intensifies a clash of cultures," *New York Times*, February 8, http://www.nytimes.com/2009/02/09/world/asia/09india.html?partner=rss&emc=rss (accessed February 9, 2009).

Shankar, B.V. Shiva. 2009. "On November 25, go home on time," *Mid-Day.com*, November 11, http://www.mid-day.com/news/2009/nov/101109-going-home-on-time.htm (accessed November 11, 2009).

———. 2006. "Lessons from Oz: Inspired by the IBM employees stir in Australia, India's IT, ITES sector renew their trade union plans," *Mid-day.com*, September 8.

Shekhar, Karthik. 2009. "Labor law holiday for IT companies," September 3, *Bpovoice.com*, http://www.bpovoice.com/profiles/blogs/labor-law-holiday-for-it (accessed August 14, 2010).

Shepherdson, David K. 2012. *Industrial Relations Outlook 2013: Embracing the 'New Normal'*. Conference Board of Canada.

Shipley, David. 2008. "Lack of employees shuts down call center," *Telegraph-Journal*, June 11, http://telegraphjournal.canadaeast.com/article/322213 (accessed June 11, 2008).

Shniad, S. 2007. "Neo-liberalism and its impact in the telecommunications industry: One trade unionist's perspective." In *Knowledge Workers in the Information Society*, edited by Catherine McKercher and Vincent Mosco, 299–310. Lanham, MD: Lexington Books.

Sify.com. 2008a. "US financial crisis not to derail India growth story: Soros," April 14, http://sify.com/finance/fullstory.php?id=14649235 (accessed April 17, 2008).

———. 2008b. "Most CEOs expect UPA to win trust vote," July 21, http://sify.com/finance/fullstory.php?id=14720515 (accessed July 21, 2008).

Silcoff, Sean. 2012. "Canadian call centers ring up new job growth," *Globe and Mail*, March 13, http://www.theglobeandmail.com/report-on-business/economy/jobs/canadian-call-centres-ring-up-new-job-growth/article533634/ (accessed June 26, 2013).

SiliconIndia. 2009. "Sacked Wipro employee alleges harassment," August 20, http://www.siliconindia.com/shownews/Sacked_Wipro_employee_alleges_harassment-nid-60537.html/1/1/error1#success (accessed August 25, 2009).

Singh, Manmohan. 2007. *PM Inaugurates the ASSOCHAM 87th Annual Session*. New Delhi: Associated Chambers of Commerce and Industry of India.

Singh, Shelley. 2007. "Rlys to kick off call center ops," *The Economic Times*, April 3, http://economictimes.indiatimes.com/News/News_By_Industry/Transportation/Shipping_Transport/Rlys_to_kick_off_call_center_ops/articleshow/1848119.cms (accessed September 5, 2007).

Smith, Adam. 2003/1776. *The Wealth of Nations*. New York: Bantam Books.

Smythe, Dallas. 1981. *Dependency Road*. Norwood, NJ: Ablex.

———. 1977. "Communications: Blindspot of Western Marxism," *Canadian Journal of Political and Social Theory*, 1:1, 1–27.

Software Human Resource Council. 2007. "The Canadian IT labor market initiatives: Labor force survey (LFS)—December 2007," The Source for LMI and Software Human Resource Council.

———. 2005. "The Canadian IT labor market initiatives: Labor force survey (LFS)—December 2005," The Source for LMI and Software Human Resource Council.

Srinivasan, N. 1989. "Growth of professional managerial unionism: The Indian experience," *Economic and Political Weekly*, 25:47, M169–M174.

St. Pierre, Denis. 2005. "Omega falls on hard times," *Sudbury Star*, February 1, A3.

———. 1999a. "Steelworkers eye Omega workers: Union starts organizing drive at call center," *Sudbury Star*, October 7, A3.

———. 1999b. "Call center employees support union," *Sudbury Star*, November 25, A1.

———. 1999c. "Call center employees invited to union event," *Sudbury Star*, September 7, A1.

———. 1999d. "Union talk makes Omega owners nervous," *Sudbury Star*, November 21, A1.

Statistics Canada. n.d.a. "North American Industry Classification (NAICS) 2007: Telephone call centers," http://stds.statcan.gc.ca/naics-scian/2007/cs-rc-eng.asp?criteria=56142 (accessed August 1, 2010).

———. n.d.b. "Search of alphabetical index in NAICS 2007: 561420," http://stds.statcan.gc.ca/naics-scian/2007/es-re-eng.asp?criteria=561420 (accessed August 1, 2010).

———. 2011. "Quarterly financial statistics for enterprises," *The Daily*, February 23. Ottawa: Statistics Canada.

———. 2008. "Outsourcing and offshoring in Canada, 1961 to 2003," *The Daily*. Ottawa: Statistics Canada.

———. 2007. "Unionization," *Perspectives on Labor and Income*, August. Ottawa: Statistics Canada, http://www.statcan.gc.ca/pub/12-501-x/12-501-x2007001-eng.pdf (accessed July 4, 2013).

———. 2006. "Trends in the telephone call center industry, 2006," *The Daily*. Ottawa: Statistics Canada.

Steedman, Mercedes. 2003. *The Changing Face of the Call Center Industry in Canada*. Toronto: United Steelworkers.

Stevens, Andrew. 2010. "Power, Production and Solidarity: Trends in Contemporary International Labor Studies." In *Renewing International Labor Studies*, edited by Marcus Taylor. New York & London: Routledge.

Stevens, Andrew, and David O. Lavin. 2007. "Stealing time: The temporal regulation of labor in neoliberal and post-Fordist work regimes," *Democratic Communiqué*, 21:2, 40–61.

Stevens, Andrew, and Elizabeth Shi. 2009. "Union responses to the offshoring of call center work," *International Journal of Interdisciplinary Social Sciences*, 4:1, 441–453.

Strauss, George. 1964. "Professional or employee-oriented: Dilemma for engineering unions," *Industrial and Labor Relations Review*, 17:4, 519–533.

Sudbury Star. 2000. "Omega workers poised to strike," April 14, A3.

Suresh, Sunayana. 2006. "This domain doesn't exist: 93 employees of Bel-Air BPO didn't know firm had shut down until they saw this message on its site," *Midday.com*, http://www.unitespro.org/uniindia/Pres%20reports%20and%20UNITES%20response.pdf (accessed October 22, 2008).

Sydney Morning Herald. 2007. "Two major airlines to shift call centers to Kenya from India, says official," February 24, http://www.smh.com.au/news/Technology/Two-major-airlines-to-shift-call-centers-to-Kenya-from-India-saysofficial/2007/02/24/1171734041660.html (accessed September 4, 2007).

Taylor, Frederick Winslow. 2005/1911. *The Principles of Scientific Management*. Fairfield: 1st World Library—Literary Society.

Taylor, Marcus. 2009. "Who works for globalization? The challenges and possibilities for international labour studies," *Third World Quarterly*, 30:3, 435–452.

———. 2005. "Opening the World Bank: International organisations and the contradictions of global capitalism," *Historical Materialism*, 13:1, 153–170.

Taylor, Michael, and Nigel Thrift. 1982. "Introduction." In *The Geography of Multinationals: Studies in the Spatial Development and Economic Consequences of Multinational Corporations*, edited by Michael Taylor and Nigel Thrift, 1–13. London: Croom Helm.

Taylor, Phil, and Peter Bain. 2008. "United by a common language? Trade union responses in the UK and India to call center offshoring," *Antipode*, 40:1, 131–154.

———. 2005. "India calling to the far away towns: the call center labor process and globalization," *Work, Employment and Society*, 19:2, pp. 261–282.

———. 2001. "Trade unions, workers' rights and the frontier of control in UK call centers," *Economic and Industrial Democracy*, 22, 39–66.

———. 1999. "An assembly-line in the head: Work and employee relations in the call center," *Industrial Relations Journal*, 30, 101–117.

Taylor, Phil, Dora Scholarios, Ernesto Noronha, and Premilla d'Cruz. 2007. *Union Formation in Indian Call Centers/BPO: The Attitudes and Experiences of UNITES Members*. Glasgow and Ahmedabad: Strathclyde Business School and Indian Institute of Management.

Tejaswi, Mini Joseph. 2009a. "Technies say 'no' to pink slips," *The Times of India*.

———. 2009b. "Tension in the air: IT union website hits rise dramatically," *The Times of India*, February 5, http://epaper.timesofindia.com/Default/Client.asp?

Daily=TOIBG&login=default&Enter=true&Skin=TOI&GZ=T&AW=1233869 242187 (accessed February 5, 2009).

The Telegraph. 2006. "Who says BPOs don't have unions?" November 5.

Thakkar, Mitul, and Mansi Bhatt. 2006. "Regional language call centers lose talent," *India Times*, September 25, http://infotech.indiatimes.com/Regional_language_call_centers_lose_talent/articleshow/2023461.cms (accessed September 3, 2007).

Thanuja, B.M. 2007. "Local BPOs get a call from home," *The Economic Times*, December 24, http://economictimes.indiatimes.com/Local_BPos_get_a_call_from_home/articleshow/2646299.cms (accessed December 24, 2007).

Thompson, E.P. 1963. *The Making of the English Working Class*. London: Penguin Books.

Thrift, Nigel. 2006. "Re-inventing invention: new tendencies in capitalist commodification," *Economy and Society*, 35:2, 279–306.

Tilly, Charles. 1978. *From Mobilization to Revolution*. New York: Addison-Wesley.

The Times of India. 2007. "Shashi on Sunday: The end of a long, enlightening journey," December 30, http://timesofindia.indiatimes.com/Opinion/Sunday_Specials/All_That_Matters/SHASHI_ON_SUNDAY_The_end_of_a_long_enlightening_journey/articleshow/2661505.cms (accessed December 30, 2007).

———. 2006. "Calling the shots!" August 25, http://timesofindia.indiatimes.com/articleshow/msid-1927454,curpg-2.cms (accessed September 3, 2007).

———. 2005. "Should unions be allowed in BPOs?" December 4.

Timmons, Heather. 2009a. "Financial scandal at outsourcing company rattles a developing country," *New York Times*, January 7, http://www.nytimes.com/2009/01/08/business/worldbusiness/08outsource.html?_r=1&partner=rss&emc=rss (accessed January 8, 2009).

———. 2009b. "Indian company in a fight to survive," *New York Times*, January 8, http://www.nytimes.com/2009/01/09/business/worldbusiness/09outsource.html?_r=1&partner=rss&emc=rss (accessed January 9, 2009).

———. 2009c. "Satyam chief is accused of falsifying size of work force, then stealing payroll," *New York Times*, January 23.

Toffler, Alvin. 1980. *The Third Wave*. New York: Morrow.

Tomlinson, Kathy. 2013a. "RBC replaces Canadian staff with foreign workers," *CBC News*, April 6, http://www.cbc.ca/news/canada/british-columbia/story/2013/04/05/bc-rbc-foreign-workers.html (accessed May 24, 2013).

———. 2013b. "Ex-RBC foreign workers say contractor controlled their lives," *CBC News*, April 11, http://www.cbc.ca/news/canada/british-columbia/story/2013/04/11/bc-igate-workers.html (accessed May 24, 2013).

Toye, John. 2003. "Introduction." In *Trade and Development: Directions for the 21st Century*, edited by John Toye, 1–15. Northampton, MA: Edward Elgar.

The Tribune. 2006. "Stolen data from Indian call centers being sold: Report," October 2, http://www.tribuneindia.com/2006/20061002/main8.htm (accessed September 3, 2007).

TUAC and OECD. 2004. "Trade, offshoring of jobs and structural adjustment: The need for a policy response," TUAC consultations with the OECD liaison committee, TUAC discussion paper, November 23.

UNCTAD see United Nations Conference on Trade and Development.

UNI see Union Network International.

UNIAPRO. 2009. "Obama to eliminate tax benefits for cos outsourcing jobs," March 2, http://www.uniglobalunion.org/Apps/UNINews.nsf/vwLkpById/818 0D86C0221BB08C125756D00267DE5 (accessed March 18, 2009).

Union Network International. 2010a. "Canada Post to privatize 300 contact center jobs across Canada," UNI Post & Logistics, March.

————. 2010b. "First time election of union delegates at IBM Argentina," January 13, http://www.uniglobalunion.org/Apps/iportal.nsf/pages/sec_20081016_gbk4En (accessed February 1, 2010).

————. 2009. "A dose of women power in uniting IT workers in India," March 28, http://www.uniglobalunion.org/Apps/iportal.nsf/pages/homeEn?Opendocu ment&exURL=http://www.uniglobalunion.org/Apps/UNINews.nsf/0/ABF72-DAC6DF952CEC12575870058BAE9 (accessed June 5, 2009).

————. 2008a. "Sustainable outsourcing standards against social dumping," UNI IBITS, January 17, http://www.uniglobalunion.org/UNIIBITSn.nsf/0/170108_EN_EC (accessed February 21, 2008).

————. 2008b. "Rolling strikes after IBM Australia refuses to talk," UNI IBITS, September 9, http://www.uniglobalunion.org/UniibitsN.nsf/0/301008_EN_C9 (accessed November 12, 2008).

————. 2007. "Breakthrough at IBM Italy," UNI IBITS, November 2, http://www. uniglobalunion.org/UNIIBITSn.nsf/0/021107_EN_D1 (accessed November 19, 2007).

————. 2006a. *You're Being Followed: Electronic Monitoring and Surveillance in the Workplace*. Nyon: Union Network International.

————. 2006b. "Unions want curbs on hi-tech snooping," UNI Press Release, June, http://www.union-network.org/uniindep.nsf/d34dbcc804498029c1256d e400420f86/304003ecc3ebbf60c1257199002f9cfd?OpenDocument (accessed August 10, 2012).

————. 2006c. *A UNI Report on Customer Service Professionals and their Unions: Global Organizing for Call Center Workers*. Nyon: Union Network International.

————. 2005. *UNI Charter on Offshore Outsourcing*. Nyon: Union Network International.

United Nations Conference on Trade and Development. 2012. Trade and Development Report, 2012.

————. 2010. *World Investment Report 2010: Investing in a Low-Carbon Economy—Overview*. New York and Geneva: United Nations.

————. 2009. *World Investment Prospects Survey, 2009–2011*. New York and Geneva: United Nations.

————. 2006. *World Investment Report 2006: FDI from Developing and Transition Economies: Implications for Development*. New York and Geneva: United Nations.

————. 2004. *World Investment Report 2004: The Shift Towards Services*. New York and Geneva: United Nations.

UNITES. 2009a. "Decisions for life project launch," June, http://www.unitespro. org/files/html/DFL%20Page/dfl_launch.htm (accessed July 30, 2009).

————. 2009b. "Request to appoint a Commission of Enquiry under Commissioner of Enquiry Act," January 7, http://itnitesunion.wordpress.com/2009/01/07/ request-to-appoint-a-commission-of-enquiry-under-commissioner-of-enquiry-act/ (accessed January 12, 2009).

Upadhya, Carol, ed. 2008a. *In an Outpost of the Global Information Economy: Work and Workers in India's Outsourcing Industry*. New York: Routledge.

————. 2008b. "Ethnographies of the global information economy: Research strategies and methods," *Economic and Political Weekly*, April 26, 64–72.

————. 2007a. "Employment and work in the Indian outsourcing industry." Revised version, paper prepared for IILS-OCSSR-IHD International Workshop on 'Global Production Networks and Decent Work: Recent Experience in India and Global Trends', November 18–20, Bangalore.

————. 2007b. "Employment, exclusion and 'merit' in the Indian IT industry," *Economic and Political Weekly*, May 19, 1863–1868.

Upadhya, Carol, and A.R. Vasavi. 2006. "Work, culture, and sociality in the Indian IT industry: A sociological study." Final report submitted to Indo-Dutch Programme on Alternatives in Development. Bangalore: National Institute of Advanced Studies.

USW (United Steelworkers). n.d. "Steelworkers Humanity Fund on the move—all over the world," http://www.usw.ca/program/content/5094.php (accessed April 1, 2009).

———. 2009. "Steelworkers form collaboration with MONDRAGON, the world's largest worker-owned cooperative," October 27, http://www.usw.org/media_center/releases_advisories?id=0234 (accessed December 6, 2009).

———. 2007. "Global solidarity: USW takes first steps to create international trade union," *USW@Work*, summer.

———. 2002. "Everybody's union everywhere," National Policy Conference, Montreal, May 14–17, http://www.steelworkers-metallos.ca/program/content/978.php (accessed July 12, 2008).

Van Jaarsveld, Danielle D. 2004. "Collective representation among high-tech workers at Microsoft and beyond: Lessons from WashTech/CWA," *Industrial Relations*, 43:2, 364–385.

Van Jaarsveld, Danielle D., Ann C. Frost, and David Walker. 2007. *The Canadian Contact Center Industry: Strategy, Work Organization, & Human Resource Management*. Global Call Center Project.

van Welsum, Desiree, and Graham Vickery. 2005. "Potential offshoring of ICT-intensive using occupations," Working Party on the Information Society, Directorate for Science, Technology and Industry, April 5. Paris: Organization for Economic Cooperation and Development.

Veltmeyer, Henry, and James Sacouman. 1998. "Political economy of part-time work," *Studies in Political Economy*, 56, 115–143.

Verma, Prachi. 2004. "Forum to tackle unfair HR policies in BPO industry," *The Financial Express*, July 29, http://www.financialexpress.com/old/fe_full_story.php?content_id=64607 (accessed December 8, 2007).

Vincent, Richard, and Larry McKeown. 2008. "Trends in the telephone call center industry," *Analytical Paper Series—Service Industries Division*. Ottawa: Statistics Canada.

Voss, Kim. 2010. "Democratic dilemmas: Union democracy and union renewal," *Transfer: European Review of Labor and Research*, 16:3, 369–382.

Wallerstein, Immanuel. 2000. "Review: Globalization, social movements and the new internationalisms," *Development and Change*, 31, 513–548.

Walsh, Conal. 2006. "New data theft scandal rocks subcontinent's call centers," *Guardian Unlimited*, September 3, http://observer.guardian.co.uk/business/story/0,,1863593,00.html (accessed September 3, 2007).

Waterman, Peter. 2010. "Beyond Polanyi and Pollyanna—Oscar Wilde?" *Global Labour Journal*, 2:1, 78–83.

———. 2008. "A trade union internationalism for the 21st century: meeting the challenges from above, below and beyond." In *Labor and the Challenges of Globalization: What Prospects for Transnational Solidarity?* edited by Andreas Bieler, Ingemar Lindberg, and Devan Pillay, 248–263. Scottsville, SA: University of KwaZulu-Natal Press.

———. 2001a. "Trade union internationalism in the age of Seattle," *Antipode*, X:X, 312–336.

———. 2001b. *Globalization, Social Movements and the New Internationalisms*. Mansell: London.

———. 1992. "The transmission and reception of international labor information in Peru." In *Democratic Communications in the Information Age*, edited by Janest Wasko and Vincent Mosco, 224–245. Toronto: Garamond Press.

Waterman, Peter, and Jane Wills. 2001. "Space, place and the new labor internationalisms: Beyond the fragments?" *Antipode*, 33:3, 305–311.

Webb, Sidney, and Beatrice Webb. 1920. *The History of Trade Unionism*. London: Longmans, Green and Co.

Weeks, John. 2001. "Globalize, Globa-lize, Global Lies: Myths of the World Economy in the 1990s." In *Phases of Capitalist Development: Booms, Crises and Globalizations*, edited by Robert Albritton, 263–282. New York: Palgrave.

Weir, Erin. 2012. "Alberta's bogus labour shortage," *The Progressive Economics Forum*, August 4, http://www.progressive-economics.ca/2012/08/04/alberta-bogus-labour-shortage/ (accessed May 27, 2013).

Whitehouse, Mike. 2001. "Steelworkers soon to have more clerks than miners," *Sudbury Star*, September 3, A3.

Wilhelm, Trevor. 2002a. "Omega-union rift deepens: Steelworkers unhappy over how call center handled layoffs," *Sudbury Star*, January 22, A3.

———. 2002b. "Slowdown idles 230 call center employees," *Sudbury Star*, January 27, A3.

Windmuller, John P. 2000. "The international trade secretariats." In *Transnational Cooperation Among Labor Unions*, edited by Michael E. Gordon and Lowell Turner, 102–119. Ithaca and London: ILR Press.

Workers Uniting. n.d.a. "Unite and USW create first global trade union," http://www.workersuniting.org/default.aspx?page=281 (accessed April 1, 2009).

———. n.d.b. "About us," http://www.workersuniting.org/default.aspx?page=280 (accessed May 7, 2009).

———. n.d.c. "About us," http://www.workersuniting.org/who (accessed August 27, 2013).

World Bank. 1999. *World Development Report: Knowledge for Development*. Washington, DC: World Bank.

Yardley, Jim, and Heather Timmons. 2010. "Telecom scandal plunges India into political crisis," *New York Times*, December 13, http://www.nytimes.com/2010/12/14/world/asia/14india.html?_r=1&partner=rss&emc=rss (accessed December 14, 2010).

Yates, Charlotte. 2006. "Women are key to union renewal: Lessons from the Canadian labor movement." In *Paths to Union Renewal: Canadian Experiences*, edited by Pradeep Kumar and Christopher Schenk, 103–112. Peterborough: Broadview Press.

Yates, Michael D. 2003. *Naming the System: Inequality and Work in the Global Economy*. New York: Monthly Review Press.

Young Professionals Collective and Focus on the Global South. 2005. *When the Wind Blows: An Overview of Business Process Outsourcing (BPO) in India*. YPC and Focus on the Global South.

Youngdahl, Jay. 2008. "Mapping the future: Cross-border unionizing strategies," *New Labor Forum*, 17:2, 71–81.

Zuboff, Shoshana. 1988. *In the Age of the Smart Machine*. New York: Basic Books.

Zureik, Elia. 2003. "Theorizing surveillance: the case of the workplace." In *Surveillance as Social Sorting: Privacy, Risk, and Digital Discrimination*, edited by David Lyon, 31–56. London: Routledge.

Zureik, Elia, Vincent Mosco, and Clarence Lochhead. 1988. "Telephone workers' perception of management strategy and union reaction to the new technology." In *Queen's Papers in Industrial Relations*. Kingston: Industrial Relations Center.

Zweig, David. 2005. "Beyond privacy and fairness concerns: Examining psychological boundary violations as a consequence of electronic performance monitoring." In *Electronic Monitoring in the Workplace: Controversies and Solutions*, edited by John Weckert, 101–122. Hershey, PA: Idea Group.

Index

Printed in the United States
by Baker & Taylor Publisher Services